JOURNEYS OF THE FORGOTTEN

JOURNEYS OF THE FORGOTTEN
THE ORPHANS OF HAMILTON COUNTY, IOWA

JILL MORELLI, CG

Copyright (c) 2024
Published Jill Morelli, CG
Cover Design by Vanessa Dormancy

All rights reserved.

The words Certified Genealogist and the designation CG are registered certification marks and Certified Genealogical Lecturer and CGL are service marks of the Board for Certification of Genealogist used under license by Associates who meet genealogical competency standards prescribe for its programs.

No part of this publication may be reduced in any form without the written permission of the author except for brief passages that a reviewer may quote.

ISBN: 979-8-9911223-0-6
Library of Congress no. 2024914233

Printed in the United States of America
First edition

For the eleven unidentified orphans who came to Hamilton County, Iowa, in the fall of 1890

The November contingent of orphans gather for a group photo on 18 November 1890, before boarding the train to take them to Hamilton County, Iowa. Eli Trott, Agent

Photo is labeled "E. Trott's Company to Iowa," dated 18 November 1890. Four girls and eleven boys arrived in that delivery according to the Iowa newspaper. Four girls and twelve boys are in this photo. No individual child is identified. It is likely that the tallest, well-dressed young man in the back was not a rider on the train, but was part of the Children's Aid Society (CAS) team, perhaps Superintendent Eli Trott's son.

Permission for publication of photo granted by the Children's Aid Society of New York. Release of photo granted by the New York Historical Society, New York City, New York.

Table of Contents

Introduction	1
The Orphans	11
William Allison	13
Fred (—?—) Ashpole	17
James G. (Johnston) Baldwin	19
Harry Bittner	25
Arther "Charles" (—?—) Bjustrom	27
George Breckfeldt	33
John (Bodger) Bringolf	39
John (Murtha) Burnett	45
Minnie Everhardina (—?—) Busing	51
Iris (McFarland) Doutrich/Harry Dawson	55
Richard Doyle	63
Lucy (Johnson) Fay	69
Henry Aeilt (—?—) Hinderks	75
Katie (Mickle) Hines	79
Clara Lavinia (Mason) Krohn	85
James Wilfred (—?—) Lyons	97
Anna (Crane) McIntyre	103
Harry Guseka Moore	109
Nelson Morris	115
George Jensen Myers	119

Edward (Graham) Pruismann	125
Lillian Florence (Lingreen) Roop	131
William Schlosshauer	137
Mary "Mayme/Mae" (—?—) Smith	141
Lulu (Knox) Strowbridge	147
Julia Mae Sumpter	153
Charles Joseph (Nolan?) Tarrant	159
William Anthony Tarrant	165
Walter M. Thompson	171
William (McEndry) Thompson	177
Jacob "Fred" Weber	179
William Louellette Weber	187
Belle (Welch) Wientjes	193
George R. (Warden) Witte	199
August Zahn	203
By the Numbers	209
Conclusion	233
Attachments	
Methodology	237
List of Hamilton County, Iowa orphans	243
Other Foster Families	247
Map, Hamilton County, Iowa	251
Bibliography	253
Index	259

Preface

I knew Belle was an Orphan Train Rider as soon as I saw her entry in the 1900 Federal census. She was just 12 years old, born in New York and lived with my childless German relatives in Iowa. My interest was piqued.

I had seen the books written about individual orphans from New York City. They invariably told happy tales of redemption and survival. The prevalence of these stories contradicted my thoughts that perhaps the stories of the orphans were not universally wonderful. Could I find a cohort large enough to study (but not too large) and determine the likelihood of a happy ending by telling their life stories?

Belle left New York City and arrived in Hamilton County, Iowa, in the fall of 1890 with forty-five other orphans. Initially no child was named; no birth dates given; no New York City parents identified; and only seventeen foster parents named. But I had my cohort!

I thank all the individuals who commented or provided photos of their ancestors, and the public historians Margaret Jane Arends and Nancy Kayser who aided in the writing and research. To Linda Lawson for going above and beyond on Clara Krohn, and to all librarians and archivists at the Kendall Young Library in Webster City—you are appreciated.

These stories do not all have happy endings, but some do, giving the reader a more balanced view of the successes and failures of a program that out-placed over one quarter of a million children, more than any single biography can.

While I hope you enjoy this journey, I only ask the reader to imagine that you are five years old, standing on the platform of the train station and some farmer walks by and picks you—or doesn't.

These are their stories.

Jill Morelli, CG

August 2024

Introduction

Webster City, Hamilton County, Iowa, Train Depot, c. 1900
Photo courtesy of Kendall Young Library, Webster City, Iowa

In August of 1890, a train left New York City with eighteen orphans. These orphans traveled multiple days and covered more than 1000 miles to their final destination of Webster City, Iowa. Two more deliveries that year brought a total of forty-six unnamed orphans to the rural farms and communities of Hamilton County.

No county history book noted their arrival, but other documents tell their stories.[1]

URLs checked July 2024. For information about sources and repositories, see the Bibliography.
[1] FamilySearch Wiki, "Hamilton County, Iowa Genealogy." Also, Jesse W. Lee, *History of Hamilton County, Iowa,* (Chicago: S.J. Publishing Company, 1912).

The Webster City train station was a two-story, brick structure with a one-story section in the rear. The wooden platform wrapped around the building on two sides forming the platform and a walkway to the street.[2]

The children, escorted by Superintendent Eli Trott of the Children's Aid Society (CAS), walked around the train station to Smith's Rink, a large assembly hall with a stage about two blocks from the train depot.

Trott introduced each child to the community. The townspeople expected all boys, but there were four girls in this first shipment,. Pre-selected farmers and townspeople inspected the children with the intention of taking one home to join their family, and more importantly, to help with the unceasing farm and house work. For these children there could not have been a starker contrast to the streets of New York City than the rural Iowa farmland and the town of Webster City.

BACKGROUND
In the mid-1800s, the Industrial Revolution created both millionaire factory owners living luxuriously in mansions and low wage factory workers eking out a living in squalid tenements. Tenement living was the norm for poor newcomers. For children, the future looked bleak. Many worked at an early age, lived on the streets selling small items like pencils and apples, or made mischief.

For two parent families, a crisis of any kind forced the out-placement of children. The family crisis could be temporary or permanent. Sickness or job loss could trigger a temporary familial crisis. The death of one parent would place extreme stress on the surviving spouse, especially if the child was an infant and no other family members resided in the area. The parents often placed their children in orphanages for the duration of these difficulties. Single parents had even fewer options.

Twenty to thirty percent of children became orphans by the age of 15, but only a third had lost both parents.[3] For the purposes of this study, we will use the term "orphan" to describe a foundling, a child with no living parents or a child with one or more parents who had released the child to an orphanage.

---

[2] Sanborn Fire Insurance Maps, Webster City, Hamilton County Iowa, 1892, map 1, bottom of page; Library of Congress.

[3] Bruce Bellingham, " 'Little Wanderers,' A Socio-Historical Study of the Nineteenth century origins of Child Fostering and Adoption Reform, Based on Early Records of the New York Children's Aid Society," (Ph.D. diss., University of Pennsylvania, 1984) 182; citing the U.S. Bureau of Education for 1884.

Even in the mid-1800s nurseries took care of children, providing 24-hour care. Industrial schools provided training, a hot meal, and a clean bed for an older child. The Newsboy Lodging Homes, first opened in 1854, provided boys with bed and board for a small fee. A similar lodging option for girls started in 1862.[4]

Laying-in hospitals provided maternity care for pregnant single mothers, but only for the first child. The mother was expected to learn the error of their ways and not repeat the transgression. There was also an expectation that the child would be given to the orphanage shortly after birth for out-placement.

When the alternatives ran out, parents sought a permanent answer—a home for their child outside of the city with an unknown family.

ORPHAN TRAIN MOVEMENT
The Orphan Train Movement, as it was called in the early 1900s, was conceived by Charles Loring Brace.[5] Brace came to NYC in 1848 after graduating from Yale University and began ministering to the terminally ill women on Blackwell Island. Shortly after arrival his wife died, and he traveled to Europe with friends. He found himself imprisoned in Hungary for seditious acts related to helping immigrants. These experiences exposed him to the plights of others and their families around the world and sparked his interest in social activism.[6]

The Children's Mission to Children of the Destitute in Boston probably served as an inspiration for Brace and the formation of the Children's Aid Society. The Children's Mission began in the early 1850s and delivered children by train to families in the west; however, the Children's Mission, treated the children as indentured servants.[7] Indentured servitude came with a contract, a practice which CAS did not employ. Children placed by the CAS could also request re-placement at any time.[8]

Believing the hard work and the bucolic environment of rural life would provide better conditions in which to raise a child, Brace met with bankers and financiers of New York City in January of 1853, to request funds to

---

[4] Stephen O'Connor, *Orphan Trains: The Story of Charles Loring Brace and the Children He Saved and Failed*, (Boston: Houghton Mifflin, 2001) 90-91.

[5] The Orphan Train Movement was called "out-placement" in the 1800s.

[6] O'Connor, *Orphan Trains: The Story of Charles Loring Brace*, 41-44.

[7] Ibid., 94.

[8] Ibid., 96.

establish the Society. He was successful, and in 1854 the first train of orphans took forty-five children to rural Michigan. Thirty-seven children were matched with foster parents and the remaining eight were taken by train to an Iowa orphanage with the hopes of finding them homes with rural farm families.[9]

The program's reliance on farmers to provide a good home was perhaps a misplaced concept; but Thomas Jefferson's ideal of "Those who labor in the earth are the chosen people of God," reinforced the commitment of the CAS founder to outplacement of children to rural America.[10]

Between 1854 and 1929, when the program ceased, upstate New York received an estimated 30,000 children, and the Midwest took in a similar number.[11] Only a few states received none.

The Secretary of the CAS reported that in 1890 2,825 children had been moved out of New York City at a cost of $28,106.77 or $9.96 per child. The Secretary compared this to the cost of almshouse housing of $140 per child. Iowa received 148 children that year.[12]

A tendency to focus on the out-placement of children to resolve a social problem of New York City and helping the children of the poor seems apparent; however the underlying reasons for removing the children were more complex and arose from a mixture of compassion and fear.

Evidence exists that many of the wealthier classes wanted the street children to go away, as they represented a broken promise— the American way of life wasn't as golden as described. The wealthy were also concerned that the poor would stay poor as adults, and the magnitude of poor might disturb their way of life in the future through the ballot box.

Charles Loring Brace echoed these fears:
> These boys and girls, it should be remembered, [form] the great lower class of our city. They will influence elections; they may shape the

---

[9] O'Connor, *Orphan Trains: The Story of Charles Loring Brace*, xvi. On the appeal of farm life, see Megan Birk, *Fostering on the Farm; Child Placement in the Rural Midwest* (Chicago: University of Illinois Press, 2015) 1. Also, "Thirty-Eighth Annual Report of the Children's Aid Society, November 1890," p. 2; *Internet Archive*, https://archive.org/details/annualreportofch00chil/mode/2up . "...the best possible place of shelter and education for the outcast and homeless children is the Farmer's Home."

[10] Megan Birk, *Fostering on the Farm: Child Placement in the Rural Midwest*, (Chicago: University of Illinois Press, 2015) 5, 19.

[11] Birk, *Fostering on the Farm*, 3.

[12] "Thirty-Ninth Annual Report of the Children's Aid Society (November 1891)," p.15, 10 ; *Internet Archive*, https://archive.org/details/annualreportofch00chil/mode/2up .

policy of the city; they will assuredly, if unreclaimed, poison the city around them.[13]

In spite of these forces swirling around him, Brace had a love and deep respect for the initiative and the leadership of the street children of New York City.

While the displacement of children from their homes seems difficult to imagine now, it represents a continuation of child-relocation as an answer to seemingly unsolvable social problems, which continues to present day. Examples include forced indenture during colonial times, slave family separations, Native American de-culturalization of children in the late 1800s into the 1900s, detention of U.S.-born Chinese children returning to the U.S. after 1882, and "home school" children taken from England to Canadian orphanages. More recently, the separation of 2500 Hispanic children from their families at the U.S.-Mexican border in 2016 and kidnapping of Ukrainian children in 2022-3 by the Russians confirms that this concept isn't a program of the past.

It is not the purpose of this book to provide the history of the Orphan Train Movement; nor is it to provide a look into Iowa farm life in the late 1800s. Many resources exist that address those subjects. This book focuses on a small subset of that mass migration—forty-six unnamed children delivered from New York City to Hamilton County, Iowa, in the fall of 1890 and the lives they lived.

To conduct this study, it was first necessary to identify the unnamed children and their foster parents. Once identified, a biography of each was written and their birth parents identified, if possible. Those findings were compared to to a 1922 study to assess the relative success of the cohort.

Our questions were the following:
1. What were the characteristics of the Hamilton County, Iowa cohort?
2. What are the characteristics of the foster parents?
3. What are the characteristics of identified NYC parents?
4. How do attributes of the orphan cohort compare with the results of the study done by Georgia G. Ralph in 1922 for CAS?
5. What observations can be made regarding the success of placement of the children in Hamilton County, Iowa?

---

[13] Steven O'Connor, *Orphan Trains: The Story of Charles Loring Brace*, 96; citing Charles Loring Brace, first publicity circular of the Children's Aid Society, New York (publisher unknown, March 1853).

Thirty-five of the forty-six children and their foster parents have been identified. Twelve of the thirty-five have identified NYC parents. Eleven remain unidentified.

HAMILTON COUNTY, IOWA

Hamilton County was established in 1850 and is located in central Iowa. Its rich soil is a result of multiple glacial intrusions and the creation of a layer of soil called "Wisconsin Drift," which when mixed with decayed vegetation, turns black. This rich soil is extremely thick in this area, resulting in high-producing farms. These glacial intrusions also formed potholes, some more like shallow lakes or swamps. The drainage of these potholes created ditching and tiling jobs for individuals as farmers aggressively drained the watery soil to gain land for agricultural purposes.[14]

In 1890, 15,164 people lived in Hamilton County, which experienced steep growth in the previous decades. Webster City was a prosperous town, the largest in the market area and the county seat.

Webster City, Second Street, "main street," about 1908
Courtesy of Kendall Young Library, Webster City, Iowa

Businesses at that time were small and relied on local markets. Many small manufacturing companies began in the area, but most were short-lived. One exception was Closz & Howard. Charles Closz invented a separator sieve for discarding the chaff from wheat as it was harvested, eliminating

---

[14] Kristen A. Gerteman, "Lost Lake: A Deep Map of a Farm Field," (MA, Diss., ISU, 2020.)

the need to stop the machine and clean it by hand.[15] They employed sixty to seventy people, even during the Great Depression.

THE ORPHANS

The Children's Aid Society of New York informed the Hamilton County community of the arrival of orphans at a yet undetermined date. The town was told to prepare for the selection of children by naming individuals to a committee to manage the selection process. The committee advertised for foster families and received the requests.[16]

In New York City, the CAS staff organized the delivery of children. They identified the children, gave them a new suit of clothes, placed them on a train, and escorted them to their new location.[17] Each child was identified by a scrap of fabric pinned to their clothing with their New York City name and birth date. The children were escorted to the train by an agent who guided them to their destination.

Identification scrap: Harry Caroon, 1888
Permission granted by Betty Jo Stockton;
original in the Orphan Train Depot Collection, Kansas.

For the three Hamilton County deliveries, individuals made more requests than available children. The specific criteria for selection of the families is

---

[15] J. W. Lee, *History of Hamilton County Iowa, vol 1* (Chicago: S.J. Clarke Publishing, 1912) 344-345.

[16] "Boys Wanting Homes," *Webster City Freeman,* 20 August 1890, p. 4, col 5. Notice posted by the Children's Aid Society.

[17] Children identified as "orphans" have no parents living; "parentally released" children implies they have one or more of their parents living, but who are unable or unwilling, to support the child.

not known; however, each household exhibited a need for help on the farm or in the home.

The first delivery of children by the CAS was 29 August:
> ... Following are the names of those who secured children in this city last Friday, as furnished by Mr. Trott: F Ashpole, H. S. Olmsted, Horace Segar, Alex. Ashpole, G. Hassebrock, John E. Young. F Pruismann, W. Pletisch, A. Hindricks, J L. Ford, W. C. Woolsey (2), John Essig, C. M. France, Jackson Mickle, Christ Krohn, P H. Dickman, A. Bussing[.] The four last named gentlemen procured girls....[18]

Following the success and demand for children in Hamilton County, Superintendent Trott promised a second delivery of children. Again, a committee managed the selection process and on 9 October at Smith's Rink, the second selection occurred.[19]

> Ten boys and three girls, from the Children's Aid Society, of New York, arrived in the city last Thursday, accompanied by Supt. E. Trott. Each child found a home among Hamilton county people, and it is hoped they will grow up useful and respected citizens. About sixty applications were sent in for children, but as Mr. Trott expects to return in a few weeks with another company those disappointed this time may then be supplied.[20]

No document names the children or foster parents for this second delivery, only that all thirteen children, ten boys and three girls, went to Hamilton County residents.

The third and last delivery of children occurred on 20 November 1890. (*See* cover photo and description on Dedication page.)

> The third and last party of children from the Children's Aid Society, of New York City, arrived as advertised, yesterday. There were four girls and eleven boys this time and no difficulty was experienced in finding good homes for them all in our county.[21]

---

[18] "E. Trott of the children's aid society...," *The Freeman,* 3 September 1890, p. 5, col. 3. If location of publication not given assume Hamilton County, Iowa.
[19] "Boys Wanting Homes," *Webster City Freeman,* 24 September 1890, p. 4, col 5.
[20] "Ten boys and three girls...", *The Freeman,* 15 October 1890, p. 5, col. 3.
[21] "The third and last party..." *The Freeman,* 21 November 1890, p. 5, col. 3.

In total, forty-six children were delivered to Hamilton County in the fall of 1890, thirty-five boys and eleven girls. No child was named at the time of delivery and only the foster parents of the first group were identified.[22]

Once out-placed, children could be shifted from family to family.[23] Two examples (Bittner, Bringolf) exist in this small cohort, but evidence exists of another. In November, N. H. Hellen, a real estate and insurance salesman, but not an identified foster parent, advertised to transfer a child to another family.[24] The child, the initial foster parents and the recipient were not identified.

Between 1890 and 1900, no additional deliveries of orphans occurred.[25] A potential foster parent could have requested and received a single child during that time. If the child was requested before 1895, it would be difficult to discern any difference between a requested child and a child who arrived in the 1890 deliveries. No newspaper articles indicated the arrival of special requested children.

NAMES
Many of the orphans used multiple names throughout their lives. The younger children usually adopted the surname of their foster parents. Older children often kept their New York name. Some foster parents changed both the given and the surname of the child (Ashpole, Hindirks). Often a child, once they reached adulthood, would change their name back to their birth name. That New York City name may not be discoverable. In a reverse example, James G. Johnson used his New York name while younger and when he became an adult took the surname of his foster parents. Names and birth dates could also be innocently misspelled, forgotten or adjusted. Foundlings, children abandoned as infants, often had no known name or birth date, except as assigned by the orphanage.

The name the child used during their adult years and, if female, before marriage, is used as the primary name in the individual biographies. A name, therefore, could be their foster family name or their New York City name. Check the name of the foster parents to determine which name is

---

[22] In the summer of 2023, CAS provided the author with a list of children and their foster parents for the October delivery only, providing New York City name, age and assigned foster parents.

[23] Birk, *Fostering on the Farm*, 8. It is estimated that 25% or more of the children placed were moved to a different household.

[24] "One of the boys...," *Webster City Tribune*, 28 November 1890, p. 5, col. 2.

[25] Searched *Advantage Archives*, Hamilton County, Iowa, from 1 January 1890 to 31 December 1900, (http://hamiltoncounty.advantage-preservation.com/viewer). No entries of deliveries to Hamilton County. Searched for "orphan train" and "children's aid."

being used. Every child made their own choice with one even adjusting the names of his foster parents to match his New York surname. (Wa. Thompson)

Seven identified male orphans disappear from the records about age 20, and probably reverted to unknown NYC names or assumed an alias.

THE ORPHANS
Each orphan's biography begins with a section devoted to the orphan's life from the time of arrival in Hamilton County using genealogical research techniques. Some children cannot be found after they reach adulthood; some can be traced to death. The second section of an individual's vignette describes the efforts used to identify the New York City parents.

In an effort to illustrate the difficulty in analyzing each orphan's status, the reader will find many inconsistencies in dates and names throughout the narrative. Each orphan has a timeline recording identifiers they used after arrival that might reflect on their New York City experience, such as name variations; names of their foster and birth parents; and age and locations of birth. These anomalies are explained by the informant making a good guess, having fuzzy recall, or transcription errors or "adjustments" for convenience. In spite of these challenges, birth parents have been identified for twelve of the orphans.

Some New York City parents cannot be identified. To maintain that effort a website was created to cotalog this research in hopes that others will share information about these orphans in the future. It will also be used to record any newly obtain information that arrived after the publication of the book. (*See* https://iowaorphans.wordpress.com)

Analysis of the cohort appears in a separate chapter after the biographies. (*See* By the Numbers). A chapter also covers the identified foster parents who did not have an orphan in their family in either the 1895 or 1900 censuses. (*See* Attachment 3)

What follows are the thirty-five biographies of the known Hamilton County orphans who arrived in the fall of 1890.

The Orphans

William Allison

B. FEBRUARY 1882 IN NEW YORK
D. UNKNOWN
BIRTH FAMILY: —?— ALLISON
FOSTER FAMILY: GEORGE/GEERD AND (M1) ETTA (BONK) HASSEBROEK;
(M2) JENNIE (BONK) HASSEBROEK

Hassebroek farm, c. 1900. William is probably the person by the horse drawn carriage with the younger girl.
Permission to use granted by Margaret Jane Arends

Superintendent E. Trott recorded G. Hassebroek as the recipient of an unnamed boy in the 29 August 1890, delivery of children to Hamilton County.[26] In 1895 William Allison, 12 years old, resided in the Geerd Hassebroek family. Geerd was 36 years old and was born in Germany. His wife, Etta, was 28 and born in Illinois. Four children under the age of 6 were born to the couple. Also living with the family was Grace Bonk, a probable sister to Etta.[27]

---

[26] "E. Trott of the children's aid society...," *The Freeman*, 3 September 1890, p. 5, col. 3.
[27] 1895 Iowa state census, Hamilton County, Iowa, population schedule, Hamilton Township, p. 405 (stamped), household 98, dwelling 9, William Allison in the household of Geerd Hassabroak.

At the time of selection, William was one year older than the oldest Hassebroek child. Geerd needed help on the farm and the young William was to provide it.

Geerd Hassebrooek became a member of the German Presbyterian Church of Kamrar in 1892. No mention of William was noted in the minutes.[28]

Harriet "Etta" (Bonk) Hassebroek died 25 February 1895, and was buried in the Presbyterian cemetery in Kamrar.[29] With four young ones and William, Geerd Hassebroek quickly married Etta's half sister, Jennie Bonk, on 19 June 1895.[30]

In 1900, William worked on the George Strever farm adjacent to the Hassebroek farm.[31]

In some locales having run-off water from an adjacent farm would be welcomed, but because of the swampy areas on farms in Hamilton County, it was not. In 1904, George Strever filed a formal complaint against Geerd and two other neighbors to stop them from draining water from their farms onto his.[32] The case was eventually found in favor of Strever.[33] Whether William was working for the Strevers at the time of the lawsuit is not known.

William Allison moved from Hamilton County, after 1900. His common name made his identification impossible without geographic placement. He was not found in the 1905 Iowa census.

Two candidates stand out.

---

[28] German Presbyterian Church, Kamrar, Hamilton County, Iowa, "Baptism Records, Burial Records, Death Certificates, Marriage Records, Religious Records, 1875-1956," *FamilySearch* > Images, baptism records, image 16 of 54. 6 November 1892. G. Hassebroek membership (6 November 1892).

[29] Ibid. ,death records, image 30 of 49. p. 75, Etty Hassebroek burial entry (25 February 1895).

[30] "Iowa, Select Marriage Index, 1758-1996," index, Hamilton County, Iowa, Hasssebroek-Bonk marriage entry (June 1895).

[31] 1900 U.S. census, Hamilton County, Iowa, population schedule, Hamilton Township, ED 107, p. 7, household 121, dwelling 121, William Elson in the household of George R. Strever. For the George Hassebroek family: Ibid., p. 6, household 108, dwelling 108, George Hassebroek.

[32] "Drainage Injunction is Asked," *Webster City Freeman*, 9 February 1904, p. 1, col. 3.

[33] "George R. Strever is Victor in Ditch Case," *Webster City Freeman*, 7 June 1907, p. 12, col. 4.

1. Was William Allison, born 1882 in New York and boarding in Chicago in 1910 with his wife of 4 years, Anna, the orphan from Hamilton County? The couple had no children. William was a laborer.[34]
2. Was William Ellison, born 1882 in New York, and incarcerated at San Quentin, Marin County, California, the orphan? Serving a sentence of 2.5 years, he entered the prison in 24 April of 1909.[35]

No additional information has been found about William Allison after 1900.

William Allison was probably the orphan's birth name. A study of known information yields little information:

Figure 1-WA
Name, location and date of birth, foster and birth parents
of William Allison/Ellison

	Name	Birth date	Birth location	Birth parents	Foster parents
1890					G. Hassebroek[a]
1895	William Alison[b]	1883	New York		Geerd Hassebroek
1900	William Elson[c]	Feb 1882	New York	b. New York	

a. "E. Trott of the children's aid society...," *The Freeman*, 3 September 1890, p. 5, col. 3.
b. 1895 Iowa state census, Hamilton County, Iowa, William Allison in the household of Geerd Hassabroak.
c. 1900 U.S. census, Hamilton County, Iowa, William Elson in the household of George R. Strever. For the Hassebroek family: Ibid., George Hassebroek.

The birth month and year given in 1900 is the date with the most credence due to his specificity, but it could be wrong.

CONCLUSION
Based on the documentary evidence, William Allison was born February 1882 or 1883 in New York.

---

[34] 1910 U. S. Census, Cook County, Illinois, population schedule, Chicago, Ward 18, ED 811, p. 6B, household 56, dwelling 127, William & Anna Allison in the household of Nellie A. Berrington.

[35] "California, Prison and Correctional Records, 1851-1950," San Quentin State Prison, prison register, 1897-1910, 21 April 1909, William Ellison, prisoner no. 23524.

William's whereabouts after 1900 is unknown. (*See* https://iowaorphans.wordpress.com for efforts to identify Williams NYC parents.)

FRED (--?--) ASHPOLE

B. NOVEMBER 1881 IN NEW YORK
D. UNKNOWN
BIRTH FAMILY: UNKNOWN
FOSTER FAMILY: FREDERICK AND ELIZABETH ASHPOLE

Superintendent Trott recorded F. Ashpole as the recipient of an orphan in the 29 August 1890 delivery of children to Hamilton County.[36] In 1895 Fred (--?--) Ashpole, age 13 and born in New York, resided in the Frederick Ashpole family, composed of Frederick, his apparent wife, and a son, age 19.[37]

Early settlers in Iowa and Hamilton County, Frederick and Lucy Ashpole emigrated from Huntingdonshire, England, and settled on a farm in Cass Township where Frederick plowed prairie land in the earliest days of Iowa history.[38]

By 1900, young Fred boarded with Frank H. Burcham in Blairsburg, and provided farm labor. He was born November 1881 in New York. Fred was one of the older orphans on the train.[39] This is the last documentation about young Fred.

The elder Frederick Ashpole died 21 May 1903 in Blairsburg at the age of 78. The orphan Fred Ashpole was not identified as a survivor in his obituary, nor was he mentioned in the probate record.[40]

---

[36] "E. Trott of the children's aid society...," *The Freeman (Webster City, Iowa)*, 3 September 1890, p. 5, col. 3.

[37] 1895 State of Iowa census, Hamilton County, Iowa, population schedule, image 8 of 681, Fred Ashpole in the household of Fred Ashpole.

[38] *The Illustrated History of Hamilton County Iowa*, (Chicago; S.J. Clarke Publishing Company, 1912) 203.

[39] 1900 U.S. census, Hamilton County, Iowa, population schedule, Blairsburg, ED 112, p. 10, household 208, dwelling 213, Fred Ashpoll in the household of Frank H. Burcham.

[40] "Iowa, U.S. Death Records, 1880-1904, register for 1903, Fredrick Ashpole death entry (May 1903). Also, "Death of Frederick Ashpole," *Daily Freeman Tribune (Webster City, Iowa)*, 22 May 1903, p. 5, col. 3. Also, Hamilton County, Iowa, Fredrick Ashpole's probate record, file 1473; Hamilton County Court, Office of the Clerk, Webster City, Iowa.

Two Fred Ashpoles resided in Hamilton County during this era, both born in 1881/1882. One was the grandson of Fred (the older); the other was the orphan. In 1905 a Frederick Ashpole, age 26 and born in Iowa, resided in Clinton County.[41] This is not the orphan Fred.

No further information has been found about Fred Ashpole. Fred possibly reverted to his birth name or an alias and left the area.

Fred Ashpole, the orphan, left no hint as to his NYC given or surname. As an older child when he arrived in Hamilton County, Fred was probably well aware of his birth name and likely reverted to it after 1900.

Figure 1-FA
Name, location and date of birth, foster and birth parents
of Fred Ashpole

	Name	Birth date	Birth location	Birth parents	Foster parents
1890					F. Ashpole[a]
1895	Fred Ashpole[b]	1882	New York		Fred Ashpole
1900	Fred Ashpoll[c]	Nov 1881	New York	b. New York	

a. "E. Trott of the children's aid society...," *The Freeman*, 3 September 1890, p. 5, col. 3.
b. 1895 State of Iowa census, Hamilton County, Iowa, population schedule, image 8 of 681, Fred Ashpole in the household of Fred Ashpole.
c. 1900 U.S. census, Hamilton County, Iowa, population schedule, Blairsburg, ED 112, p. 10, household 208, dwelling 213, Fred Ashpoll in the household of Frank H. Burcham.

CONCLUSION
Fred was likely born in November 1881 or 1882 in New York City. Fred disappeared from the records after 1900. With no known birth name and without any other unique identifiers, Fred (—?—) Ashpole cannot be identified beyond the 1900 census.

(*See* https://iowaorphans.wordpress.com for efforts to identify Fred's NYC parents and new information about him.)

---

[41] 1905 Iowa state census, Clinton County, Iowa, population schedule, Lyons Township, card no. A71, Fredrick Ashpole.

JAMES GARFIELD (JOHNSTON) BALDWIN

B. 22 OCTOBER 1883 OR 1884, NEW YORK CITY, NEW YORK
D. 4 FEBRUARY 1938, SAN FRANCISCO, CALIFORNIA
BIRTH FAMILY: —?— JOHNSON/JOHNSTON
FOSTER FAMILY: PERRY O. & LAVANCHE (WOODWARD) BALDWIN

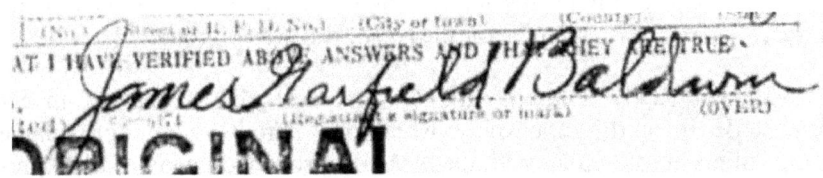

WWI draft registration

James Johnston, age 7, arrived in Hamilton County in the October delivery of children and was selected by the Perry O. Baldwin family of Webster City.[42] James G. Johnson, identified as the Baldwin's ward, was born October 1883 in New York. He attended school as late as 1900.[43]

James and the Baldwin family moved to Merced, California, in early 1895 with $2,700, which is "all [Perry] could scrape together after forty years of life in Iowa." What the newspaper failed to mention was that Baldwin sold the half section of farmland for $13,500.[44] After the move to California, he purchased 30 acres and began dairy farming. In 1910, Perry O. Baldwin purchased an additional 19.9 acres in Dos Palos, California.[45] In a 1915 article highlighting successful farmers in the Merced area, Baldwin gave each daughter twenty acres; retained 120 acres; and had farm land in

---

[42] Kialy Carson, Kansas, [(CURATOR@ORPHANTRAINDEPOT.COM),] to Jill Morelli, email, 7 March 2023, "Info from the CAS," OTR folder, privately held by Morelli, [(E-ADDRESS) & STREET ADDRESS FOR PRIVATE USE], Seattle, Washington, 2023. The email referred to an email from the archivist Paul Clark [(archivist@ChildrensaidNYC.org)] of the CS to the Depot. Email listed the agent's name (Trott); the thirteen children by name and gender; the name of their foster parent and the location of residence of the foster parents.

[43] 1900 U.S. census, Merced, California, population schedule, Township 3, ED 47, P. 3, household 49, dwelling 50, Perry O. Baldwin.

[44] "Culp & Lee have sold…," *Webster City Freeman*, 5 December 1894, p. 5, col 3.

[45] "Instruments Files-19 August 1910," *Merced (California) Sun-Star*, 25 August 1910, p. 3, col. 3; *California Digital Newspaper Collection*, https://cdnc.ucr.edu/.

Mexico; and a town lot in Oakland.[46] No mention of James was made in any of these transactions.

After the move to California, James G. Johnson (without the "t") informally changed his name to James G. Baldwin, a name he used for the rest of his life and indicative of close familial ties with the Baldwin family. Perry Baldwin called James his adopted son. Whether this was an official adoption or one of convenience is not known.[47]

James G. Baldwin registered for the World War I draft in September 1918 in San Francisco, California. He stated he was born 22 October 1884 and listed Lavanche Baldwin, his foster mother, as his closest contact. James was employed as a messenger for the A. M. Railway Company.[48]

In 1920 James G. Baldwin, age 34 and still single, resided in San Francisco. James did not know where his parents were born. James continued his employment with the A. M. Railroad Company as an express messenger, an occupation he followed his whole life.[49] James resided in San Francisco at least between 1918 and 1938.[50]

James G. Baldwin married Loretta A. McCabe in San Francisco on 26 July 1920 in the Catholic Church.[51]

Perry Baldwin died 28 March 1921 at his home is Dos Palos. His obituary mentioned that he left Webster City for Dos Palos in March 1895 and noted the he built "one of the largest and best ranches in this section."
    Mr. Baldwin is survived by his son, Frank, two daughters…all of Dos Palos and an adopted son James.[52]

---

[46] "What the Small Farmer Is Doing in Merced County; Successful Dairying," *Merced County Sun (California)*, 20 March 1915, p. 18, col. 5.

[47] "Pioneer Resident Passes Away," *The Dos Palos Star (CA)*, p. 1, col. 6.

[48] "World War I Draft Registration Cards, 1917-1918," 12 September 1918, San Francisco, San Francisco County, California Local Board for Division 12, for James G. Baldwin.

[49] James was enumerated twice: 1920 US. Census, San Francisco County, California, population schedule, San Fransisco, Assembly District 28, ED 297, household 13, dwelling 14, James G. Baldwin in the household of James C. Rayburn. Also, Ibid., Assembly District 28, ED 297, household 97, dwelling 98, James G. Baldwin in the household of Emanuel Worthheimer. The entries are identical.

[50] "CaliforniaVoter Registrations, 1900-1968," various years, James G. Baldwin.

[51] "California, San Francisco County Records, 1824-1997," database with images, *FamilySearch* (https://familysearch.org/ark:/61903/3:1:33SQ-G56G-F2T), Marriages > Marriage Certificates, Vol. 49, 1920 > image 62 of 511, James G. Baldwin-Loretta A. McCabe marriage entry (26 July 1920).

[52] "Pioneer Resident Passes Away," *The Dos Palos Star (CA)*, p. 1, col. 6. No formal adoption has been located for James.

In 1930 James and Loretta lived in San Francisco with Anna McCabe, a widowed aunt; Myrtle Caneo, a sister-in-law; and Frank and James Lindland, nephews. James owned the house valued at $8000 and a radio. James was an express messenger for Express Company. Loretta was a shipping clerk. They couple had no children.[53]

James G. Baldwin died 4 February 1938 at age 53 and was buried in Holy Cross Catholic Cemetery in San Mateo County, California.[54] At the time of his death his estate was valued at less than $5000. Loretta was the administratrix of his estate.[55] Loretta died in 1966 in San Francisco.[56] She is buried next to James; however, the joint tombstone does not have her name or birth/death information engraved on the stone.[57]

A summary of known information of the life of James G. Johnson/Baldwin which might help us identify James's birth parents follows:

---

[53] 1930 US. census, San Francisco County, California, population schedule, San Fransisco, Assembly District 28, ED 38-232, p. 3B, household 54, dwelling 58, James G. Baldwin.

[54] "California Death Index, 1905-1939," database with images, *FamilySearch* (https://familysearch.org/ark:/61903/3:1:33S7-81S5-4P3), 1930-1939 > Aabel, Arnold-Hetterman, John > image 84 of 819, James G Baldwin death entry (4 February 1938). Also "Baldwin," obituary, The San Francisco Examiner, 7 February 1938, p. 13, col 6.

[55] "Estates Filed for Probate-Baldwin," *The San Francisco Examiner*, 16 February 1938, p. 15, col. 5.

[56] "Social Security Death Index, 1935-2014," 556-09-9922, Loretta A. Baldwin.

[57] Find a Grave, database and images (https://www.findagrave.com/memorial/189858658/loretta_a-baldwin: accessed July 7, 2024), memorial page for Loretta A. Baldwin (29 Oct 1885–28 Jun 1966), Find a Grave Memorial ID 189858658, citing Holy Cross Catholic Cemetery, Colma, San Mateo County, California, USA; Maintained by Renee (contributor 48423945).

Figure 1- JGB
Name, location and Date of birth, foster parents and birth parents of James G. Johnson

	Name	Birth date	Birth location	Birth parents	Foster parents
1890	James Johnston[a]	1883			Perry O. Baldwin
1900	James G. Johnson[b]	Oct 1883	New York	b. New York	Perry Baldwin
1918	James Garfield Baldwin[c]	22 Oct 1884			Lavanche Baldwin
1920	James G. Baldwin[d]	1885	New York	b. Unknown	
1920	James Garfield Baldwin[e]	1885	New York, New York	P. O. Baldwin & Lavanche Woodward	
1921	James[f] [Baldwin]				Perry Baldwin
1930	James G. Baldwin[g]				
1937	James Garfield Baldwin[h]	22 Oct 1884	New York, New York	Perry Baldwin	
1938	James G. Baldwin[i]				

a. Kialy Carson, Kansas, [(curator@orphantraindepot.com),] to Jill Morelli, email, 7 March 2023, "Info from the CAS," OTR folder.
b. 1900 U.S. census, Merced, California, population schedule, Township 3, ED 47, P. 3, household 49, dwelling 50, Perry O. Baldwin.
c. "World War I Draft Registration Cards, 1917-1918," 12 September 1918, San Francisco, San Francisco County, California Local Board for Division 12, for James G. Baldwin.
d. 1920 US. Census, San Francisco County, California, population schedule, San Fransisco, Assembly District 28, ED 297, household 13, dwelling 14, James G. Baldwin in the household of James C. Rayburn.
e. "California, San Francisco County Records, 1824-1997," database with images, *FamilySearch* (https://familysearch.org/ark:/61903/3:1:33SQ-G56G-F2T), Marriages > Marriage Certificates, Vol. 49, 1920 > image 62 of 511, James G. Baldwin-Loretta A. McCabe marriage entry (26 July 1920).
f. Pioneer Resident Passes Away," *The Dos Palos Star (CA)*, p. 1, col. 6.
g. 1930 US. census, San Francisco County, California, population schedule, San Fransisco, Assembly District 28, ED 38-232, p. 3B, household 54, dwelling 58, James G. Baldwin.
h. Security Applications and Claims Index, 1936-2007," James Garfield Baldwin, SS#: 714101038.
i. "California Death Index, 1905-1939," database with images, *FamilySearch* (https://familysearch.org/ark:/61903/3:1:33S7-81S5-4P3), 1930-1939 > Aabel, Arnold-Hetterman, John > image 84 of 819, James G Baldwin death entry (4 February 1938).

The CAS recorded the name of James Johnston upon his arrival in Webster City, Iowa. The middle initial 'G' may have been added later by James to differentiate between same-named men. After the move to California James went by James Garfield Baldwin.

The birth parents of James Johnston Baldwin cannot be determined with extant records.

CONCLUSION

James Johnston, his probable birth name, was born 22 October 1883 or 1884 in New York City, New York. He arrived in the October delivery of children to Webster City, Iowa, and was fostered into the family of Perry O. Baldwin. In early 1895, the family moved to Merced, California with James and established a farm.

After his arrival in California, James used the name James G. Baldwin. Perry Baldwin identified James as an adopted son. It is not known if a formal adoption occurred or if it was an informal surname change.

James worked as an express messenger for companies that specialized in quick deliveries of goods. James, age 37, married Loretta McCabe in 1920. He died 4 February 1938, age 53, in San Francisco.

James Garfield (Johnson) Baldwin had no descendants. (*See* https://iowaorphans.wordpress.com for efforts to identify James's NYC parents.)

Harry Bittner

B. 13 November 1885, New York
D. 25 February 1900, Hamilton County, Iowa
Birth family: —?— Bittner
Foster Family: Hiram S. & Lucy Olmsted, then Charles H. & Harriet Young

Superintendent Trott recorded H. Olmstead as the recipient of an out-placed orphan in the 29 August 1890 delivery of children to Hamilton County.[58] Harry was
"one of those New York boys brought to Webster City with several other children about ten years ago [1890]."[59]

By 1892 Harry moved from the Olmstead family to the Charles H. Young family.[60] While the reason for this shift is not known, Hiram's wife Lucy died in 1891.[61] By 1900 Hiram and his new wife, also named Lucy, had moved to Calhoun County, Iowa.[62]

In 1895 Harry Bittner resided with the Young family, composed of Charles, age 68; apparent wife Harriet, age 59; two adult children; and Harry, age 9 and born in New York.[63]

Harry died on 25 February 1900, at age 14, of an unknown illness. He was described as "rugged and healthy" until he became sick a few days before

---

[58] "E. Trott of the children's aid society...," *The Freeman,* 3 September 1890, p. 5, col. 3.
[59] "Obituary," *Daily Freeman Tribune,* 28 February 1900, p. 8, col. 3.
[60] "Obituary," *Daily Freeman Tribune,* 28 February 1900, p. 8, col. 3.
[61] Find a Grave, database and images (https://www.findagrave.com/memorial/63203580/lucy-a-olmstead: accessed 01 February 2023), memorial page for Lucy A. Baker Olmstead (1828–28 Jul 1891), Find a Grave Memorial ID 63203580, citing Graceland Cemetery, Webster City, Hamilton County, Iowa, USA; Maintained by From the Heart (contributor 47715879).
[62] 1900 U.S. census, Calhoun County, Iowa, population schedule, Jackson, ED 24, p. 2, household 40, dwelling 42, Hiram S. Olmstead.
[63] 1895 State of Iowa census, Hamilton County, Iowa, population schedule, image 311 of 681, Harry Bittner in the household of Charles H. Young.

his death. He was baptized in the Baptist faith just five weeks before and was buried in the Homer Baptist Church cemetery. [64]

Harry Bittner did not assume the name of either of his foster parents and probably kept his birth name.

Figure 1-HB
Name, location and date of birth, foster and birth parents of Harry Bittner

	Name	Birth date	Birth location	Birth parents	Foster parents
1890					H. Olmstead[a]
1895	Harry Bitner[b]	1886	New York		Charles Young
1900	Harry Bittner[c]	13 Nov 1885	New York	b. Unknown	Charles Young

a. "E. Trott of the children's aid society…," *The Freeman*, 3 September 1890, p. 5, col. 3.
b. 1895 State of Iowa census, Hamilton County, Iowa, population schedule, image 311 of 681, Harry Bittner in the household of Charles H. Young.
b. "Obituary," *Daily Freeman Tribune*, 28 February 1900, p. 8, col. 3.

Harry Bittner was probably born in New York City on 13 November 1885. Candidates were investigated with no conclusion reached as to Harry's NYC parents.

CONCLUSION
Harry Bittner was born 13 November 1885 in New York City and came to Hamilton County in 1890. He was initially placed with the Hiram Olmstead family, but quickly moved to the Charles Young family. Harry died on 25 February 1900, in Hamilton County, Iowa, at age 14 of an unidentified illness.

(*See* https://iowaorphans.wordpress.com for efforts to identify Harry's NYC parents and any new information received.)

---

[64] "Obituary," *Daily Freeman Tribune*, 28 February 1900, p. 8, col. 3.

CHARLES ARTHUR (MULLER) BJUSTROM

B. 18 AUGUST 1884, NEW YORK CITY, NEW YORK
D. 12 AUGUST 1941, BOONE, BOONE COUNTY, IOWA
BIRTH FAMILY: —?— MULLER
FOSTER FAMILY: JOSEPH AND MATILDA (NELSON) BJUSTROM

Signature from WWI Draft Registration Card

Arthur Muller, age 6, arrived in Hamilton County in the October delivery of children and was placed with the Joseph Bjustrom family of Stratford.[65] In 1895 nine year-old Arthur Bjustrom resided with Joseph and Mathilda Bjustrom.[66] By 1900 Arthur was a farm laborer on the Bjustrom farm and was enumerated as Joseph and Mathilda's son. Arthur could read and write, but had not attended school the past year as he was required to do. The Bjustroms had been married for 12 years with no biological children.[67]

Arthur's interest in photography was sparked by the time he was a young man. In 1905 Joseph, Mathilda and Arthur attended the anniversary gathering of Mathilda's grandparents. Special note was made that Arthur took photos of the attendees.[68]

In April 1902, Joseph sold the farm in Hamilton County for $2,200 and the family moved to Webster City.[69] By 1910, Arthur was described as a stepson. He was a tile ditcher, operating the machinery that digs the

---

[65] Kialy Carson, Kansas, [(CURATOR@ORPHANTRAINDEPOT.COM),] to Jill Morelli, email, 7 March 2023, "Info from the CAS," OTR folder.

[66] 1895 State of Iowa census, Hamilton County, Iowa, population schedule, image 530 of 681, Charles Bjustrom in the household of Joseph Bjustrom.

[67] 1900 U.S. census, Hamilton County, Iowa, population schedule, Marian Township, ED 112, p. 10, household 208, dwelling 213, Arthur Bjustrom in the household of Joseph Bjustrom.

[68] "Marian," *Daily Freeman Tribune*, 11 July 1905, p. 4, col. 3.

[69] "Real Estate Transfers," *Daily Freeman Tribune,* 9 April 1902, p. 8, col 3. Property was described as "se qr ne qr 34-24-86," or the southeast quarter of the north east quarter, section 34, township 24, principal meridian.

trenches within which to lay drainage tile. He was out of work and had been unemployed for 12 weeks.[70]

Probably to avoid confusion with another Arthur Bjustrom in the area of approximately the same age, Arthur assumed the name of Charles as his given name.

In 1915 Charles A. Bjustrom, age 29, stated he was born in New York, but his parents were born in Iowa, obviously referring to his foster parents. He came to the state in 1891, and had 3 years of common school. Charles was a photographer with earnings of $300, but had been out of work for four months in 1914.[71]

By September 1917 Charles Arthur Bjustrom had given up on his love of photography and was a molder at the Quinn Wire and Iron Works in Boone, Iowa.[72] The Quinn Wire and Iron Works manufactured automatic hog and poultry waterers, calf weaners, and chimney tops.[73] Charles was one of 174 Boone County men who were classified as 1-A for the draft.[74] He did not serve.[75]

Charles A. Bjustrom married Lucy (Allison) Hayes, her second marriage, on 28 January 1919 in Boone County, Iowa.[76] One year later Charles and Lucy rented their home at 522 Story Street in Boone. Lucy's son, Isaac, from her first marriage lived with them. Charles was a brakeman on a steam railroad; Lucy was a waitress in a restaurant; and Isaac worked as a messenger for a telegraph office.[77]

---

[70] 1910 U.S. census, Webster County, Iowa, population schedule, Hardin Township, ED 208, p. 7A, household 129, dwelling 129, Arthur Bjustrom in the household of Joseph Bjustrom.

[71] 1915 State of Iowa census, Hamilton County, Iowa, population schedule, card no. 127, Charles A. Bjustrom.

[72] "U.S. World War I draft registration cards, 1917-1918," Local Board of Boone County, Boone, Iowa, serial no. 3516, Charles Arthur Bjustrom.

[73] *Boone County City Directory, 1940* (Boone, Iowa : Keiter Directory Company, 1940) p. 2.

[74] "Part of Class One Men Given in Long List," *Boone News-Republican (Boone, Boone County),* 24 October 1918, p. 2, col. 3.

[75] 1930 U.S. census, Boone County, Iowa population schedule, Boone, ED 8-14, p. 11A, household 260, dwelling 265, Chas. A. Bjustrom.

[76] "Iowa, U.S. Marriage Records, 1880-1951," vol. 478, Boone County, entry 9540, Charles A. Bjustrom-Lucy (Allison) Hayes marriage entry (28 January 1919).

[77] 1920 U.S. census, Boone County, Iowa, population schedule, Boone, Ward 2, ED 8, p. 3A, household 18, dwelling 32, Charles A. Bjustrom.

Joseph, Matilda's husband, abandoned her and in 1921 Mathilda filed for divorce. The couple had married in 1888. Because of his assets, Matilda applied for alimony of a fixed amount of $1500.[78] She was granted a divorce in October 1921.[79] How this affected Charles is not known, but undoubtedly there was unsettlement in the home prior to the formal decree issued by the court.

By December 1920 Charles and Lucy lived in Kossuth County, Iowa, but this must have been a short stay, because by 1925 Charles and Lucy had purchased a home at 1727 Monona Street in Boone. Again, his parents were recorded as Joseph and Matilda Bjustrom.[80]

In November 1921 Lucy was diagnosed with diphtheria and the members of the household were quarantined. The doctors said the outbreak was waning.[81]

Just five years later, Charles and Lucy owned their own home at 1727 Monona Street with a radio, an indicator of wealth. Isaac, his wife, and their two children lived with the couple. Charles was a laborer; Lucy was a charwoman in private homes; and Isaac was a laborer on road crews.[82]

Joseph Bjustrom died April 1926.[83] His probate documents did not mention his foster son, Charles.

As the country came out of the Depression, Charles and Lucy continued living on Monona Street. Charles, a laborer who did interior cleaning, had no earned income, but had worked 42 hours the previous month. Charles also had other unidentified income. Matilda, described as "mother" to Charles, lived with Charles and Lucy. Neither Lucy nor Matilda worked outside the home.[84]

---

[78] "Wants Alimony with Divorce from Courts," *Boone County Pioneer*, 17 August 1921, p. 2, col. 1.

[79] "Default Divorces," *Boone News-Reppublican,* 19 October 1921, p. 1, col 4.

[80] For Kossuth County: "Personal and Brief," *Boone News-Republican*, 6 December 1920, p. 6, col. 4. Also, 1925 Iowa state census, Boone County, Iowa, population schedule, Boone, Chas. A. Bzustrom..

[81] "Quarantined," *Boone News-Republican*, 3 November 1921, p. 6, col. 5.

[82] 1930 U.S. census, Boone County, Iowa population schedule, Boone, ED 8-14, p. 11A, household 260, dwelling 265, Chas. A. Bjustrom.

[83] "Iowa, U.S. Death Records 1880-1972," certificate 40-844, Joseph Bjustrom.

[84] 1940 U.S. census, Boone County, Iowa, population schedule, Boone, Ward 2, ED 8-14, p. 1B, household 14, Chas. Byustrogs. Charles was the informant.

Charles Arthur Bjustrom suffered a heart attack and died on 12 August 1941 in Boone. His wife Lucy, the informant, provided the information that Charles was born 18 August 1885 in New York City, New York. His parents were recorded as his foster parents, Joseph and Matilda.[85] Lucy died in 1961 and the two share a tombstone in Rose Hill Cemetery in Boone where Charles is engraved as Arthur Bjustrom. [86]

---

[85] "Iowa, U.S. Death Records 1920-1967," certificate 8C-102, Charles Arthur Bjustrom.

[86] *Find a Grave*, database and images (https://www.findagrave.com/memorial/38925429/lucy_ann-bjustrom: accessed June 26, 2024), memorial page for Lucy Ann Allison Bjustrom (1885–1961), Find a Grave Memorial ID 38925429, citing Rose Hill Cemetery, Boone, Boone County, Iowa, USA; Maintained by Cathy (contributor 47100569).

Only at the time of arrival in 1890, did Charles or any of his family members identify his birth parents as "Muller." A summary of all known information that relates to his life before Hamilton County follows:

Figure 1-CAB
Name, location and date of birth, foster and birth parents
of Charles Arthur (Muller) Bjustrom

	Name	Birth date	Birth location	Birth parents	Foster parents
1890	Arthur Muller[a]	1884			Joseph Bjustrom
1895	Arthur Bjustrom[b]	1885	New York		Joseph Bjustrom
1900	Arthur Bjustrom[c]	Aug 1886	New York	b. Unknown	Joseph Bjustrom
1915	Charles A. Bjustrom[d]	1886	New York	b. Iowa	
1917	Charles Arthur Bjustrom[e]	18 Aug 1885			Nearest relative: Matilda Bjustrom
1919	Charles A. Bjustrom[f]	1884	New York City	Joseph & Matilda (Nelson) Bjustrom	
1920	Charles A. Bjustrom[g]	1886	New York	b. Unknown	
1925	Chas. A. Bjustrom[h]	1886	New York	Joe Bjustrom & Matilda Nelson, b. Sweden, b. Iowa	
1930	Chas. A. Bjustrom[i]	1886	Unknown	b. Unknown	
1940	Chas. Bjustrom[j]	1886	New York		
1941	Charles Arthur Bjustrom[k]	18 Aug 1885	Nw York, New York	Joseph & Matilda (Nelson) Bjustrom	

a. Kialy Carson, Kansas, [(CURATOR@ORPHANTRAINDEPOT.COM),] to Jill Morelli, email, 7 March 2023, "Info from the CAS,"[(ARCHIVIST@CHILDRENSAIDNYC.ORG)] of the CAS to the Depot, OTR folder.
b. 1895 State of Iowa census, Hamilton County, Iowa, population schedule, image 530 of 681, Charles Bjustrom.
c. 1900 U.S. census, Hamilton County, Iowa, population schedule, Marian Township, ED 112, p. 10, household 208, dwelling 213, Arthur Bjustrom.
d. 1915 State of Iowa census, Hamilton County, Iowa, population schedule, card no. 127, Charles A. Bjustrom.
e. U.S. World War I draft registration cards, 1917-1918," Local Board of Boone County, Boone, Iowa, serial no. 3516, Charles Arthur Bjustrom.
f. "Iowa, U.S. Marriage Records, 1880-1951," vol. 478, Boone County, entry 9540, Charles A. Bjustrom-Lucy (Allison) Hayes marriage entry (28 January 1919).
g. 1920 U.S. census, Boone County, Iowa, population schedule, Boone, Ward 2, ED 8, p. 3A, household 18, dwelling 32, Charles A. Bjustrom.
h. 1925 Iowa state census, Boone County, Iowa, population schedule, Boone, Chas. A. Bjustrom.
i. 1930 U.S. census, Boone County, Iowa population schedule, Boone, ED 8-14, p. 11A, household 260, dwelling 265, Chas. A. Bjustrom.
j. 1940 U.S. census, Boone County, Iowa, population schedule, Boone, Ward 2, ED 8-14, p. 1B, household 14, Chas. Byustrogs.
k. "Iowa, U.S. Death Records 1920-1967," certificate 8C-102, Charles Arthur Bjustrom.

Charles knew he was born in New York City, but never indicated that he knew the names of his New York parents or their birth location. The CAS provided his New York City name and age at the time of his arrival. When given the opportunity to identify his birth parents, Charles consistently indicated that his parents were unknown or named his foster parents. There was obviously a close relationship between Charles and his foster parents.

Arthur was probably his given name at birth.

CONCLUSION

Arthur Muller, age 6, arrived in Hamilton County in the October delivery of children and was placed with the Joseph Bjustrom family of Stratford.

Arthur "Charles" Bjustrom married Lucy (Allison) Hayes (her second marriage) on 28 January 1919, in Boone County, Iowa. Lucy's son Isaac lived with the couple but Charles and Lucy had no children of their own. Charles Arthur Bjustrom died of a heart attack on 12 August 1941 in Boone.

With no descendants, DNA will not help to identify his birth parents. (*See* https://iowaorphans.wordpress.com for efforts to identify Charles's New York City parents and for any new information.)

GEORGE BRECKFELDT

B. 29 JUNE 1885, NEW YORK CITY, NEW YORK
D. 28 NOVEMBER 1921, CHEROKEE, CHEROKEE COUNTY, IOWA
BIRTH FAMILY: GEORGE & MARY (CUSICK) BRECKFELDT
FOSTER FAMILY: OLAF F. AND EVA ANGSTROM

Signature from WWI Draft Registration Card

George Breckfeldt was abandoned at birth:
> George Breckfeldt was born in the Children's Home in New York City June 29[,] 1885…He lived at the home until Nov. 20, 1890 at which time he was adopted by Mr. and Mrs. O. F. Angstrom.[87]

Although George Breckfeldt was not enumerated with the Angstrom family in 1895, by 1900 George resided in Stratford in the household of Olaf and Eva Angstrom and their son, Benjamin. George was born January 1886 in New York, and identified as a "son."[88] No record of a formal adoption of George exists.

---

[87] "George Breckfeldt Passes Away Monday at Cherokee," *Stratford Courier [Iowa]*, 1 December 1921, p. 1, col. 6. Also, N. Y., N. Y., U. S., Index to Birth Certificates, 1866-1909. Certificate no. 430717, George Brckfeldt birth entry (29 June 1885).

[88] 1895 Iowa State census, Hamilton County, Iowa; population schedule, image 546 of 681, Olaf Angstrom. And, 1900 U. S. census, Hamilton County, Iowa, population schedule, Stratford, ED 112, p. 4, household 97, dwelling 99, George Breckfeldt in the household of Olaf Angstrom.

In 1910 24 year-old George was recorded as "George Angstrom, son" of Olaf and Eva Angstrom. George was born in New York to unknown parents. He worked in a restaurant as a waiter.[89]

George married between 1910 and 1914 then was quickly divorced by Rosa Breckfeldt, birth name unknown, for "cruelty and inhuman treatment." The divorce was granted on 24 September 1914 in Story County, Iowa.[90] No record of the marriage has been found.[91]

By 1915 George, a laborer, resided in Cambridge, Story County, Iowa. He was 29 years old and had been in Iowa for 24 years. His father was born in the United States and George did not know the location of birth of his mother. George was not married.[92] Arriving in Iowa when he was five years old places his year of arrival as 1890, confirming his status as a member of the Hamilton County cohort.

One year later, George considered opening a restaurant in Spencer, Nebraska, but couldn't find a suitable location and returned to Stratford.[93] That same year, he started a lunch room called the Busy Bee, "in the building one door down from the meat market" in Stratford. He had managed a similar operation the previous winter. George remodeled the interior with a counter built across the space to provide more eating area, and created a "neat and up-to-date lunchroom."[94]

George's entrepreneurial entry into business didn't last long. In the early morning on 25 February 1917, a fire started in downtown Stratford. Three buildings were burned to the ground, including the one occupied by the Busy Bee. The fire was first spotted in the barber shop. Unfortunately, the town's fire alarm did not work. George estimated the loss to his interior

---

[89] 1910 U.S. census, Hamilton County, Iowa Population schedule, Marion, ED 121, household 77, dwelling 81, George Angstrom in the household of Olaf F. Angstrom.

[90] "Record for the Divorces of Story County [Iowa], for the fiscal year ending June 30, 1915," p. 114, case no. 9271, George Breckfeldt vs. Rosa Breckfeldt, effective 24 September 1914.

[91] Searched for a marriage of George Breckfeldt and Rosa —?—, prior to September 1914 was conducted in Ancestry, FamilySearch and the newspapers of Story and Hamilton County, Iowa. No findings reported.

[92] 1915 Iowa state census, Story County, Iowa, population schedule, Cambridge, card no. 271, George Brecffeldt.

[93] "Local Items," *Stratford Courier*, 14 September 1916, p. 3, col. 2. The location is probably in error and should be Spencer, Iowa.

[94] "New Lunchroom is now in Operation," *Stratford Courier,* 26 October 1916, p. 1, col. 4.

furnishings was $500, $300 of which was covered by insurance. While others found temporary locations for their businesses, George had no other place to reestablish his business and no way to furnish it.[95] By June 1919, George left the restaurant business and found work as a cook for the Northwestern railroad bridge crew.[96]

George registered for the draft on 12 September 1917, stated his birth date was 25 June 1885, and identified Olaf Angstrom as the person to notify. George was now a farmer working with Olaf.[97]

In late 1919, with an obvious desire to run his own business and the completion of the railway bridge, George resigned his position with the Northwestern bridge crew and purchased an existing vacant restaurant in Dayton, Iowa. The newspaper reported that George was an experienced short-order cook, and it was anticipated that he would bring his skills to Dayton in a positive way.[98] George moved to Dayton and lived alone, but declared he was married.[99]

In 1920 Olaf and Eva managed a "hostelry" in Stratford, which provided room and board for its customers. The restaurant closed immediately after World War I due a shortage of fuel. The Angstroms decided to take an extended vacation that summer and left the management of the hotel to George.[100] George continued to describe himself as married, yet no wife resided with him.[101]

After a lingering illness and admission to the Cherokee Hospital in Cherokee County, Iowa, George Breckfeldt, age 36, died on 28 November 1921, of general paresis, progressive dementia, or paralysis that in the past was associated with syphilis. George was the informant upon admission. The record indicates he was married (name of wife not stated), a common

---

[95] "Three Business Buildings Destroyed by Flames" *Stratford Courier*, 1 March 1917, p. 1, cols. 3 & 4.

[96] "Local Happenings," *Stratford Courier*, 19 June 1919, p. 3, col 3.

[97] "U.S. World War I draft registration cards, 1917-1918," Local Board of Hamilton County, Webster City, Iowa, serial no. 2146, George Breckfeldt.

[98] " New Highway Overhead Bridge is Completed," and "Has Purchased a Restaurant in Dayton," *Stratford Courier*, 27 November 1919, p. 1, col. 4.

[99] 1920 U.S. census, Webster County, Iowa, population schedule, Dayton, ED 224, p. 3B, household 68, dwelling 68, George Breckfeldt.

[100] "Hotel Quits Services Meals on Account of a Shortage of Fuel," *Stratford Courier*, 3 June 1920, p. 1 col. 2.

[101] 1920 U.S. census, Webster County, Iowa, population schedule, Dayton, ED 224, p. 3B, household 68, dwelling 68, George Breckfeldt.

laborer, and born in New York. His parents were unknown.[102] His death came as a shock to the Stratford community. "George had a sunny disposition and was friendly to all."[103]

◈

Because he kept his New York name and his birth date was consistent, George represents one of a few orphans whose parents can be identified using documentary evidence.

Figure 1-GB
Birth Return for George Brchfeldt, b. 29 June 1885[104]

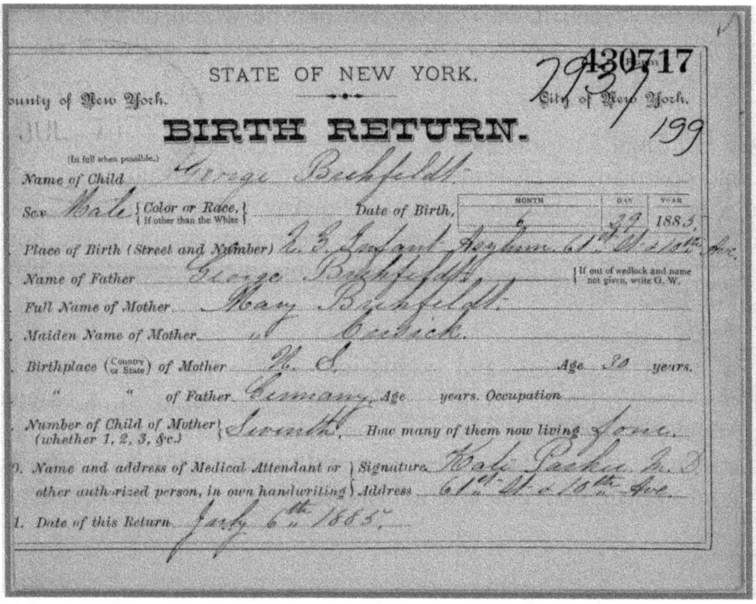
430717 7937
STATE OF NEW YORK.
County of New York. City of New York.
BIRTH RETURN. 199
Name of Child (In full when possible.) George Brchfeldt
Sex Male Color or Race, (If other than the White) Date of Birth, Month 6 Day 29 Year 1885
Place of Birth (Street and Number) U. S. Infant Asylum 61st St & 10th Ave
Name of Father George Brchfeldt (If out of wedlock and name not given, write O. W.)
Full Name of Mother Mary Brchfeldt
Maiden Name of Mother Cusick
Birthplace (Country or State) of Mother U. S. Age 30 years.
" " of Father Germany Age years. Occupation
Number of Child of Mother (whether 1, 2, 3, &c.) Seventh How many of them now living Three
Name and address of Medical Attendant or other authorized person, in own handwriting Signature Kate Parker M. D. Address 61st St & 10th Ave
Date of this Return July 6th 1885

George was born to George and Mary (Cusick) Breckfeldt and was Mary's seventh child, three of which were still living. Mary gave birth at the New

---

[102] "Iowa Death Records, 1904-1951," original standard Certificate of Death, certificate no. 18-083, George Breckfeldt death certificate (28 November 1941).

[103] "George Breckfeldt Passes Away Monday at Cherokee," *Stratford Courier*, 1 December 1921, p. 1, col. 6.

[104] Ibid.

York Infant Asylum at 61st and 10th Avenue on 29 June 1885. She was 30 years old, born 1855 in the United States.[105]

The economic situation of the Breckfeldt family may have led George and Mary to leave the infant George with the orphanage and ultimately release him to be fostered into a farm family in the Midwest. Another document supports this motivation.

Figure 2-GB

Record of Inmates, Kings County Alms House: Mary Breakfeld[106]

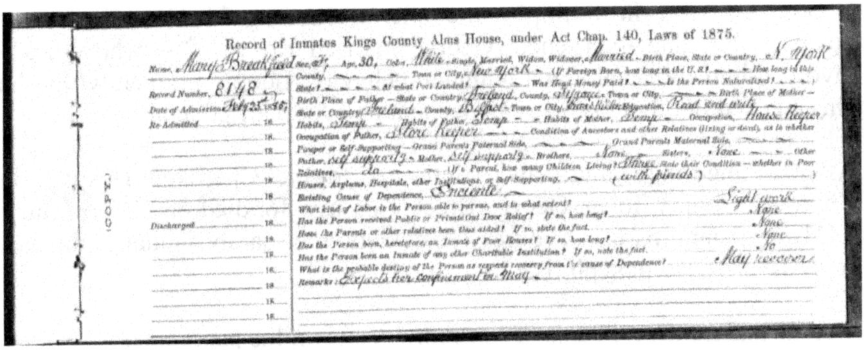
Record of Inmates Kings County Alms House, under Act Chap. 140, Laws of 1875.

Name, Mary Breakfield Sex, F, Age, 30, Color, White, Single, Married, Widow, Widower, Married. Birth Place, State or Country, N. York

County, Town or City, New York (If Foreign Born, how long in the U. S.? How long in this State? At what Port Landed? Was Head Money Paid? Is the Person Naturalized?)

Record Number, 8148

Date of Admission, Feb 25 1885

Re-Admitted 18

Birth Place of Father — State or Country, Ireland, County, Tyrone, Town or City. Birth Place of Mother — State or Country, Ireland, County, Belfast, Town or City. Education, Read and write

Habits, Temp. Habits of Father, Temp. Habits of Mother, Temp. Occupation, House Keeper

Occupation of Father, Store Keeper. Condition of Ancestors and other Relatives (living or dead), as to whether Pauper or Self-Supporting — Grand Parents Paternal Side, Grand Parents Maternal Side, Father, self supporting, Mother, self supporting, Brothers, None, Sisters, None, Other Relatives, do. (If a Parent, how many Children Living? Three. State their Condition — whether in Poor Houses, Asylums, Hospitals, other Institutions, or Self-Supporting. (with friends))

Existing Cause of Dependence, Enceinte

What kind of Labor is the Person able to pursue, and to what extent? Light work

Has the Person received Public or Private Out Door Relief? If so, how long? None

Have the Parents or other relatives been thus aided? If so, state the fact. None

Has the Person been, heretofore, an Inmate of Poor Houses? If so, how long? None

Has the Person been an Inmate of any other Charitable Institution? If so, note the fact. No

What is the probable destiny of the Person as regards recovery from the cause of Dependence? May recover

Remarks: Expects her confinement in May

Discharged 18

Mary completed her pregnancy in the Kings County Alms House, before giving birth in the Infant Asylum.

George's birth certificate and the Mary's Record of Inmates in the Alms House align the name, marital status, birth year, and location of the mother. The mother declared she had three children, which if Gorge is added to the total makes four as recorded on the birth record. Mary entered the almshouse in February 1885 with an expected delivery of a child in May. George was born in early June. Little is asked about the father of the child, but Mary's parents were born in Ireland.

The Breckfeldt/Cusick family has not been found in subsequent censuses or indexes for birth, marriage, or death.

---

105 New York City Municipal Archives, "Historical Vital Records," Birth Return, certificate no. 430717, George Brckfeldt birth entry (29 June 1885).

106 "New York, U.S., Census of Inmates in Almshouses and Poorhouses, 1830-1920, Kings County, New York, 1885, image 159 of 760, record no. 8148, Mary Breakfeld.

CONCLUSION

George Breckfeldt was born 29 June 1885 at the Infant Asylum at 61st Street & 10th Avenue in New York City, New York. His parents were the married couple, George Breckfeldt, the German shopkeeper and Mary (Cusick) Breckfeldt, age 30, born in the United States. George was Mary's seventh child, but only four, counting George, were still living.

George and Mary released George to the CAS to travel to the Midwest. In 1890 he arrived in Hamilton County and was fostered into the Angstrom family.

George engaged in multiple attempts at running his own restaurant business, but fate intervened. George married Rosa —?— who quickly divorced him for cruelty and inhuman behavior. George frequently said he was married but there is no evidence that he ever married again.

After a lingering illness and admission to the Cherokee Hospital in Cherokee County, Iowa, George Breckfeldt, age 36, died on 28 November 1921, of general paresis, progressive dementia, or paralysis that in the past was associated with syphilis.

George had no descendants; DNA cannot confirm his parentage.

John Bodger Bringolf

B. 4 May 1887 in New York
D. 14 November 1945, Long Beach, California
Birth Family: —?— Bodger
Foster Family: Philip Morris then William and Clara Bringolf

WWII Draft Registration Card

John Bodger, age 4, arrived in Hamilton County in the October delivery of children. He was initially placed with the Philip Morris family of Webster City.[107] No subsequent record places John with the Morris family.[108] Between 1890 and 1895, John moved to the William H. And Clara Bringolf family.[109]

During his early years, John had multiple run-ins with the law. As a teenager, he stole a watch and chain and sold it for $1.25. He confessed and the watch was returned to its owner. It was felt that "a term in the reform school might do Johnnie some good." This was not the first incident with the law that Bringolf had experienced.[110] John was sent to the Eldora Training School for Boys in Eldora, Iowa.[111]

William Bringolf circulated a petition requesting the governor release John, because he deemed the trial unfair. The arresting officers and many

---

[107] Kialy Carson, Kansas, [(CURATOR@ORPHANTRAINDEPOT.COM),] to Jill Morelli, email, 7 March 2023, "Info from the CAS,"OTR folder.

[108] Both the 1895 and 1900 censuses were searched.

[109] 1895 State of Iowa census, Hamilton County, Iowa, population schedule, image 42 of 681, John Bringolf in the household of William Bringolf. For Clara's birth name, Iowa, U.S., Marriage Records, 1880-1945, 1881 > 302 (Dubuque-Henry), Return of Marriages in the County of Hamilton, fiscal year ending, 1 October 1881, p. 40-432, Bringolf marriage entry (4 October 1881).

[110] "Young Bringolf, the adopted son...," *Webster City Freeman*, 11 September 1895, p. 6, col 2.

[111] "Personal and Social Gossip," *Webster City Freeman*, 22 November 1895, p. 6, col. 6.

townspeople signed the petition encouraging the release.[112] The governor granted John Bringolf a pardon in February 1896.[113] In 1904 John was charged with stealing a revolver. A jury trial was held, and he was acquitted.[114] In August of 1914, John, having taken a load of grain into Webster City for sale for his foster father, engaged in a poker game with two other young men from the community and lost all the money. The two young men stated they did not play poker and instead were holding money for John. William filed with the court forcing the issue; the court outcome was not apparent.[115] But, the boys returned the money. William had choices; he chose to advocate for his foster child, John.

Throughout this time, John lived with the Bringolfs. By 1900, William and Clara had been married 18 years, and Clara had given birth to no children.[116]

As a young man, John participated in the life of the county. He played on the amateur "Golden Eagles" baseball team and received special mention for his hits against the Metropolitans. The Golden Eagles still lost 7 to 5.[117]

John and the Bringolf family began a series of moves over the next twenty years. By 1910 John and the William Bringolfs had left Hamilton County and moved to Twin Lake, Carlton County, Minnesota, where the family farmed. William owned the farm with a mortgage.[118] On 4 August 1914, John Bodger Bringolf married Emma Marie Angell in Carlton County.[119]

By 1915 John and his wife had moved back to Hamilton County, doing general farm labor. The enumerator noted "This man was adopted."[120] Just two years later, John Bodger Bringolf, registered for the draft in

---

[112] "Webster City Warblings," *Saturday Mail*, 7 December 1895, p. 1, col 5

[113] "John Bringolf Pardoned," *Webster City Freeman*, 5 February 1901, p. 5, col. 7.

[114] "John Bringolf charged...," *Daily Freeman Tribune*, 26 January 1904, p. 8, col 2.

[115] "Gambling Case in Police Court," *Daily Freeman Tribune*, 3 January 1914, p. 5, col. 5. Criminal records are not extant in Hamilton County and Bringolf was not mentioned in the civil cases of the county.

[116] 1900 U.S. census, Hamilton County, Iowa, population schedule, Independence, ED 101, p. 10, household 216, dwelling 221, John Bringolf in the household of William Bringolf.

[117] "Our professional ball team...," *Daily Freeman Tribune*, 20 August 1901, p. 5, col 2.

[118] 1910 U.S. census, Carlton County, Minnesota, population schedule, Twin Lake, ED 35, p. 7B, household 152, dwelling 157, William Bringolf.

[119] Carlton County, Minnesota, marriage license and certificate, certificate G-215, John Bodger Bringoth-Emma Marie Angell marriage entry (4 August 1914); Carlton County Recorder, Carlton County, Minnesota.

[120] "Iowa, U.S. census collection, 1836-1925," 1915, Hamilton County, Fremont Township, card no. 377, John B. Bringolf.

Yellowstone, Montana.[121] By 1922 John and family had moved back to Hamilton County, next door to his foster father, and stayed until after the spring of 1926.[122]

Between 1926 and 1930, John and fthe amily moved again, this time to Wichita, Sedgwick County, Kansas, where they rented a house for $16 a month. John was a laborer doing odd jobs.[123] They continued their residence there for the next ten years. The economic condition of the family seemed to improve during this time. In spite of having gone through the Depression, John now owned his own home valued at $1000, which they purchased prior to 1935. By 1940 William lived with John, Emma and their four children in Wichita. All members of the family had earned income, and William had additional income to contribute.[124]

In 1942 John registered for the World War II draft, and declared his birth date and place as 4 May 1886, New York City.[125]

The family had one move left. In 1944 John and Emma moved to Long Beach, California, probably to live near their daughter, Ida Louise.[126] On 14 November 1945, John died in Long Beach, survived by his wife, a daughter, and three sons.[127]

---

[121] U.S., WWI Draft Registration Cards, 1917-1918," 12 September 1917, Montana, Yellowstone, serial no. 527, John Bodger Bringolf.

[122] 1940 U.S. census, Sedgwick County, Kansas, Wichita, ED 107-67, p. 5A, household 109, John Bringolf. The timing of the move to Montana is based on the location of birth of the two children born in the state. Iowa entry year is based on the birth of the third and fourth children in Iowa. For residence location, 1925 Iowa state census, Hamilton County, Iowa, population schedule, Marian Township, lines 83-88, John Bringolf.

[123] 1930 U.S. census, Sedgwick County, Kansas, population schedule, Wichita, Kansas, ED 42, p. 21A, household 256, dwelling 527, John Bringolf.

[124] 1940 U.S. census, Sedgwick County, Kansas, Wichita, ED 107-67, p. 5A, household 109, John Bringolf.

[125] U.S., WWII Draft Registration cards, 1942," Kansas, Beene, John-Brockway, Howard, serial no. 1307, John Bodger Bringolf.

[126] U.S., WWII Draft Registration cards, 1942," Kansas, Beene, John-Brockway, Howard, serial no. 1307, John Bodger Bringolf. Ida Louise Bringolf of Los Angeles, "daughter" was relative who would know his location.

[127] "Get Word of Death," *The Wichita Eagle (Wichita, Kansas)*, 15 November 1945, p. 6 col. 8. Also, California, U.S., Death Index, 1940-1997, Los Angeles, John B. Bringolf death entry (14 November 1944).

John's New York name was Bodger or some variation. Lending credence to the surname, Bodger also appeared in the names of two of John and Emma's children:

- Clarence Bodger Bringolf, born 7 September 1919;[128]
- Charles Wesley Bodger Bringolf, born 24 September 1921.[129]

Multiple documents indicate birth dates and locations of John and his New York City parents.

Figure 1-JBB
Name, location and date of birth, foster and birth parents
Of John (Bodger) Bringolf

	Name	Birth date	Birth location	Birth parents	Foster parents
1890	John Bodger[a]	1886		—?— Bodger	Philip Morris
1895	John Bringolf[b]	1887	New York		William Bringolf
1900	John Bringolf[c]	May 1887	New York	b. England; b. England	William Bringolf
1910	John B. Bringolf[d]	1887	New York	b. Ireland; b. England	William Bringolf
1914	John Bodger Bringolf[e]				
1915	John B. Bringolfd[f]	1887	New York		
1925	John Bringolf[g]	1886	New York	Bodger, b. Ireland; b. England	
1930	John B. Bringolf[h]	1887	New York	b. US; b. US	
1940	John Bringolf[i]	1887	New York	William Bringolf	
1942	John Bodger Bringolf[j]	4 May 1886	New York City, NY		

---

[128] "Montana, U.S. Birth Records 1897-1988," Yellowstone, Yellowstone County, Montana > Delayed Births, Standard Certificate of Live Birth, file no. 5319, Clarence Bodger Bringolf birth (7 September 1919).

[129] "Iowa, U.S., Births (series) 1880-1904, 1921-1944 and Delayed Births (series), 1856-1940," >birth Records > Hamilton County > 1921-1930, no. 40-088, Charles Weley Bodger Bringoff; image, Ancestry (https://www.ancestry.com : accessed 21 December 2022).

a. Kialy Carson, Kansas, [(CURATOR@ORPHANTRAINDEPOT.COM),] to Jill Morelli, email, 7 March 2023, "Info from the CAS," OTR folder.
b. 1895 State of Iowa census, Hamilton County, Iowa, population schedule, image 42 of 681, John Bringolf in the household of William Bringolf.
c. 1900 U.S. census, Hamilton County, Iowa, population schedule, Independence, ED 101, p. 10, household 216, dwelling 221, John Bringolf in the household of William Bringolf.
d. 1910 U.S. census, Carlton County, Minnesota, population schedule, Twin Lake, ED 35, p. 7B, household 152, dwelling 157, William Bringolf.
e. Carlton County, Minnesota, marriage license and certificate, certificate G-215, John Bodger Bringoth-Emma Marie Angell marriage entry (4 August 1914); Carlton County Recorder, Carlton County, Minnesota.
f. "Iowa, U.S. census collection, 1836-1925," 1915, Hamilton County, Fremont Township, card no. 377, John B. Bringolf.
g. 1925 Iowa state census, Hamilton County, Iowa, population schedule, Marian Township, lines 83-88, John Bringolf.
h. 1930 U.S. census, Sedgwick County, Kansas, population schedule, Wichita, Kansas, ED 42, p. 21A, household 256, dwelling 527, John Bringolf.
i. 1940 U.S. census, Sedgwick County, Kansas, Wichita, ED 107-67, p. 5A, household 109, John Bringolf.
j. U.S., WWII Draft Registration cards, 1942," Kansas, Beene, John-Brockway, Howard, serial no. 1307, John Bodger Bringolf

The names of John Bodger Bringolf's NYC parents were not identified.

CONCLUSION

John Bodger Bringolf was born 4 May 1886, in New York City. His parents are unknown, but their surname was Bodger or some variation. John arrived in Hamilton County, Iowa, in the October 1890 delivery of children from New York City. He was initially assigned to the Philip Morris family, but moved to join William and Clara Bringolf. John married Emma Angell on 4 August 1904, in Carlton County, Minnesota.

The couple had four children: Ida Louise, Clarence B., Charles W. and Merlyne G. Bringolf. John died 14 November 1945, in Long Beach, California.

DNA may assist the identification of the parents of John.
(*See* https://iowaorphans.wordpress.com for efforts to identify John's NYC parents.)

John Henry (Murtha) Burnett

B. 8 June 1883 in Manhattan, New York
D. 6 November 1957, Dallas Center, Dallas County, Iowa
Birth Family: Patrick & Emily (Lee) Murtha
Foster Family: John & Mary Burnett

Image from "John H. Burnett Dies; Hold Rites," *Dallas Center Times*, 14 November 1957; courtesy of Dallas Center Public Library

Signature from WWII draft Registration card

John Murtha, age 7, arrived in Hamilton County in the October delivery of children and fostered into the John Burnett family of Stanhope.[130]

In January 1892 John's foster father sold their farm.[131] By March of that same year, John had loaded his remaining farm implements and household goods with the intent to move to the southwestern part of Iowa.[132] Instead, the Burnett family, with John Murtha Burnett, moved to Jacksonville,

---

[130] Kialy Carson, Kansas, [(CURATOR@ORPHANTRAINDEPOT.COM),] to Jill Morelli, email, 7 March 2023, "Info from the CAS," OTR folder.

[131] "Real Estate Transfers," *Webster City Freeman*, 27 January 1892, p. 5, col. 8.

[132] "Stanhope," *Webster City Tribune*, 4 March 1892, p. 4, col 1.

Randolph County, Missouri.[133] By 1900 John was a farmer on a mortgaged farm and "Johnny," age 17, attended school.[134]

John M. Burnett married Eva Butler, both of Huntsville, Randolph County, Missouri, on 28 July 1904 at Macon, Macon County, Missouri. Both were under the age of majority, requiring that their fathers give their consent to marry.[135]

The young Burnett family moved to Dallas Center, Iowa, in August of 1908.[136] By 1910 Eva had given birth to two children, but neither survived. John was a salesman for a lumber yard. The family owned their home free of mortgage.[137]

By 1920 the family included two sons, John M., age 9, and M. Burton, age 7, both born in Iowa. John was the manager of a grain elevator.[138] During this time, John appeared to have obtained information concerning the name of his birth mother. In 1925 he declared he was born in New York in 1894. His father's name and where he was born was unknown; but his mother was Emily Lee or Fee who was born in England.[139]

In 1930 Eva's mother, Fannie M. Butler, lived with John, Eva, and their two sons. John was a buyer of grain, born in New York, with parents born in Ireland and England.[140]

The Burnett family weathered the agricultural crisis of the 1920s and the worst of the Depression. John became the owner of the grain elevator with

---

[133] Negative search: 1895 State of Iowa census, Hamilton County, Iowa, population schedule, search for John Burnett in Iowa; index, *FamilySearch*. Also, "John H. Burnett Dies; Hold Rites," *Dallas Center Times*, 14 November 1957, p. 1, col 2.

[134] 1900 U.S. census, Randolph County, Missouri, population schedule, ED 131, p. 1, household 13, dwelling 13, John Burnett.

[135] "Missouri, County Marriage, Naturalization, and Court Records, 1800-1991," database with images, *FamilySearch* (https://familysearch.org/ark:/61903/3:1:3QS7-998M-B9RR) Macon > Marriage records 1902-1905, vol 8-9 > image 235 of 423, John H. Burnett Jr.- Eva Butter marriage license and certificate (28 July d1904).

[136] "John H. Burnett Dies; Hold Rites," *Dallas Center Times*, (Iowa)," 14 November 1957, p. 1, col 2.

[137] 1910 U.S. census, Dallas County, Iowa, population schedule, Dallas Center, ED 2, p. 2A, household 37, dwelling 37, John H. Burnett.

[138] 1920 U.S. census, Dallas County, Iowa, population schedule, Adel Township, ED 2, p. 16A, household 209, dwelling 219, John H. Burnett.

[139] 1925 Iowa state census, Dallas County, Iowa, population schedule, Dallas Center, image 130 of 156, lines 134-137, John H. Burnett.

[140] 1930 U.S. census, dDallas County, Iowa, population's schedule, Adel Township, ED 3, p. 3B, household 89, dwelling 92, John H. Burnett.

a steady and larger income than most. The children no longer lived in the household, but Eva's mother still resided with them.[141]

In 1942 John Henry Burnett registered for the World War II draft, stating that he was born 8 June 1883 in New York City, New York. Eva Burnett, his wife, was a person who would always know his address.[142]

John H. Burnett died 6 November 1957;[143] Eva died 4 February 1969. Both were buried in Dallas County, Iowa.[144]

A summary of known information of John Henry (Murtha) Burnett follows:

---

[141] 1940 U.S. census, Dallas County, Iowa, populations schedule, Dallas center, ED 25-3, dwelling 49, John H. Burnett. John was the informant.

[142] World War II Draft Registration Cards, 1942, Iowa > Thomas, Burke-Frank, Bush, image 674 of 2099, Dallas County, Iowa, serial number U447, John Henry Burnett.

[143] "John H. Burnett Dies; Hold Rites," *Dallas Center Times*, (Iowa)," 14 November 1957, p. 1, col 2.

[144] *Find a Grave,* database and images (https://www.findagrave.com/memorial/14748380/john-h-burnett), memorial page for John H Burnett (8 Jun 1883–6 Nov 1957), Find a Grave Memorial ID 14748380, citing Brethren Cemetery, Dallas Center, Dallas County, Iowa.

Figure 1-JHB
Name, location and date of birth, foster and birth parents of John Henry (Murtha) Burnett

	Name	Birth date	Birth location	Birth parents	Foster parents
1890	John Murtha[a]	1883			John Barnett
1900	Johnny Burnett[b]	Mar 1883	New York	f.. New York; m. Scotland	John Burnett
1910	John H. Burnett[c]	1883	New York	b. Ireland	
1917	John Henry Burnett[d]	8 June 1883	New York City, NY		
1920	John H. Burnett[e]	1884	New York City	f. Ireland; m. England	
1925	John H. Burnett[f]	1894	New York	f. Unknown; m. Emily Lee, England	
1930	John H. Burnett[g]	1883	New York	f. Ireland; m. England	
1940	John H. Burnett[h]	1883	New York		
1942	John Henry Burnett[i]	8 June 1883	New York City, NY		
1957	John H. Burnett[j]	8 June 1883	Brooklyn, New York	Mr. & Mrs. Patrick H. Murphy	John Burnett

a. Kialy Carson, Kansas, [(CURATOR@ORPHANTRAINDEPOT.COM),] to Jill Morelli, email, 7 March 2023, "Info from the CAS," OTR folder.
b. 1900 U.S. census, Randolph County, Missouri, population schedule, ED 131, p. 1, household 13, dwelling 13, John Burnett.
c. 1910 U.S. census, Dallas County, Iowa, population schedule, Dallas Center, ED 2, p. 2A, household 37, dwelling 37, John H. Burnett.
d. U.S. World War I draft registration cards, 1917-1918," Local Board of Dallas County, Adel, Iowa, serial no. 663, John Henry Burnett.
e. 1920 U.S. census, Dallas County, Iowa, population schedule, Adel Township, ED 2, p. 16A, household 209, dwelling 219, John H. Burnett.
f. 1925 Iowa state census, Dallas County, Iowa, population schedule, Dallas Center, image 130 of 156, lines 134-137, John H. Burnett.
g. 1930 U.S. census, Dallas County, Iowa, population schedule, Adel Township, ED 3, p. 3B, household 89, dwelling 92, John H. Burnett.
h. 1940 U.S. census, Dallas County, Iowa, population schedule, Dallas Center, ED 25-3, dwelling 49, John H. Burnett.
i. World War II Draft Registration Cards, 1942, Iowa > Thomas, Burke-Frank, Bush, image 674 of 2099, Dallas County, Iowa, serial number U447, John Henry Burnett.
j. "John H. Burnett Dies; Hold Rites," *Dallas Center Times*, (Iowa)," 14 November 1957, p. 1, col 2.

John seemed to have obtained information concerning his birth parents before 1925. A search was conducted for all males with a surname of

Murphy or Murtha, born in 1883, with a father named Patrick, and possibly with a mother named Emily. One candidate stood out.

Figure 1-JHB
Birth return for male Murtha born 8 June 1883[145]

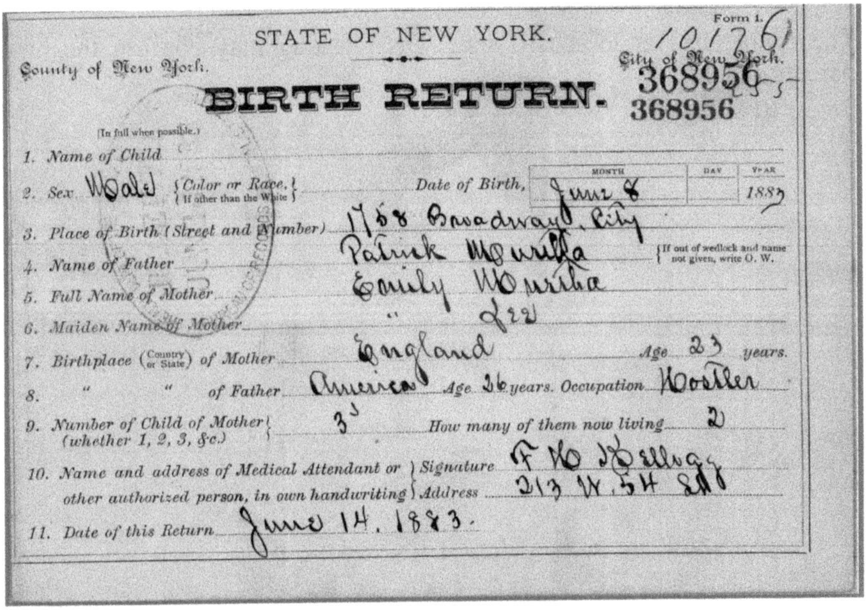
Form 1. 101761

STATE OF NEW YORK.

County of New York. City of New York.

BIRTH RETURN. 368956 368956

[In full when possible.]

1. Name of Child
2. Sex Male {Color or Race, If other than the White} Date of Birth, MONTH June DAY 8 YEAR 1883
3. Place of Birth (Street and Number) 1758 Broadway, City
4. Name of Father Patrick Murtha {If out of wedlock and name not given, write O. W.
5. Full Name of Mother Emily Murtha
6. Maiden Name of Mother " [illegible]
7. Birthplace (Country or State) of Mother England Age 23 years.
8. " " of Father America Age 26 years. Occupation Hostler
9. Number of Child of Mother (whether 1, 2, 3, &c.) 3 How many of them now living 2
10. Name and address of Medical Attendant or other authorized person, in own handwriting Signature F. W. Kellogg Address 213 W. 54 St.
11. Date of this Return June 14. 1883.

While the child is not named, the gender, birth date, name of the parents, and birth place of the mother align with known information. In conflict is that the child was born in the City of New York rather than in Brooklyn, and the father was born in the United States and not Ireland. The family possibly resided in Brooklyn, but gave birth in New York City or this could be a mistake. These are minor issues that do not affect the conclusion.

Although Emily Murthagave birth to three children (minimum span of time approximately 3 years prior to 1883), the family was not found in the 1880 or in the 1900 federal censuses. A death certificate for Emily was not found in New York City in the years following the birth.

145 New York City Municipal Archives, "Historical Vital Records," Birth Return, certificate 368956, unnamed male Murtha birth entry (8 June 1883).

CONCLUSION

John Henry (Murtha) Burnett was born 8 June 1883 in Manhattan, New York. His birth parents were Patrick and Emily (Lee) Murtha. John married Eva Butler, both of Huntsville, Randolph County, Missouri, on 28 July 1904, at Macon, Macon County, Missouri. John died 6 November 1957;[146] Eva died 4 February 1969. Both are buried in Dallas County, Iowa.[147]

The couple had at least two sons. DNA testing may confirm the birth parents of John.

---

[146] "John H. Burnett Dies; Hold Rites," *Dallas Center Times*, (Iowa)," 14 November 1957, p. 1, col 2.

[147] *Find a Grave,* database and images (https://www.findagrave.com/memorial/14748380/john-h-burnett), memorial page for John H Burnett (8 Jun 1883–6 Nov 1957), Find a Grave Memorial ID 14748380, citing Brethren Cemetery, Dallas Center, Dallas County, Iowa.

Minnie Everhardina (—?—) Busing

B. 4 July 1883 in New York
D. 21 June 1918, East Moline, Rock Island County, Illinois
Birth family: unknown
Foster family: (M1) Aalderk and Grietje/Grace (Bloem) Busing;
(M2) John Grensberg and Grietje/Grace (Bloem) Busing Grensberg

Superintendent Trott recorded A. Busing as a recipient of an orphan in the 29 August 1890 delivery of children to Hamilton County.[148]

Life in the rural Midwest of a religious family like the Busings began rather typically. Minnie was baptized in the German Presbyterian Church in Kamrar, Hamilton County, Iowa, on 13 August 1893, witnessed by her foster parents, Aldrich Busing and his wife, Grietje, born Bloem.[149] Aalderk Busing died on 25 January 1894, and left a widow and an "adopted" daughter, Minnie.[150] Aalderk willed his entire estate to his wife Grietje A. Busing. No accommodation was made in the will for the care of Minnie.[151]

In 1895, Minnie Busing appeared in the household of the widow Mrs. [Grietje] Busing. Minnie was 12 years old and born in New York. No other children resided in the household.[152] Grace (Bloem) Busing married second Johan Grensberg on 13 November 1895.[153] In 1900 Minnie Busing,

---

[148] "E. Trott of the children's aid society...," *The Freeman,* 3 September 1890, p. 5, col. 3.

[149] German Presbyterian Church, Kamrar, Hamilton County, Iowa, "Baptism Records, Burial Records, Death Certificates, Marriage Records, Religious Records, 1875-1956," *FamilySearch* > Images, baptism records, image 44 of 49. p. 108, Minni Everhardina Busing baptized (13 August 1893).

[150] "A. Bussing," *Webster City Freeman,* 31 January 1894, p. 5, col. 5

[151] "Iowa, U.S. Wills and Probate Record, 1758-1997," Hamilton county, Iowa, Will Record, vol 1-4 (1865-1901), image 729 of 947, Aalderk Busing will dated 10 December 1883. Also, German Presbyterian Church, Kamrar, Hamilton County, Iowa, "Baptism Records, Burial Records, Death Certificates, Marriage Records, Religious Records, 1885-1956," *FamilySearch* > Images, burial records, image 30 of 49. p. 75, Ahdrick Busing burial record (29 January 1894).

[152] 1895 State of Iowa census, Hamilton County, Iowa, population schedule, image 384 of 681, Minnie Bussing in the household of Mrs. Bussing, widow.

[153] Iowa, Select Marriages Index, 1758-1996, Grensberg-Brevour marriage entry (13 November 1895. While the Brevour indexed name is far off, all other characteristics are aligned for this to be Grace (Bloem) Busing, including the names of her parents.

resided in the household of John Grensberg as a "servant," with her foster mother, Grace Grensberg.[154]

Minnie (—?—) Busing married John Meyer from near Freeport, Stephenson County, Illinois, on 24 February 1904 in Webster City. Minnie declared her parents were Alderk and Grace (Bloem) Busing. The Busings were likely related to Minnie's new husband, as his parents were John and Anna (Busing) Meyer.[155]

In 1910 the Meyer family composed of John, Minnie, and daughters Viola (age 1 year and 8 months) and Carrie Riemtema (age 1 year, probably Rietema), resided in Ogle County, Illinois. Minnie had been married for six years and had given birth to one child who survived[156] The relationship oto Carrie is not known; but based on the age of Viola, the two could not have been born of the same mother.

Minnie died 21 June 1918 at Watertown State Hospital, a hospital for the insane, located in Rock Island County, Illinois. Her cause of death was dementia (pellagra).[157] Minnie was born in New York and was 35 years old at the time of her death. Burial was in Crane's Cemetery, Stephenson County, Illinois.[158] John Meyer died 22 December 1932 in Freeport, Stephenson County. John was survived by his daughter, Viola.[159]

Grietje Grensberg died in Hamilton County 3 January 1922. She was specific in her will about what should be placed on her tombstone, but was equally specific that her granddaughter Viola Meyer should receive $600 from her estate. Other heirs got $100. John J. Meyer was Viola's

---

[154] 1900 U.S. census, Hamilton County, Iowa, population schedule, Independence, ED 106, p. 9, household 176, dwelling 175, Minnie Busing in the household of John Greinsberg.

[155] "Iowa, County Marriages, 1838 to 1934," index, Meyer-Busing marriage entry (24 February 1904); index, *FamilySearch* (https://familysearch.org).

[156] 1910 U.S. census, Ogle county, Illinois, population schedule, Lincoln Township, ED 75, p. 3B, household 58, dwelling 59, John Meyer. It is likely the spelling of Carrie's surname is Reemtsma.

[157] Illinois Department of Public Health, Rock Island County, Illinois, certificate of death, Minnie Meyer death entry (21 June 1918). John Meyer was the informant. Birth date, location of birth, parent's names or parent's location of birth are blank.

[158] "Illinois, Deaths and Stillbirths Index, 1916-1947," Minnie Myer death entry (21 June 1918); index, *FamilySearch* (https://familysearch.org), FHL # 1544382. Also, "Funeral of Mrs. Meyer," *Freeport (Illinois) Journal-Standard*, 24 June 1918, p. 8, col. 5. Also, *FindAGrave*, database and images (http://findagrave.com), memorial page for Minnie Meyer (1883-1918), Memorial no. 47855961, citing Cranes Grove Cemetery, Stephenson County, Illinois; the accompanying tombstone by Gary Monigold provides a legible image. John J. and Viola Meyer are buried in the same row.

[159] "John Meyer, Silver Creek," *Freeport [Illinois] Journal-Standard*, 22 December 1932, p. 16, col. 2.

designated guardian.¹⁶⁰ This is a rare example of where the orphan or their descendent was identified as an heir by the foster parent.

Viola never married and had no descendants.¹⁶¹

Clues to Minnie's New York life are few, and she never named her New York parents.

Table 1-MB
Name, location and date of birth, foster and birth parents
of Minnie (—?—) Busing

	Name	Birth date	Birth location	Birth parents	Foster parents
1893	Minni Everhardina Busing[b]	4 July 1882			Ahlderk & Grietje (Bloem) Busing
1894	Minnie Busing[a]				Alderk & Grietje Busing
1895	Minnie Busing[c]	1883	New York		Mrs. Busing
1900	Minnie Busing[c]	July 1882	New York	b. New York	John & Grace Griensburg
1904	Minnie Busing[e]	1883	New York City, New York	Alderk Busing & Grace Bloom Busing	
1910	Minnie Meyers[f]	1884	Illinois	b. Unknown	
1918	Minnie Meyer[g]	1883			

---

¹⁶⁰ Hamilton County, Iowa, probate file number #2380, probate file, Grietje Grensberg, will dated 14 June 1917; Office of the Court Clerk.
¹⁶¹ "Deaths: Miss Viola Meyer," *Freeport (Stephenson County, Illinois) Journal-Standard*, 2 August 1972, p. 12, col. 6.

a. "A. Bussing," *Webster City [Iowa] Freeman*, 31 January 1894, p. 5, col. 5.
b. German Presbyterian Church, Kamrar, Hamilton County, Iowa, "Baptism Records, Burial Records, Death Certificates, Marriage Records, Religious Records, 1875-1956," *FamilySearch* > Images, baptism records, image 44 of 49. p. 108, Minni Everhardina Busing baptized (13 August 1893).
c. 1895 State of Iowa census, Hamilton County, Iowa, population schedule, image 384 of 681, Minnie Bussing in the household of Mrs. Bussing, widow.
d. 1900 U.S. census, Hamilton County, Iowa, population schedule, Independance, ED 106, p. 9, household 176, dwelling 175, Minnie Busing in the household of John Greinsberg..
e. "Iowa, County Marriages, 1838 to 1934," index, Meyer-Busing marriage entry (24 February 1904). Also, "Iowa, U.S. Marriage Records, 1880-1945," Iowa, vol. 416 (Emmett - Lyon), Hamilton County, Iowa, 4th entry, John Meyer-Minnie Busing marriage entry (24 February 1904).
f. 1910 U.S. census, Ogle County, Illinois, population schedule, Lincoln Township, ED 75, p. 3B, household 58, dwelling 59, John Meyer.
g. "Illinois, Deaths and Stillbirths Index, 1916-1947," Minnie Myer death entry (21 June 1918). Also, *FindAGrave*, database and images (http://findagrave.com), memorial page for Minnie Meyer (1883-1918), Find A Grave memorial no. 47855961, citing Cranes Grove Cemetery, Stephenson County, Illinois; the accompanying photograph by Gary Monigold provides a legible image.

Few documents yield clues to identify Minnie's parents. Busing was Minnie's adopted name and not the surname of her New York parents. Because of her short life, only a birth month and year are identified, which may be wrong.

CONCLUSION

Minnie Busing was born July 1882 or 1883 in New York. Her birth parents, and their year and location of birth, are unknown. Minnie (—?—) Busing married John Meyer from near Freeport, Stephenson County, Illinois, on 24 February 1904 in Webster City. Minnie died 21 June 1918, at Watertown State Hospital, a hospital for the insane, located in Rock Island County, Illinois.

Viola, her only daughter, never married and had no known descendants.

Iris (McFarland) Doutrich
AKA Harry Dawson

B. March 1885, New York
D. Unknown
Birth family: —?— Doutrick/Doutrich
Foster family: David and Eliza McFarland

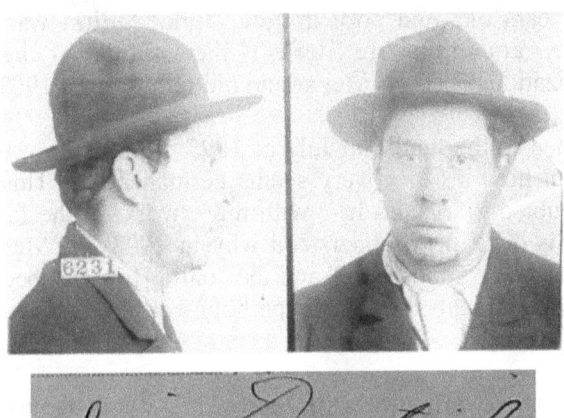

Iris Doutrich, alias McFarland, Case File, US Penitentiary, Leavenworth, Kansas

David McFarland received a child probably in the November delivery, as Iris was not on the manifest for October and McFarland was not an allocated foster parent in August.

> [Iris McFarland] was born in New York and being left an orphan was adopted by Mr. and Mrs. David McFarland, who lived near here...[162]

> Dentrich [sic] is a foundling sent west from New York. He was one of two carloads of children sent out by the benevolent organization

---

[162] "Stanhope Thief Caught At Last," *Webster City Journal*, 6 September 1906, p. 2, col. 1.

to find homes in Iowa. ....He was...adopted by a well-to-do farmer by the name of McFarland.[163]

A court record of an adoption does not exist.

Just three years after Iris joined the family, David McFarland was identified as "threatened with insanity."[164] A year later Eliza appealed to the county to provide support for David's extended stay in the asylum. Her request was granted; the county ageeed to pay half if the family paid half.[165]

In 1895 Eliza McFarland, 58 years old, identified herself as a widow and headed the household composed of two adult children and Iris, identified as male, 8 years old, and born in New York.[166] Eliza was a widow by convenience, attempting to deflect the stigma of her husband's institutionalization, as David McFarland did not die until 1903.[167]

David returned to the family in July of 1895. Initially he was pronounced incurable, but now his "recovery seems permanent."[168] This crisis in the family undoubtedly affected Iris, with more work on the farm or loss of affection. It is difficult to understand why in 1908, the McFarland home was described as a "good home" and the "child [Iris] has been surrounded by best of environments."[169] This hyperbole was not, however, uncommon in local newspapers.

He had a history of difficulty with the law. In 1899 at age twelve, Iris was sent to the Eldora Training School for Boys in Eldora, Iowa, and stayed at the industrial school for three years.[170]

> He became incorrigible and it was finally decided to send him to the reform school. He spent two to three years in the industrial school and

---

[163] "Iowa News," *Jewell Record*, 12 November 1908, p. 6, col 4.

[164] "We regret very much...," *Webster City Freeman*, 15 February 1893, p. 5. Col. 3.

[165] "County Legislation, Fourth Day," *Webster City Freeman*, 13 Jun 1894, p. 4, col 3.

[166] 1895 Iowa state census, Hamilton County, Iowa, population schedule, Clear Lake Township, p. 35/276, image 265 of 681, Iris McFarland in the household of Eliza McFarland.

[167] *Find a Grave*, database and images (https://www.findagrave.com/memorial/34385409/david-mcfarland), memorial page for David McFarland (28 Apr 1829–7 Feb 1903), Find a Grave Memorial ID 34385409, citing Saratoga Cemetery, Stanhope, Hamilton County, Iowa, USA; Maintained by Mike Mc (contributor 47104460). Also, "Saratoga," *Webster City Journal*, 12 February 1903, p. 12, col. 2.

[168] "Webster City," *Stratford Courier*, 18 July 1895, p. 4, col. 5.

[169] "Criminal By Nature," *Daily Freeman Tribune*, 7 November 1908, p. 8, col. 3.

[170] "Stanhope Thief Caught At Last," *Webster City Journal*, 6 September 1906, p. 2, col 1.

after his release from that institution he returned to Stanhope, where for a time he worked at odd jobs.[171]

The Eldora Training School for Boys was established by the legislature in 1868 to provide education and training in a trade. At first it admitted both boys and girls between the ages of 7 and 16. Almost immediately another institution was established for the girls.

> This is not a prison, but a compulsory educational institution. It is a school where wayward boys are brought under the influence of Christian instruction...[172]

In 1904 Eliza posted a personal notice that she would no longer be responsible for the debts, nor would she collect the wages of her adopted son, Iris Doutrich.[173] Iris would have been 19 years old. During this time he traveled to Harrold, South Dakota, but returned.[174]

In June of 1906, Iris stole $25 from the Williams Harness Shop in Stanhope. He was captured, confessed, and agreed to pay the retribution. Once paid and feeling his obligation was complete, he left the area. An informant spotted him in Des Moines and the sheriff arrested and brought him back to Hamilton County to await the grand jury's determination.[175] The court found him guilty.

Between October 1906 and February 1908, Iris was an inmate of the Iowa State Penitentiary in Anamosa, Iowa, serving an 18 month sentence for grand larceny. He entered prison on 12 October 1906 at age 21. He was of medium complexion; listed his occupation as tailor; and was temperate (not addicted to alcohol), with no religion. Iris served his complete sentence and was released 2 November 1908.[176]

After his Anamosa experience, Iris started adopting aliases. A letter was received inquiring about a Harry Dawson, but...

---

[171] "Stanhope Thief Caught At Last," *Webster City Journal*, 6 September 1906, p. 2, col. 1.

[172] Hon. William J. Moir, editor, *Past and Present of Hardin County Iowa*, (Indianapolis : B.F. Bowen, 1911) p. 104-105.

[173] "Time Notice," *Stanhope Mail*, 22 September 1904, p. 4, col. 3. Record of a formal adoption does not exist.

[174] "The Weekly Roundup," *Stanhope Mail*, 20 October 1904, p. 5, col 1.

[175] "Accused Robber Landed in Jail," *Webster City Freeman*, 4 September 1906, p. 3, col. 4.

[176] "Iowa, U.S. Consecutive Registers of Convicts, 1867-1970, Book 1, Men's Reformatory: Alamosa, 1876-1907 p. 130, inmate no. 5620, Iris Doutrich; Iowa State Historical Society, Des Moines, Iowa. Why Iris served two years of an 18 month sentence is not known. Also, "Stanhope Thief Caught at Last," *Webster City Journal*, 6 September 1906, p. 2, col. 1.

... a [letter] informed Mr. Johnson that the prisoner confessed that his name was Harry Dountrich, but said since he was released from Anamosa, that he had assumed the name of Dawson.[177]

On 3 February 1908, Iris using the name of Harry Dawson, broke into the Post Office in Thorton, Iowa, a federal crime. He pleaded guilty in the Northern District Court in Fort Dodge on 21 November 1908, and was sentenced to pay a $100 fine and serve six months in the Federal Penitentiary in Leavenworth, Kansas.[178] His sentence started on 21 November 1908, and he was to be released on 20 May 1909.[179] Iris was 24 years old, a clerk by occupation, of German background, 5 feet 5 inches tall, used tobacco but not liquor, and had a vaccination scar.[180]

While in Leavenworth, Iris committed three recordable infractions. In January Iris quarreled with his competitor over a game of checkers and threatened to "knock the block off" of prisoner #5557. A scuffle ensued where Iris shoved the other prisoner, hit him over the head with the checker board, and caused injury. In early February Iris stole a state form but was caught by an attendant. Later that month, he was given the task of cleaning the windows. He was indifferent to the task and by his carelessness, broke the window.[181]

Iris received no letters while he was incarcerated and sent only one to Washington, DC. He was released on 20 April 1909.[182] Upon his release, Iris requested $5, a sum he would have received if he had served a term of one year; his request was denied. Iris appealed the decision, but was again denied as he had not been held in Leavenworth for one full year.[183]

In 1910 Harry Dawson appeared in Woonsocket, Sanborn County, South Dakota. Harry, single, age 26 (b. 1884), and born in New York, was a clerk

---

[177] "Interesting Bits of Local Information," *Stratford Courier*, 19 November 1908, p. 6, col. 3. Also, "Criminal By Nature," Daily Freeman Tribune, 7 November 1908, p. 8, col 3.

[178] "Confessed Burglar Brought to City," *Fort Dodge (Webster County, Iowa) Messenger*, 5 November 1908, p. 1, col 7. Ivis Dentrick is probably a misspelling.

[179] "Inmate Case Files, 7/3/1895 - 11/5/1957," Department of Justice, U.S. Prisons, U.S. Penitentiary, Leavenworth, Kansas, Iris Doutrick, alias Iris McFarland, case file.

[180] "Inmate Case Files, 7/3/1895 - 11/5/1957," Iris Doutrick, alias Iris McFarland, case file.

[181] "Inmate Case Files, 7/3/1895 - 11/5/1957," Iris Doutrick, alias Iris McFarland, case file.

[182] "Inmate Case Files, 7/3/1895 - 11/5/1957," Iris Doutrick, alias Iris McFarland, case file.

[183] United States, Decisions of the Comptroller of the Treasury, "Gratuities Paid to United States Prisoners Upon Discharge from Penal Institutions," Iris Doutrich (September 1909), Decision rendered 26 October 1909; citing Section 6, Act of March 3, 1891 (26 Stat., 840.)

for a hotel. His parents were born in Ireland.[184] At the same time another Hamilton County orphan, Anna (Crane) McIntyre resided in Woonsocket.[185] This cannot be a coincidence.

Harry obtained employment with a tailor, soliciting business in Madison, South Dakota, a town a few miles west of Woonsocket. On 1 August 1912 the tailor relieved Harry of his duties.[186] The alignment of name and occupation with his prison record indicates this is the same man as the out-placed orphan Iris Doutrich.

Iris/Harry cannot be identified after 1912.

David McFarland died in February 1903 in the Cherokee Hospital, and Eliza died in 1921. Neither obituary mentioned Iris/Harry.[187] The probate documents of Eliza McFarland did not mention Iris/Harry.[188]

Few sources provide clues to the origins of Iris Doutrich, and his multiple aliases create problems. Names he assumed included Iris McFarland, Iris Doutrich/Dietrich/Dountrich, Harry Doutrich, and Harry Dawson. The fact he was a founding may indicate there was no formal birth registration, no identified New York name or date and all were assigned to him. Without descendants, we may never know the parents of Iris.

---

[184] 1910 U.S. census, Sanborn County, South Dakota, Woonsocket, Ward 1, ED 386, p. 4B, household 92, dwelling 96, Harry Dawson in the employment of Fredrick H. Davis, proprietor.

[185] 1910 U.S. census, Sanborn County, South Dakota, Woonsocket, Ward 1, ED 386, p. 2A, household 37, dwelling 38, Anne McIntyre in the household of Harry M. Lucas.

[186] "The City: Local News," *The Madison (SD) Daily Leader*, 3 August 1912, p. 3, col 3.

[187] "Satatoga," David McFarland, *Webster City Journal*, 12 February 1903, p. 12, col. 2. Also, "Obituary," Eliza Francis McFarland, *Jewell Record*, 17 March, 1921, p. 2, col. 4.

[188] Hamilton County, Iowa, probate file number #2324, file, Eliza McFarland. The record for David McFarland was unavailable as he was judged insane at the time of death.

Figure 1-IMD
Name, location and date of birth, foster and birth parents
of Iris (McFarland) Doutrich

	Name	Birth date	Birth location	Birth parents	Foster parents
1895	Irs McFarland[a]	1887	New York		Eliza McFarland
1900	Iris Dountrick[b]	Mar 1885	New York	b. New York	
1906	Iris Doutrich[c]	1885	New York		
1908	Harry Dawson[d]				
1908	Ivis Dentrick[e]		New York		McFarlands
1909	Irs Doutrich[f] & Iris McFarland	1884	New York	b. Unknown	E.F. McFarland
1910	Harry Dawson[g]	1884	New York		
1912	Harry Dawson[h]				

a. 1895 Iowa state census, Hamilton County, Iowa, population schedule, Clear Lake Township, p. 35/276, image 265 of 681, Iris McFarland in the household of Eliza McFarland.
b. 1900 U.S. census, Hardin County, Iowa, population schedule, Industrial School for Boys, Eldora, ED 170, p. 3, line 79, Iris Dountrick.
c. "Iowa, U.S. Consecutive Registers of Convicts, 1867-1970, Book 1, Men's Reformatory: Alamosa, 1876-19.; Iowa State Historical Society, Des Moines, Iowa.
d. "Interesting Bits of Local Information," *Stratford Courier*, 19 November 1908, p. 6, col. 3.
e. "Iowa News," *Jewell Record*, 12 November 1908, p. 6, col 4.
f. "Inmate Case Files, 7/3/1895 - 11/5/1957," Department of Justice, U.S. Prisons, U.S. Penitentiary, Leavenworth, Kansas, Iris Doutrick, alias Iris McFarland, case file.
g. 1910 U.S. census, Sanborn County, South Dakota, Woonsocket, Ward 1, ED 386, p. 4B, household 92, dwelling 96, Harry Dawson in the employment of Fredrick H. Davis, proprietor.
h. "The City: Local News," *The Madison (SD) Daily Leader*, 3 August 1912, p. 3, col 3.

Iris was described as a foundling and the likelihood of a birth record is small. A search was made in the following with no results or too many results to be useful:
- NYC Historical Vital Records website for births of any Doutrick/ Doutrich/Dou*tr* born in New York City or the available boroughs between 1883 and 187.[189]
- Ancestry public and private trees for a male named Iris, born c. 1885 in New York.[190]
- Ancestry Search and FamilySearch search for a male named Harry Dawson, born 1884-1886 and born in New York.
- Newspapers.com for Iris Doutrick/Doutrich.[191]

---

[189] New York City Municipal Archives, "Historical Vital Records," searched with no findings for Doutrich, Doutrick,and Dontrich and Dontrick.

[190] Public and Private Trees, *Ancestry,* searched for Iris, b. 1885 in New York.

[191] *Newspapers.com*. Searched for Iris Doutrick between 1900 and 1930 in any location. Doutricks primary location in Pennsylvania; no one named Iris.

- The World War I draft registrations yielded too many options for Harry Dawson.
- Harry Dawson appeared in no other Madison, South Dakota edition of their newspaper.
- Doutrich is a name found in Pennsylvania.

This investigation revealed no additional evidence of the identification of Iris Doutrich's parents nor the whereabouts of Iris/Harry after 1912.

CONCLUSION

Iris Doutrich was probably born in New York City in March 1884-1887 and was a foundling. He served nine months in Leavenworth Federal Prison.

In 1910, using the alia Harry Dawson, Iris resided in Woonsocket, South Dakota, the same location as fellow orphan Anna (Crane) McIntyre. In 1912 his employer relieved Harry Dawson of his duties in Madison, South Dakota. His whereabouts after 1912 are not known.

No known marriage or descendants have been identified.

(*See* https://iowaorphans.wordpress.com for any new information that may be found about Iris/Harry.)

Richard Doyle

B. 12 October 1878/1879, Cuba
D. 17 November 1933, Cherokee County, Cherokee, Iowa
Birth Family: John & Annie (Newall) Doyle
Foster Family: W. R. Wilson

Permission to use the photo of his great grandfather granted by Ken Norstrud

Richard Doyle, age 11, arrived in Hamilton County in the October delivery of children, just days before his twelfth birthday, and was selected by W. R. Wilson of Stanhope.[192] W. R. Wilson, an early pioneer to the area and Stanhope's postmaster, died four years later.[193] As an older foster child who could work independently, Richard, age 16, worked on his own as a laborer on the Leonard Hill farm.[194]

Richard was the oldest identified child delivered to Hamilton County.

---

[192] Kialy Carson, Kansas, [(CURATOR@ORPHANTRAINDEPOT.COM),] to Jill Morelli, email, 7 March 2023, "Info from the CAS," OTR folder.

[193] "A Pioneer Gone," *Saturday Mail (Stanhope)*, 10 November 1894, p. 1, col. 4.

[194] 1895 State of Iowa census, Hamilton County, Iowa, population schedule, image 514 of 681, Richard Doyle in the household of Leonard Hill.

Richard's great grandson shared a family tradition,

> Richard was born in Cuba. ... His mother Annie (Newall) died and his father remarried. That is when he was sent to Iowa with his sister Sadie. Family lore has it that when his father, an attorney in New York, died he left $50 for each of the children. Richard refused to return to get the money.[195]
>
> Sadie moved back to New York City. ...the last address that we had was in Brooklyn.[196]

As with most family stories there is a mix of fact and family lore. Richard and his two siblings, Sadie and William, were born in Cuba. Based on the birth year of William, the family came to the United States after 1882.[197] John was enumerated as a machinist, not a lawyer.[198]

It is unlikely that Sadie was an out-placed orphan. She was not enumerated by CAS as traveling with her brother in 1890.[199] And by 1892 she was living with her father, stepmother, and brother in Brooklyn.[200]

Richard was placed with the William R. Wilson family of Stanhope, Hamilton County, Iowa.[201] Only the manifest provided by the CAS places him with the family. This is understandable. W. R. Wilson, an early pioneer to the area and Stanhope's postmaster, died in late 1894 before 1895 Iowa census.[202] Richard, now age 16 or 17, was old enough to work on his own.[203]

---

[195] Ken Norstrud, [(E-ADDRESS FOR PRIVATE USE),] to Jill Morelli, e-mail, 12 March 2023, "Richard Doyle," OTR file.

[196] Ibid.

[197] "1892, New York state Census, Kings County, New York, population schedule, Brooklyn, Ward 17, ED 21, bottom of second column, John Doyle; database with images, *FamilySearch* (https://familysearch.org/ark:/61903/3:1:S3HY-6PT4-FV).

[198] New York City Municipal Archives, "Historical Vital Records," Certificate of Death, certificate 11318, John Doyle death entry (2 July 1896).

[199] Kialy Carson, Kansas, [(CURATOR@ORPHANTRAINDEPOT.COM),] to Jill Morelli, email, 7 March 2023, "Info from the CAS," OTR folder.

[200] "1892, New York state Census, Kings County, New York, population schedule, Brooklyn, Ward 17, ED 21, bottom of second column, John Doyle; database with images, *FamilySearch* (https://familysearch.org/ark:/61903/3:1:S3HY-6PT4-FV).

[201] Ibid.

[202] "A Pioneer Gone," *Saturday Mail (Stanhope)*, 10 November 1894, p. 1, col. 4.

[203] 1895 State of Iowa census, Hamilton County, Iowa, population schedule, image 514 of 681, Richard Doyle in the household of Leonard Hill.

In July of 1896, John Doyle died intestate in Brooklyn. John's second wife, Martha, was named administratrix. In the probate file, five children of the previous wife were identified as heirs: Richard Doyle of Stanhope, Iowa; Sadie Valentine (William); and three other siblings. The personal property of the estate did not exceed $8000 and there was no real estate.[204] According to New York law, Martha was due the entire estate because it was less than $50,000.[205] While the amount offered to Richard cannot be confirmed, Martha determined how much, if any, she gave to each of the five children. The lack of relationship between Richard and Martha might explain why he never returned to NYC to receive the $50 gift.

Richard Doyle, age 22, married Minnie Runyon on 7 August 1899 in Hamilton County.[206] A year later the couple resided in Webster County. The family farmed and took in boarders.[207] Richard came to the United States in 1884 from Cuba and had lived in Iowa for 14 years.[208]

The family continued their residency in Webster County, and in 1917 Richard registered for the World War I draft. Richard Doyle declared he was born 12 October 1879. He was tall, medium build with dark blue eyes and dark brown hair.[209] Richard purchased war bonds in support of the war effort.[210]

In July 1919 Richard saved Sammie Michaelson from drowning in the Des Moines River and attempted to save two other boys who had been caught in an undertow. Few of the boys who went to the river that day knew how to swim, but Richard was noted as an excellent swimmer.[211]

---

[204] "New York, Wills & Probate records, 1659-1999," Kings County, Admin Records Deverman-Cocoran, 1896, John Doyle probate filed 17 August 1896.

[205] *Collateral Inheritance and Transfer Tax Law of the State of New York: Containing Original Act of 1885 with All Amendments, the Revision of 1892 with All Subsequent Amendments Prior to 1896, and the Codification of 1896 with All Subsequent Amendments* (New York: Baler. Voorhis & Company, 1903;) permalink: https://search.library.doc.gov/permalink/01USDOC_INST/k7eb2i/alma991000299913104716.

[206] "Iowa, U.S., Marriage Records, 1880-1945," 1915-1916 > 463 (Payette-Lee), Return of Marriages in the County of Hamilton, fiscal year ending, 31 December 1899 p. 123, Richard Doyle- Minnie Runyon marriage entry (7 August 1899).

[207] 1900 U.S. census, Webster County, Iowa, population schedule, Washington Township, ED 189, p. 13, household 193, dwelling 195, Richard Doyle.

[208] 1905 Iowa state census, Hamilton County, Iowa, population schedule, Fremont Township, image 2880 of 6894, card no. 565, Richard Doyle.

[209] "World War I Draft Registration Cards, 1917-1918," 12 September 1918, Fort Doge, Webster County, Iowa, Local Board, for Richard Doyle.

[210] "Lehigh Buys $48,200.00 Second Liberty Bonds," *Lehigh Valley Argus (Fort Dodge, Webster County, Iowa)*, 1 November 1917, p. 1, col. 2.

[211] "Two Drown in River Sunday," *Lehigh Valley Argus*, 31 July 1919, p. 1, col. 1.

Richard signaled his intent to move to Winnebago County, Iowa, by holding a public auction on 20 December 1919. He had accumulated a significant amount of personal property and placed it for sale—78 head of livestock, including 16 horse and mules; 38 head of cattle, 12 of which were cows; and 24 head of sheep. Eleven turkeys and many pieces of farm machinery were also auctioned. Similar to every farm auction in this area, the more expensive items would be offered last; and a free hot lunch would be served. Richard outlined the deal points expected for payment in his advertisement.[212]

Moving Day for farmers is the first of March. Richard moved two carloads of equipment and animals by rail. Like others, he was detained, like others, by the snow fall, said to be three feet deep.[213] By the end of that month he and the family were settled in their new home on the farm near Leland, Winnebago County, Iowa.[214]

By April 1921, the family had moved back to Webster County.[215]

In 1925 Richard declared he was 48 years old and born in Cuba. His father was John Doyle. His mother's name and birthplace were unknown.[216] By 1930 the family owned their home valued at $2000 and no longer lived on a farm; Richard worked as a laborer in a gypsum plant. Their divorced daughter Irene lived with them with her daughter.[217]

Richard Doyle died 17 November 1933 in the Cherokee State Hospital, Cherokee County, Iowa of a perforated gastric ulcer.[218]

Richard's great grandson identified Richard's father as John W. Doyle, born in 1848 in Ireland and died in 1896 in Brooklyn. Richard's mother

---

[212] "Public Auction!," *Fort Dodge Messenger and Chronicle*, 17 December 1919, p. 11, col. 2-4.

[213] "——News was received... ," *Lehigh Valley Argus*, 11 March 1920, p. 5, col. 3. For "moving day" see "Moving Day A Big Event," Lehigh valley aRgus, 4 March 1920, p. 1, col. 1.

[214] "——Richard Doyle came down...," *Lehigh Valley Argus*, 25 March 1920, p. 5, col. 4.

[215] Ibid.

[216] 1925 Iowa state census, Hamilton County, Iowa, population schedule, Webster Township, image 206 of 862, lines 114-115, Richard Doile.

[217] 1930 U.S. census, Webster County, Iowa, population schedule, Fort Dodge, ED 43, p. 21B, household 481, dwelling 504, Richard Doyle.

[218] "Iowa, Death Records, 1904-1951," database with images, *FamilySearch* (https://familysearch.org/ark:/61903/3:1:3Q9M-CSQ7-Y9PS-S > image 4039 of 4702.

and first wife of John was Annie Newall, born 1857 in an unknown location and died in 1890 in Brooklyn, New York.[219]

Multiple records document the life of Richard Doyle.

Table 1-RD
Name, location and date of birth, foster and birth parents of Richard Doyle

Year	Name	Birth date	Birth location	Birth parents	Foster parents
1890	Richard Doyle[a]	1878			W.R. Wilson
1895	Richard Doyle[b]	1879	Spain		
1899	Richard Doile[c]	1877	Cuba	F. John Doile	
1900	Richard Doyle[d]	Feb 1878	New York	b. NY & NY	
1905	Richard Doyle[e]	1879	Cuba	fb. England; mb. Ireland	
1915	Richard Doyle[f]	1879		fb. England; mb. Ireland	
1917	Richard Doyle[g]	12 Oct 1879			
1920	Richard Doyle[h]	1879	Cuba	fb. England; mb. Ireland	
1925	Richard Doile[i]	1880	Cuba	f. John Doile; m. Unknown	
1930	Richard Doyle[j]	1879	Cuba	b. Unknown	
1933	Richard Doyle[k]	12 Oct 1878	Spain	Fb & mb: Spain; names unknown	

[219] "Public Member Trees," database, Ancestry (https://wwww.ancestry.com: accessed 12 Mary 2023)," "Judy Norstrud" family tree by Judy Norstrud, profile for Richard Doyle (1878-1933, d. Cherokee County, Iowa) undocumented data. In email with Ken Norstrud, great grandson of Richard, he outlined how his uncle, Richard Linn Doyle, had gathered the data. Ken mentioned that he had visited the graves of John and Anne (Newall) Doyle personally.

a. Kialy Carson, Kansas, [(CURATOR@ORPHANTRAINDEPOT.COM),] to Jill Morelli, email, 7 March 2023, "Info from the CAS," OTR folder.
b. 1895 State of Iowa census, Hamilton County, Iowa, population schedule, image 514 of 681, Richard Doyle in the household of Leonard Hill.
c. "Iowa, U.S., Marriage Records, 1880-1945," 1915-1916 > 463 (Payette-Lee), Return of Marriages in the County of Hamilton, fiscal year ending, 31 December 1899 p. 123, Richard Doyle - Minnie Runyon marriage entry (7 August 1899).
d. 1900 U.S. census, Webster County, Iowa, population schedule, Washington Township, ED 189, p. 13, household 193, dwelling 195, Richard Doyle.
e. 1905 Iowa state census, Hamilton County, Iowa, population schedule, Fremont Township, image 2880 of 6894, card no. 565, Richard Doyle.
f. 1915 Iowa state census, Webster County County, Iowa, population schedule, Webster Township, image 142 of 426, card no. 63, Richard Doyle.
g. "World War I Draft Registration Cards, 1917-1918," 12 September 1918, Fort Doge, Webster County, Iowa, Local Board, for Richard Doyle.
h. 1920 U.S. census, Webster County, Iowa, population schedule, Webster Township. ED 256, p. 6A, household 51, dwelling 51, Richard Doyle.
i. 1925 Iowa state census, Hamilton County, Iowa, population schedule, Webster Township, image 206 of 862, lines 114-115, Richard Doile.
j. 1930 U.S. census, Webster County, Iowa, population schedule, Fort Dodge, ED 43, p. 21B, household 481, dwelling 504, Richard Doyle.
k. "Iowa, Death Records, 1904-1951," *FamilySearch* (https://familysearch.org/ark:/61903/3:1:3Q9M-CSQ7-Y9PS-S > image 4039 of 4702. Richard Doyle death certificate (13 November 1933).

The conflict of the birth location of Richard is easily explained. Spain ruled Cuba until 1896, well after Richard was born. The name of the island was Cuba.[220]

John Doyle and a likely second wife, Martha, resided at 171 Norman Avenue, in Brooklyn, New York, in 1892. Living with them were Sadie, age 21, and William, age 10, both born in Cuba.[221] John Doyle was a machinist and not a lawyer, and Sadie was not an out-placed orphan like Richard.

There will be no record of John's birth in the NYC Historic Vital Records.

CONCLUSION

Richard's father was John Doyle and his mother was Anne (Newall) Doyle. Richard was born in Cuba on 12 October 1878. The birth places of John and Anne are unknown, but probably England and Ireland, respectively.
Richard, age 22, married Minnie Runyon on 7 August 1899 in Hamilton County, Iowa. Richard died 13 November 1933 at Cherokee State Hospital.

Richard and Minnie had children who had children. DNA may confirm John and Anne (Newell) Doyle as Richard's parents.

---

[220] José M. Hernandex, "Cuba in 1898," Library of Congress, research guide, https://guides.loc.gov/world-of-1898/cuba-overview.

[221] 1892 New York state census, Kings County, New York, population schedule, Brooklyn, Ward 17, ED 21, p. 12, col 2 (bottom); John Doyle.

Lucy (Johnson) Fay

B. 17 April 1882, Brooklyn, New York
D. 26 March 1974, Medford, Wisconsin
Birth family: William Henry and Hester (Parisen) Fay/Fee
Foster family: Thea Johnson

Lucy (Fay/Johnson) Johnson Brigham Cannon
FindAGrave memorial 11079962, maintained by KT (46789591).

Lucy Fay, age 8, arrived in Hamilton County in the October delivery of children. According to the manifest, Lucy was placed with the J. L. Johnson family of Kamrar; however, John L. Johnson had died in 1888.[222] Lucy was allocated to his widow, Thea Johnson.

In 1900 Lucy Johnson, described as a "daughter," resided in the household of Thea Johnson.[223] Thea was the only known woman to receive an orphan.

---

[222] Kialy Carson, Kansas, [(CURATOR@ORPHANTRAINDEPOT.COM),] to Jill Morelli, email, 7 March 2023, "Info from the CAS," OTR folder. For death, "Iowa, Armed Forces Grave Registrations, ca. 1835-1998," database, *FamilySearch*, Webster City, Iowa, John L Johnson, 19 Feb 1888.

[223] 1900 U. S. census, Hamilton County, Iowa, population schedule, Kamrar, ED 106, p. 14, household 267, dwelling 266, Lucy Johnson in the household of Thea Johnson.

Lucy and August Zahn, both New York orphans, visited the Johnson home in Kamrar on 28 April 1901.[224] This is a rare instance of two orphans having a mutually documented event and implies that Lucy was no longer living with Thea at the time.

Thea died prior to 23 September 1913, in Edmundson, North Dakota, at the home of her daughter, Mrs. Walter Layne.[225]

Lucy Johnson married first Nels Johnson in 1902, location unknown. The couple first moved to Nebraska. By 1910 they resided in Money Creek, Houston County, Minnesota, with their two children, Alta and Johanna. The children's birth locations give clues to the movement of this family. The move from Nebraska to Minnesota occurred between 1905 and 1909.[226]

Nels probably died or the couple divorced between 1910 and 1912.[227] On or before 24 July 1912, Lucy (Johnson) Johnson of Belmont, Lafayette County, Wisconsin, and Wilfred J. Brigham of Marathon, Wisconsin, applied for a marriage license.[228] At least one child was born to this marriage, Irene Brigham in 1914.[229] Wilfred died 15 January 1915.[230]

Lucy Brigham married third Benjamin E. Cannon on 21 May 1917 in Waupaca County, Wisconsin.[231] In 1920 Lucy and her husband, enumerated as Edward Cannon, lived in Wisconsin with their two children, Ben and Glenn Cannon, both toddlers. Residing with the family were Johanna Johnson, age 10, and Irene Brigham, age 6, step-daughters to Edward and children of Lucy's two previous marriages.[232]

---

[224] "Neighborhood Notes-Independence," *Daily Freeman Tribune*, 30 April 1902, p. 4, col. 1.

[225] "Old Resident Dead," *Webster City Freeman*, 23 September 1913, p. 3, col. 6.

[226] 1910 U. S. census, Houston County, Minnesota, population schedule, Moneycreek township, ED 71, p. 6B, household 173, dwelling 214, Nels Johnson.

[227] "Mrs. B. Cannon," obituary, *Marshfield News-Herald* (Wisconsin), 28 March 1974, p. 4, col. 7.

[228] "Marriage Licenses," *Gazette (Stevens Point, Wisconsin)*, 24 July 1912, p. 1, col. 3.

[229] 1920 U. S. census, Waupaca County, Wisconsin, population schedule, Waupaca, Ward 1, ED 152, p. 7B, household 115, dwelling 115, Edward Cannon.

[230] Find a Grave, database and images (https://www.findagrave.com), memorial page for Wilfred J. Brigham (1882–16 Jan 1915), memorial 84942949, citing Pine River Cemetery, Pine River, Waushara County, Wisconsin, USA; Maintained by KT (contributor 46789591).

[231] Wisconsin, U.S., Marriage Records, 1820-2004," index, Cannon-Johnson marriage record.

[232] 1920 U. S. census, Waupaca County, Wisconsin, population schedule, Waupaca, Ward 1, ED 152, p. 7B, household 115, dwelling 115, Edward Cannon.

By 1930 the family had moved to Rib Lake, Wisconsin, with their five children and Benjamin's step-daughter, Irene Brigham, now age 16. Benjamin was a watchman for a lumber company.[233] In 1940 the family continued residence in Taylor County, but lived on a rental farm in Greenwood Township.[234]

In 1944 the Cannon family joined the Borea Evangelical Lutheran Church of Superior, Wisconsin. Lucy registered her name as Lucy (Fay) Cannon.[235]

Benjamin Edward Cannon died 7 August 1946 in Medford.[236] Their son, Benjamin, assumed responsibility for the farm and the care and support of his widowed mother. Lucy was born in New York, but the birth location of her parents was unknown. She attended five years of elementary school.[237]

Lucy (Johnson) Fay Johnson Brigham Cannon died 26 March 1974 in Marshfield, Wood County, Wisconsin.[238]

The analysis of Lucy (Fay/Johnson) Johnson Brigham Cannon's birth dates and locations yields some consistency:

---

[233] 1930 U. S. census, Taylor County, Wisconsin, population schedule, Rib Lake, ED 24, p. 7B, household 146, dwelling 169, Benjamin Cannon.

[234] 1940 U.S. census, Taylor County, Wisconsin, population schedule, Greenwood Township, ED 60-9, p. 6, Benjamin Common.

[235] "U.S., Evangelical Lutheran Church in America Church Records, 1781-1969," congregational records, Superior, Wisconsin, Borea Lutheran, p. 14,1944, entry 15, registrants Emma Lucy Cannon, stating the names of her parents.

[236] "Cannon Rites Will Be Held Saturday," *Marshfield News-Herald (Marshfield, Wisconsin)*, 9 August 1946, p. 2, col. 1.

[237] 1950 U.S. census, Price County, Wisconsin, population schedule, Prentice Township, ED 60-9, p. 6, Benjamin Common.

[238] "Mrs. B. Cannon," obituary, *Marshfield News-Herald (Wisconsin)*, 28 March 1974, p. 4, col. 7.

Figure 1-LJ
Name, location and date of birth, foster and birth parents of Lucy (Fay/Johnson) Johnson Brigham Cannon

	Name	Birth date	Birth location	Birth parents	Foster parents
1890	Lucy Fay[a]	1882	New York		J. L. Johnson
1900	Lucy Johnson[b]	April 1883	New York	Unknown	Thea Johnson
1910	Lucy Johnson[c]	1883	New York	b. New York	
1920	Lucy Cannon[d]	1886	New York	b. New York	
1930	Lucy Cannon[e]	1884	New York	b. Unknown	
1940	Lucy Cannon[f]	1883	New York		
1944	Lucy (Fay) Cannon[g]				
1950	Lucy Cannon[h]	1883	New York	b. Unknown	
1974	Lucy Cannon[i]	12 April 1883	Brooklyn, New York		

a. Kialy Carson, Kansas, [(CURATOR@ORPHANTRAINDEPOT.COM),] to Jill Morelli, email, 7 March 2023, "Info from the CAS," OTR folder.
b. 1900 U. S. census, Hamilton County, Iowa, population schedule, Kamrar, ED 106, p. 14, household 267, dwelling 266, Lucy Johnson in the household of Thea Johnson.
c. 1910 U. S. census, Houston County, Minnesota, population schedule, Moneycreek township, ED 71, p. 6B, household 173, dwelling 214, Nels Johnson.
d. 1920 U. S. census, Waupaca County, Wisconsin, population schedule, Waupaca, Ward 1, ED 152, p. 7B, household 115, dwelling 115, Edward Cannon.
e. 1930 U. S. census, Taylor County, Wisconsin, population schedule, Rib Lake, ED 24, p. 7B, household 146, dwelling 169, Benjamin Cannon.
f. 1940 U.S. census, Taylor County, Wisconsin, population schedule, Greenwood Township, ED 60-9, p. 6, Benjamin Cannon
g. "U.S., Evangelical Lutheran Church in America Church Records, 1781-1969," congregational records, Superior, Wisconsin, Borea Lutheran, p. 14, 1944, entry 15, registrant Emma Lucy Cannon, stating the names of her parents.
h. 1950 U.S. census, Price County, Wisconsin, population schedule, Prentice Township, ED 60-9, p. 6, Benjamin Common.
i. "Mrs. B. Cannon," obituary, *Marshfield News-Herald (Wisconsin)*, 28 March 1974, p. 4, col. 7.

When Lucy recorded her birthday associated with a day and month, she used the year 1883; however the 1882 year was as recorded by the CAS upon her arrival.

Lucy Fay, born 17 April 1882 to William Henry Fay and Hester (Parisen) Fay, is a candidate for Lucy Johnson.

Figure 2-LJ
Birth certificate of Lucy Fay (17 April 1882)[239]

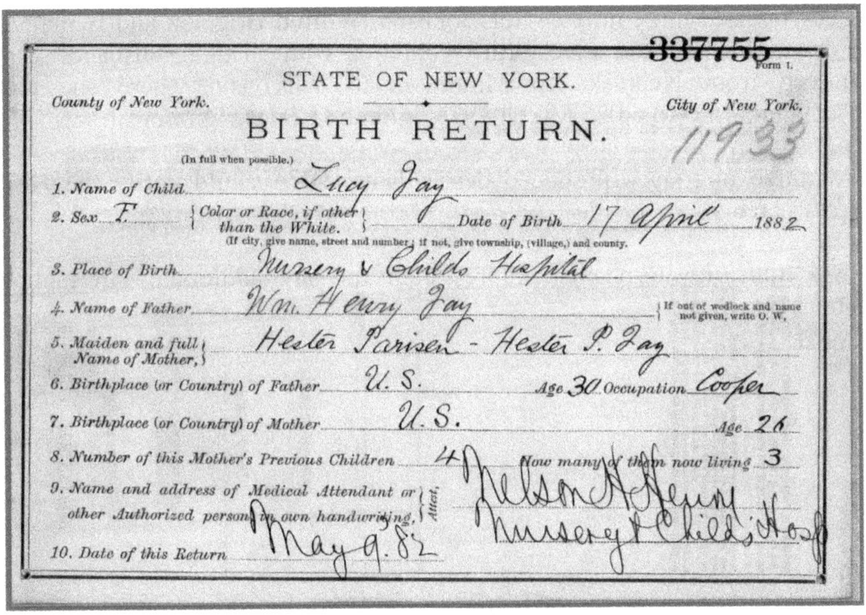

337755 Form 1.

STATE OF NEW YORK.

County of New York. City of New York.

BIRTH RETURN. 11933

(In full when possible.)

1. Name of Child Lucy Fay
2. Sex F { Color or Race, if other than the White. } Date of Birth 17 April 1882

(If city, give name, street and number; if not, give township, (village,) and county.)

3. Place of Birth Nursery & Childs Hospital
4. Name of Father Wm. Henry Fay { If out of wedlock and name not given, write O. W.
5. Maiden and full Name of Mother, Hester Parisen - Hester P. Fay
6. Birthplace (or Country) of Father U. S. Age 30 Occupation Cooper
7. Birthplace (or Country) of Mother U. S. Age 26
8. Number of this Mother's Previous Children 4 How many of them now living 3
9. Name and address of Medical Attendant or other Authorized person, in own handwriting, Attest. Nelson H. Henry Nursery & Child's Hosp
10. Date of this Return May 9. 82

In agreement with known information is the name of the child and the month of birth. The year is consistent with her age upon arrival in Hamilton County but in conflict with the year she used throughout her life. Also in conflict is the exact date. The 17 possibly looked like a 12 on the information that Thea Johnson received in 1890.

At the time of Lucy's birth, Hester Fay had given birth to three other children. One of those children was Florence Fee, born 2 February 1879 at Brooklyn Maternity hospital. Her father was the cooper William Fee.[240]

CONCLUSION

Lucy Fay was born to the married couple William Henry and Hester (Parisen) Fay on 17 April 1882. Lucy was their fourth child of whom three were still living.[241] In 1900 William Henry Fay, married, resided with his

---

239 New York City Municipal Archives, "Historical Vital Records," Birth Return, certificate 397755, Lucy Fay birth entry (17 April 1882).

240 "New York, new York City births, 1866-1909," Birth Return, certificate 1069, Florence fee birth entry (2 February 18790); digital image, *MyHeritage* (https://myheritage.com)

241 Ibid.

mother. Hester and the children were not enumerated.[242] William died February 1934 in New York.[243] No death record has been found for Hester.

Lucy married three times—Nels Johnson, Wilfred Brigham and Benjamin Edward Cannon and gave birth to children with all three husbands. She moved from Nebraska to Minnesota to Wisconsin where she met Benjamin. Lucy died 26 March 1974, in Wood County, Wisconsin.

All three marriages produced descendants; DNA could verify the New York parents.

(See https://iowaorphans.wordpress.com *for any additional information about Lucy.)*

---

[242] 1900 U.S. census, Kings County, New York, population schedule, Brooklyn, Ward 16, ED 224, p. 8, household 66, dwelling 205, William H. Fee in the household of Eliza Fee.
[243] New York City Municipal Archives, "Historical Vital Records," Death Return, certificate 3373, William H. Fee death entry (February 1934).

HENRY AEILT (—?—) HINDERKS

B. MAY 1885 OR 4 AUGUST 1884, NEW YORK
D. 8 OCTOBER 1936, KAMRAR, HAMILTON COUNTY, IOWA
BIRTH FAMILY: UNKNOWN
FOSTER FAMILY: AEILT AND HILKE HINDERKS

Signature from WWI Draft Registration Card

Superintendent Trott recorded A. Hinderks as a recipient of an orphan in the 29 August 1890 delivery of children to Hamilton County. Hinderks was also on the local selection committee for allocation of the children for both the August and October deliveries.[244] There was no identifiable orphan enumerated in the Aeilt Hinderks household in 1895.[245]

Henry's obituary makes his participation as one of the orphans clear.
> Mr. [Henry A.] Hinderks was born in New York August 4, 1884 and came to Kamrar at the age of 4 [1888].[246]

Even with the discrepancies of age and date, a male child of an unknown name arrived in Hamilton County in the August 1890 delivery of children and was chosen by Aeilt Hinderks. In 1900 one male child confirmed this assessment—Henry Hinderks, age 14, resided with Aeilt, age 57, and Hilke, age 64. The enumerator noted Iowa as his location of birth. The birth locations of Henry's parents matched that of his foster parents. Henry was a farm laborer and had not attended school the past year, even though required by the CCAS to do so.[247]

The Hinderks were members of the Kamrar First Presbyterian Church and Aeilt served as one of three Elders managing the religious activities of the church. On 1 May 1893, Aeilt was excommunicated from the church for having "committed a

---

[244] "E. Trott of the children's aid society...," *The Freeman*, 3 September 1890, p. 5, col. 3. For October: "Boys Wanting Homes," *Webster City Freeman*, 24 September 1890, p. 5, col. 5.

[245] 1895 State of Iowa census, Hamilton County, Iowa, population schedule, image 401 of 681, R. Hinderks. Kamrar Township records are lost.

[246] "Injury Fatal to Kamrar Man," *Daily Freeman Journal*, 9 October 1936, p. 1, col. 5.

[247] 1900 U.S. census, Hamilton County, Iowa, population schedule, Liberty, ED 98, p. 1, household 20, dwelling 20, Henry Hinderks in the household of Aeilts Hinderks.

great sin by breaking the seventh commandment"—adultery.[248] Rremoval from the family's religious community and the stigma associated with adultery must have caused an upheaval in the household. In spite of the accusation and removal from their religious community, the family stayed together.[249]

Henry Aeilts Hinderks married Lulu Pearl Kennedy on 30 June 1909 in Marshalltown, Iowa. It was a first marriage for both. Henry identified his parents as his foster parents.[250] Lulu's son attended the event. After the marriage, the couple moved near Lulu's parents, Robert and Margaret Kennedy.[251] By 1910 Henry and Lulu Hinderks and their two children lived with Lulu's parents. Again, Henry declared his birth location similar to those of his foster parents. He was a laborer doing odd jobs.[252]

By 1915 Henry and Lulu moved to Hamilton County and lived on the second floor of the building that housed the restaurant managed by Ed Pruismann, another out-placed orphan. Lulu cooked and assisted in Pruismann's lunch room.[253]

At the start of World War I, Henry A. Hinderks registered for the draft in Webster City. He declared he was born 4 August 1884 and labored on a nearby farm. Pearl Hinderks would know his address. He was of medium height and build with blue eyes and dark hair.[254]

By 1920 the family, now composed of Henry, Pearl, and four children, continued living in Hamilton County. Henry was a harness maker with his own shop.[255] Probably due to decreasing demand, Henry left harness making between 1920 and 1930.

---

[248] "Kamrar, Hamilton, Iowa, German Presbyterian records, images, FamilySearch (https://www.familysearch.org/ark:/61903/3:1:3Q9M-CSVY-Y94Z-M), pages no numbered, image 20 of 54, 1 May 1893.

[249] 1905 State of Iowa census, Hamilton County, Liberty Township, image 5872 of 6894, card 242 for Henry Hinderks.

[250] "Iowa, U.S., Marriage Records, 1880-1945," 1908-1909, vol 433 (Emmet-Montgomery), Hinderks-Kennedy marriage (30 June 1909).

[251] "Hinderks-Kennedy," marriage notice, *Evening Times-Republican (Marshalltown, Iowa)*, 1 July 1909, p. 6, col 2.

[252] 1910 U.S. census, Cerro Gordo County, Iowa, population schedule, Grimes, ED 25, p. 10B, household 190, dwelling 191, Henry Hinderks residing in household of Robert Kennedy.

[253] "The Kamrar Record," *Jewell Record*, 13 May 1915, p. 6, col 1.

[254] "U.S., World War II Draft Registration Cards, 1917-1918," Iowa, Hamilton County, Henry A. Hinderks.

[255] 1920 U.S. census, Hamilton County, Iowa, population schedule, Kamrar, ED 130, p. 3A, household 61, dwelling 61, Henry A. Hinderks.

The family moved to Independence Township before 1930 where they rented their home for $8 a month. Henry provided labor for a trucking group. His birth location was New York and that of his parents was in the United States.[256]

Henry died 8 October 1936 of an aneurism on a construction site while lifting heavy timbers.[257]

Henry Hinderks was an adopted name and not the name of the New York parents. His New York name is not known.

Figure 1-HAH
Name, location and date of birth, foster and birth parents
of Henry Aeilts (—?—) Hinderks

	Name	Birth date	Birth location	Birth parents	Foster paren
1900	Henry Hinderks[a]	1885	Iowa	b. Germany	Aielts Hinderks
1905	Henry Hinderks[b]	1888	Iowa	b. Germany	
1909	Henry Aielts Hinderks[c]	1885	Iowa	Aielts & Nettie (Telkamp) Hinderks	
1910	Henry Hinderks[d]	1886	Iowa	b. Germany	
1915	Henry Henderks[e]	1886	New York	b. New York	
1917	Henry A. Hinderks[f]	4 Aug 1884			
1920	Henry A. Hinderks[g]	1886	New York	b. Unknown/U.S.	
1925	Henry A. Hinderks[h]	1886	New York	b. Unknown	
1930	Henry A. Hinderks[i]	1886	New York	b. United States	
1936	Henry Aielts Hinderks[j]	4 Aug 1884	Unknown	b. Unknown	

---

[256] 1930 U.S. census, Hamilton County, Iowa, population schedule, Independence Township, ED 15, p. 2B, household 48, dwelling 49, Henry A. Hinderks.

[257] "Iowa, U.S., death Records, 1880-1904, 1921-1952, death certificate, n 40-161, death certificate G40-164, Henry Aielt Hinderks; digital image, *Ancestry*. Also, "Injury Fatal to Kamrar Man," *Daily Freeman Journal*, 9 October 1936, p. 1, col. 5.

a. 1900 U.S. census, Hamilton County, Iowa, population schedule, Liberty, ED 98, p. 1, household 20, dwelling 20, Henry Hinderks in the household of Aeilts Hinderks.
b. 1905 State of Iowa census, Hamilton County, Liberty Township, image 5872 of 6894, card 242 for Henry Hinderk.
c. "Iowa, U.S., Marriage Records, 1880-1945," 1908-1909, vol 433 (Emmet-Montgomery), Hinderks-Kennedy marriage (30 June 1909).
d. 1910 U.S. census, Cerro Gordo County, Iowa, population schedule, Grimes, ED 25, p. 10B, household 190, dwelling 191, Henry Hinderks residing in household of Robert Kennedy.
e. 1915 State of Iowa census, Hamilton County, Kamrar, image of card 4601 of 5178, no. 79, Henry Henderks.
f. "U.S., World War II Draft Registration Cards, 1917-1918," Iowa, Hamilton County, Henry A. Hinderks.
g. 1920 U.S. census, Hamilton County, Iowa, population schedule, Kamrar, ED 130, p. 3A, household 61, dwelling 61, Henry A. Hinderks.
h. 1925 State of Iowa census, Hamilton County, Jewell, image 109 of 125, Henry Hinderks.
i. 1930 U.S. census, Hamilton County, Iowa, population schedule, Independence Township, ED 15, p. 2B, household 48, dwelling 49, Henry A. Hinderks.
j. "Iowa, U.S., death Records, 1880-1904, 1921-1952, death certificate, n 40-161, death certificate G40-164, Henry Aielt Hinderks (8 October 1836).

Henry was possibly his given name in New York. When asked to give his full birth date, Henry consistently gave his Iowa name. The Hinderks followed the advice of the CAS, urging children to assimilate into their new living environment and leave memories and memorabilia behind.

Without a New York given or surname, this investigation revealed no additional evidence of Henry Aeilts Hinderks's New York parents.

CONCLUSION

Henry A. Hinderks was born 4 August 1884 in New York. His NYC parents are unknown. Henry Aeilts Hinderks married Lulu Pearl Kennedy on 30 June 1909 in Marshalltown, Iowa. On 8 October 1936, Henry died of an aneurism on a construction site while lifting heavy timbers.

Henry and Pear had four children. DNA test results may identify Henry's parents.

(*See* https://iowaorphans.wordpress.com for any new information about Henry.)

KATIE (MICKLE) HINES

B. 13 JUNE 1882 IN NEW YORK CITY, NEW YORK
D. 6 FEBRUARY 1966, CLINTON COUNTY, IOWA
BIRTHPARENTS: FRANK AND ELLEN (LEAHY) HINES
FOSTER FAMILY: N. JACKSON AND ELSIE J. MICKLE

Superintendent Trott recorded Jackson Mickle as a recipient of a female orphan in the 29 August 1890 delivery of children to Hamilton County.[258] In 1895 Katie Hines, age 10 and born in New York, lived with N. J. and Elise J. Mickle, an elderly couple with no other children in the household.[259] Katie was born June 1882; she and her parents were born in New York. Katie was a servant.[260]

By 1905 Katie worked as a dressmaker.[261] In 1910 Katie F. Mickle, "adopted daughter," continued living in the household of Jackson and Elsia J. Mickle.[262] No evidence exists that the Mickles formally adopted Katie.

Katie made the news when a piece of a sewing needle which had lodged in her foot for two years festered, and she had to have it surgically removed.[263]

Jackson Mickle died in 1913. In his obituary, Katie was described as being "not a daughter," but raised by the Mickle family since 1889. N. J. Mickle was born in Oneida County, New York.[264]

---

[258] "E. Trott of the children's aid society...," *The Freeman*, 3 September 1890, p. 5, col. 3.

[259] 1895 State of Iowa census, Hamilton County, Iowa, population schedule, image 376 of 681, Katie Hines in the household of N. J. Mickle.

[260] 1900 U.S. census, Hamilton County, Iowa, population schedule, Independence, ED 106, p. 9, household 186, dwelling 186, Katie Hines in the household of N. J. Mickle.

[261] 1905 State of Iowa census, Hamilton County, Iowa, population schedule, Webster City, card 924, Katie Mickel.

[262] 1910 U.S. census, Hamilton County, Iowa, population schedule, Webster City, ED 112, p. 3B, household 70, dwelling 71, Katie Mickle in the household of Jackson Mickle.

[263] "Piece of Needle in Foot for Two Years," *Daily Freeman Tribune*, 4 November 1911, p. 5, col. 5.

[264] "N.J. Mickle is Called to Rest," *Webster City Freeman*, 18 March 1913, p. 5, col. 5.

Like many other orphans, either Katie or the Mickles contacted the CAS to obtain information about Katie's NYC parents.

Katie married Joe Goulden, a tailor, on 24 December 1914, in Hamilton County. Katie Hines, described as a niece of Mr. Mickle, worked as dressmaker; Joe was a tailor with Cash and Lenhard.[265] Katie was 29 years old and born in New York City, New York. Her father's surname was Hines, but she did not know her mother's name or the given name of her father.[266]

In 1915 John was a tailor and earned $900 in the past year in spite of being out of work for three months. Katie came to Iowa when she was 4 years old; had 9 years of common school; and followed the Baptist faith.[267] By 1920 the fortunes of the Goulden family stabilized. They owned their own home in Webster City free of mortgage. Two children had joined the family, a toddler and an infant. Joe worked as a tailer.[268]

In 1925 Joe and Katie Goulden and their four children continued living in Hamilton County, Iowa. Katie declared her father's name was Francis Hines, but the name of the mother was unknown. Francis Hines and Katie's unknown mother were born and married in New York.[269]

In 1929 Dr. M.B. Galloway sued Mrs. Joe Goulden related to her dressmaking. The judge found for the plaintiff for $27.[270]

Between 1925 and 1930 the Goulden family moved from Hamilton County to Clinton County, Iowa, and rented the house at 708-1/2 South Second Street for $20 a month. The three boys, John, Fredrick, and Dean attended school. The family did not own a radio.[271]

The family fortunes seemed to have declined sharply through the Depression years. The family continued to reside in Clinton, but now the

---

[265] "Hines-Golden," *Webster City Journal*, 31 December 1914, p. 4, col. 5.

[266] "Iowa, U.S., Marriage Records, 1880-1951," Hamilton County, vol 459, Goulden-Hines marriage entry (24 December 1914).

[267] 1915 state of Iowa census, Hamilton County, Iowa, population schedule, Webster City, cards no. 81 and 82, J. H. Golden, Katie Golden.

[268] 1920 U.S. census, Hamilton County, Iowa, population schedule, Webster Township, Ward 4, ED 124, p. 12B, household 298, dwelling 305, Jo H. Goulden.

[269] 1925 Iowa state census, Hamilton County, Iowa, population schedule, Scott-Webster City, image 230 or 884, entry 932, Joseph H. Goulden.

[270] "Grant Judgement," *Daily Freeman Journal*, 26 Jun 1929, p. 6, col. 6.

[271] 1930 U.S. census, Clinton County, Iowa, population schedule, Clinton, ED 12, p. 24A, household 607, dwelling 676, Joseph Goulden.

family rented their home for $10 per month, at the low end compared to other renters in the neighborhood. But there was hope. Joe had worked 52 weeks in the previous year as a tailor, and the boys were now old enough to bring in some income by clerking in an auto supply store and doing odd jobs. A son informed the enumerator that his mother was born in Iowa.[272]

By 1950 Joe and Katie still lived in Clinton, but all the children had moved on. Joseph was a tailor in a men's store and Katie, enumerated as Katherine, was a kitchen helper in the local Veteran's Administration Hospital. Both had worked in excess of 40 hours the previous week. Katherine's parents were born in the United States and she had completed the 8th grade.[273]

In 1953 Joseph and Katie still lived at 708 1/2 Second Street in Clinton, and Joe continued his trade as a tailor.[274]

Kathryn was active in her community as a member of WOTM (Women of the Moose service auxiliary), the Rebekahs (auxiliary of the Independent Order of Odd Fellows), and two Ladies Auxiliaries of two Veterans of Foreign Wars posts.[275]

Joseph H. Goulden, age 76, died 11 June 1965 in Clinton;[276] Kathryn F. (Hines) Goulden died 6 February 1966. She was born 13 June 1883 in New York City.[277] Both are buried in Clinton Township, Clinton County, Iowa.[278]

---

[272] 1940 U. S. census, Clinton County, Iowa, population schedule, Clinton, ED 23-14A, p. 2B, household 32, Joe Golden.

[273] 1950 U. S. census, Clinton County, Iowa, population schedule, Clinton, ED 23-26, p. 71, dwelling 21, Joseph H. Goulden.

[274] "Clinton, Iowa, City Directory, 1953" Joe Goulden, (Chillocothe, Ohio : Mullin Killes Co., 1953) p. 500.

[275] "Mrs. Kathryn F. Goulden," *Clinton (Iowa) Herald*, 7 February 1966, p. 8, col 1 & 2; Clinton (Iowa) Public Library, Clinton Iowa.

[276] "Joseph H. Goulden," *Quad City Times (Davenport, Iowa),* 12 June 1965, p. 11, col. 6.

[277] "Mrs. Kathryn F. Goulden," *Clinton Herald*, 7 February 1966, p. 8, col 1 & 2.

[278] *FindAGrave,* database and images (https://findagrave.com), memorial page for Joseph H. Goulden (1883-1965), memorial no. 6195671and Kathryn Goulden (1888-1966) memorial no. 6195672, citing Springdale cemetery, Clinton, Clinton County, Iowa; no accompanying image; originally created by Alberta Daniels Withrow.

Multiple sources provide differing information about critical identifiers.

Figure 1-KMH
Name, location and date of birth, foster and birth parents
of Kathryn "Katie" Hines

	Name	Birth date	Birth location	Birth parents	Foster parents
1895	Katie Hines[a]	1885	New York		N.J. Mickle
1900	Katie Hines[b]	June 1882	New York	b. New York	N.J. Mickle
1905	Katie Mickel[c]	1884	New York	b. Unknown	
1910	Katie F. Mickle[d]	1888	New York	b. New York	Jackson Mickle
1914	Katie Hines[e]	1886	New York City	F: —?— Hines M: Unknown	
1915	Katie Golden[f]	1887	New York	b. New York	
1920	Katie Goulden[g]	1884	New York	b. New York	
1925	Katie Goulden[h]	1884	Iowa	F: Frances Hines, b. NY; M: unknown	
1930	Katie Goulden[i]	1890	New York	b. New York	
1940	Katie Goulden[j]	1890	New York	b. New York	
1950	Katherine Goulden[k]	1893	Iowa	b. U.S.	
1966	Mrs. Kathryn Francis Goulden[l]	13 June 1883	New York City		

a. 1895 State of Iowa census, Hamilton County, Iowa, population schedule, image 376 of 681, Katie Hines in the household of N. J. Mickle.
b. 1900 U.S. census, Hamilton County, Iowa, population schedule, Independence, ED 106, p. 9, household 186, dwelling 186, Katie Hines in the household of N. J. Mickle.
c. 1905 State of Iowa census, Hamilton County, Iowa, population schedule, Webster City, card 924, Katie Mickel.
d. 1910 U.S. census, Hamilton County, Iowa, population schedule, Webster City, ED 112, p. 3B, household 70, dwelling 71, Katie Mickle in the household of Jackson Mickle.
e. Iowa, U.S., Marriage Records, 1880-1945," Hamilton County, vol 459, Goulden-Hines marriage entry (24 December 1914).
f. 1915 state of Iowa census, Hamilton County, Iowa, population schedule, Webster City, cards no. 81 and 82, J. H. Golden, Katie Golden.
g. 1920 U.S. census, Hamilton County, Iowa, population schedule, Webster Township, Ward 4, ED 124, p. 12B, household 298, dwelling 305, Jo H. Goulden.
h. 1925 Iowa state census, Hamilton County, Iowa, population schedule, Scott-Webster City, image 230 or 884, entry 932, Joseph H. Goulden.
i. 1930 U.S. census, Clinton County, Iowa, population schedule, Clinton, ED 12, p. 24A, household 607, dwelling 676, Joseph Goulden.
j. 1940 U. S. census, Clinton County, Iowa, population schedule, Clinton, ED 23-14A, p. 2B, household 32, Joe Golden.
k. 1950 U. S. census, Clinton County, Iowa, population schedule, Clinton, ED 23-26, p. 71, dwelling 21, Joseph H. Goulden.
l. Iowa, Death Records, 1880-1972, certificate no. 116-66-02821, Mrs. Kathryn Frances Gulden death entry (6 February 1966). Also, "Mrs. Kathryn F. Goulden," *Clinton (Iowa) Herald*, 7 February 1966, p. 8, col 1 & 2; Clinton (Iowa) Public Library, Clinton Iowa.

Based on the documentary evidence, Katie (Hines) Goulden was born 13 June 1882 or 1883 in New York City. Her father may have been Frances

Hines; both parents were probably born in New York. Mickle was an adopted name and not the name of the New York parents or child.

Catherine Frances Hines, born 1 August 1883, to Frank and Ellen (Leahy) Hines is a likely candidate.[279]

Image 2-KMH
NYC Birth return for
Catherine Francis Hines, 1 August 1883.[280]

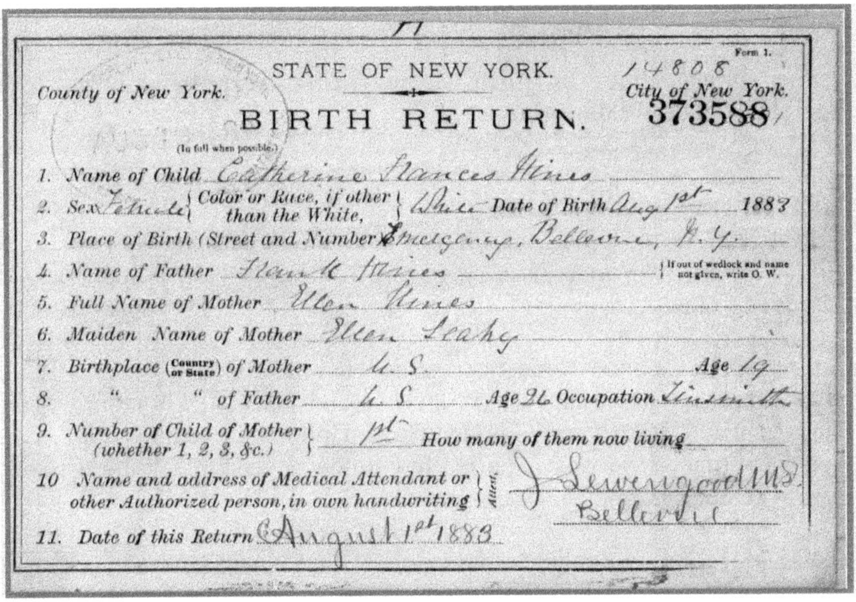

Form 1.

STATE OF NEW YORK. 14808

County of New York. City of New York.

BIRTH RETURN. 373588

(In full when possible.)

1. Name of Child Catherine Frances Hines
2. Sex Female Color or Race, if other than the White, White Date of Birth Aug 1st 1883
3. Place of Birth (Street and Number) Emergency, Bellevue, N.Y.
4. Name of Father Frank Hines (If out of wedlock and name not given, write O. W.)
5. Full Name of Mother Ellen Hines
6. Maiden Name of Mother Ellen Leahy
7. Birthplace (Country or State) of Mother U S Age 19
8. " " of Father U S Age 26 Occupation Tinsmith
9. Number of Child of Mother (whether 1, 2, 3, &c.) 1st How many of them now living
10. Name and address of Medical Attendant or other Authorized person, in own handwriting Attest. J Sewengood MD Bellevue
11. Date of this Return August 1st 1883

While the birth date does not match exactly, the child's name and the father's name of Frank Hines is consistent with information given in the 1925 Iowa census. Katie also used the middle initial of F. throughout her life and later used Kathryn/Katherine, instead of Katie.

Frank Hines and Ellen Leahy married on 27 December 1881 in Calvary Church, Manhattan, New York. Frank was a tinsmith. Ellen Leahy would

279 NYC, Department of Records & Information Services, Historical Vital Records, (https://a860-historicalvitalrecords.nyc.gov/browse-all), certificate 373588, Catherine Frances Hines birth entry (1 August 1883).

280 Ibid.

be 18 at her next birthday on 27 October 1882 (b. 1864), and was born in Jamaica, Long Island. Catherine was the first child of this family.[281]

Frank Hines died on 16 January 1884 in Manhattan. His estimated birth year was 1854; he was born in New York City; married at the time of his death; and worked as a tinsmith. He was buried at Calvary Cemetery on 22 January 1884.[282]

As a widow, Frank's death may have precipitated Ellen's decision to release her daughter to the orphanage, and ultimately to the CAS for out-placement.

Neither Frank Hines or Ellen (Leahy) Hines can be confirmed as individuals in the 1880 census.

CONCLUSION

Catherine Frances Hines was born to Frank and Ellen (Leahy) Hines on 1 August 1883 in the Emergency Room at Bellevue Hospital in New York City, New York. When Frank died the following year, Ellen released Catherine to the CAS.

Catherine, now called Katie, arrived in Hamilton County in August of 1890 and was fostered into the N. Jackson and Elsie Mickle family. Katie Hines married Joseph/Joe Goulden/Golden on 24 December 1914. She died 6 February 1966 and is buried in Clinton Township, Clinton County, Iowa with her husband.

The DNA of her descendants may confirm the parents of Katie and their whereabouts.

(See https://iowaorphans.wordpress.com for any additional information about Katie.)

---

[281] NYC, Department of Records & Information Services, Historical Vital Records, digital image (https://a860-historicalvitalrecords.nyc.gov/browse-all), certificate M-M-1881-0009214, Frank Hines- Ellen Leahy marriage entry (27 December 1881).

[282] "New York, New York City Municipal Deaths, 1795-1949," database, *FamilySearch* (https://www.familysearch.org/ark:/61903/1:1:2WJV-XZ8 : 2 June 2020), certificate no. 479325, Frank Hines death entry (16 Jan 1884).

Clara Lavinia (Mason) Krohn

Photo provided and permission given
by Randall Kuchenreuther, grandson of Clara.
Photo restored by Snapseed

B. 16 January 1884 in New York City, New York
D. 2 July 1978, Seattle, Washington
Birth Mother: Father: unknown; Mother: Sarah Lavinia Mason
Foster Family: Christ & Charlotte "Lottie" (Roseneau) Krohn

Recent Wisconsin migrants to Hamilton County, the Christ Krohn family was allocated a female child in the August delivery of children.[283] Before 1895 the family moved to Kossuth County, Iowa, with their "daughter" Clara, age eleven. All were born in Wisconsin.[284] The family still lived in Kossuth County in 1900. Clara was born January 1884 in New York and now sixteen years old. The birth location of her parents was unknown. Christ and Lottie were younger than most foster parents, but Lottie had given birth to nine children, all deceased.[285]

---

[283] For prior location of residence: 1885 Wisconsin state census, Iowa County, Wisconsin, population schedule, Pulaski, roll 4, p. 7 (verso), Christian Krohn. The family was composed of 2 males and 3 females; 3 were born in the U.S. and 2 were born in Germany. Also, "E. Trott of the children's aid society…," *The Freeman,* 3 September 1890, p. 5, col.

[284] 1895 State of Iowa census, Kossuth County, Iowa, population schedule, image 375 of 733, Clara Krohn in the household of Chris Krohn.

[285] 1900 U.S. census, Kossuth County, Iowa, population schedule, German Township, ED 135, p. 9, household 158, dwelling 159, Clara Krohn in the household of Chris Krohn.

Wedding photo, Henry & Clara (Krohn) Kuchenreuther, Randall Kuchenreuther, used with permission

Clara L. Krohn, age eighteen, married thirty-three year-old Henry J. Kuchenreuther on 27 February 1901 in Kossuth County. She declared her birth location as New York City and her parents as Christian and Charlotte (Rosenow) Krohn, her foster parents.[286]

In 1908 Heinrich Kuchenreuther and Clara had their infant, Lena, baptized in the Lutheran Church of Lakota, Kossuth County. Clara again declared that her birth name was Krohn.[287] Between 1908 and 1910 Clara and Henry relocated to Whatcom County, Washington. In 1910 Clara, twenty-six, had been married for nine years and had given birth to four children. The birth location of Clara's parents was not known. Henry was a farmer, born in Germany, and a naturalized citizen. The two oldest children, Ervin and Lottie, attended school.[288]

After the summer of 1910 and before February 1911, the Christ Krohn family followed Henry and Clara to Whatcom County where they purchased property.[289] In December of 1916 they conveyed that same property (ten and a quarter acres, minus the road) to Clara Kuchenreuther for $400 who was to assume the mortgage.[290]

In mid-March 1917 Clara Kuchenreuther took ill and was hospitalized at St. Luke's Hospital in Bellingham, Washington. By mid-April, while still hospitalized, she was declared to be recovering from a long and severe

---

[286] Iowa, U.S., Marriage Records, 1880-1947, 1901, 404 (Emmet-Lyon), Return of Marriages in the County of Kossuth, fiscal year ending, 31 December 1901, p. 33, Kuchenenthen-Krohn marriage entry (27 February 1901).

[287] Evangelical Lutheran church in America church Records, 1781-1969," congregational records, St. Paul's Lutheran Church, Lakota, Iowa, Lena Mabel birth and baptism entry (1 February / 19 April, 1908).

[288] For 1907 residency see: "Notice of Hearing on Drainage Petition," *Algona Advance (Kossuth County, Iowa)*, 10 January 1907, p. 4, col 4. For 1910 residency see: 1910 U. S. Census, Whatcom County, Washington, population schedule, Delta, ED 342, household 114, dwelling 114, Henry Kuchenreuther.

[289] "Whatcom, Washington, United States records," images, *FamilySearch* (https://www.familysearch.org/ark:/61903/3:1:3Q9M-C9R4-MQ5X : 29 March 2024), image 132 of 642; Washington State Archives. Northwest Regional Branch.

[290] For 1916: "Whatcom, Washington, United States records," images, *FamilySearch* (https://www.familysearch.org/ark:/61903/3:1:3Q9M-C9RH-YQLD-6 : 29 March 2024), image 282 of 642; Washington State Archives. Northwest Regional Branch.

illness. She was frequently visited by various family members, including her "parents" Mr. and Mrs. C. Krohn.[291] In October the family thanked the community for their "kind aid and assistance" during Clara's illness.[292]

By 1920, the Kuchenreuther family had grown to seven children Irvin, Charlotte "Lottie," Anna, Lena, Julia, Mason and Dorothy Levinia. Henry continued farming in Whatcom County.[293] In 1923, Lottie, Clara and Henry's daughter, married. Lottie gave her mother's birth surname as 'Mason.'[294] This is a possible birth name. The fact that Clara named a son Mason in 1914 and a daughter Dorothy Lavinia (b. 1919) is significant.

On the verge of the Great Depression, Clara and Henry were starting to see the children leave—only Mason, Dorothy, and Eleanor were at home. The family now owned their farm.[295]

Christ Krohn died in 1931 in Whatcom County and included "Clara Kuchenreuther, adopted daughter" as an heir.[296] In 1932, Lottie Krohn, Clara's mother, exercised a Warranty Deed that transferred 15 acres of land to Clara.[297]

Mrs. Krohn believed that Clara had been formally .adopted. In November of 1935, Lottie Krohn swore before a Notary Public that Clara L. (Krohn) Kuchenreuther was adopted by court decree. Unfortunately, no credible information was provided in the affidavit as to which court or when this proceeding would have occurred, and Lottie stated that all other evidence

---

[291] "West Delta," *The Lyndon (WA) Tribune*, 15 March 1917, p. 5, col 2 and 19 April 1917, p. 5, column 3 & 4; *NewspaperArchive*.

[292] "Card of Thanks," *The Lyndon Tribune,* 16 October 1917, p. 9, col. 3.

[293] 1920 U.S. census, Whatcom County, Washington, population schedule, Delta, ED 250, p. 7A, household 161, dwelling 161, Henry Kuchensenther.

[294] "Washington, Marriage Records, 1854-2013," Marriage Return, no. 65-18, Amos W. Ameden-Lottie B. Kuchenreuther marriage card (21 May 1924.)

[295] 1930 U.S. census, Whatcom, Washington, population schedule Delta, ED 29, p. 10B, household 223, dwelling 223, Henry Kuchenreuther.

[296] Superior Court of the State of Washington, Whatcom County, no. 7792, filed 4 May 1931, 'Petition for Letters of Administration," probate packet, Christ Krohn, deceased.

[297] Washington State Board of Health, Bureau of Vital Statistics, Certificate of Death, record no. 91, registered no. 14, Christian S. Krohn death entry (25 April 1931.) Also, "Courthouse Records: Files for September 30, 1932," *The Bellingham Herald (Washington)*, 4 October 1932, p. 10 col. 5.

had been lost.[298] Clara is only one of two individuals, both girls, who were adopted, or considered so, by their foster parents.

Henry died at Lynden, Whatcom County, on 19 February 1938. He was described as a progressive farmer; a member of the Whatcom County Dairymen's Association; and a member of the Washington Co-operative Egg & Poultry Association. He also served as the registration officer for Delta Township, precinct No. 1.[299] In 1939 Clara leased out the 40 acre farm and moved to the home of her foster mother, Lottie, providing more evidence of a close relationship with her foster family.[300]

In 1940 Clara headed the household that now included only her son, Mason. They had no income and rented their house for $8 per month. Clara stated she resided in New York in 1935, but in 1940 was back in Whatcom County. Credence is given to this statement because Clara was the informant.[301]

In September of 1942, Clara fell on a defective sidewalk on Grover Street. She received facial cuts, body bruises, and was 20% permanently disabled. On 27 January 1943, Clara filed a lawsuit against the City of Lynden for the defective sidewalk, requesting $5000 in damages.[302] The outcome of the case is not known.

In 1944 Clara again traveled to New York to spend "the summer with her daughter in New YorkCity."[303] Clara visited her youngest daughter, June Eleanore, who had married a US Navy officer, Hugh E. Hoover Jr. The New York birth location of June's youngest child, Joyce June in 1944, coincides with her extended trip to the East Coast.[304] The child in the photo at the beginning of this chapter is Hugh and June's child, Joyce June, with

---

[298] Sworn statement by Lottie Krohn sworn to Notary Public, Clara Temsland, Lynden, Whatcom County, Washington, copy of original, dated 26 October 1935, identifying Clara L. (Mason) Kuchenreuther, born 16 January 1884 as her adopted daughter. Document in the family papers of Randall Kuchenreuther, Bellingham, Washington, and the Whatcom County Historical Society, and collected by Linda Lawson, 16 November 2023.

[299] Washington State Board of Health, Bureau of Vital statistics, Certificate of Death, no. 39, Lynden, Whatcom County, Washington, Henry Kuchenreuther death entry (19 February 1938.) Also, "Sunrise," obituary of Henry Kucherreuther, T*he Bellingham Herald*, 24 February 1938, p. 2, cols. 4-6.

[300] "Sunrise," *The Bellingham Herald* (Washington), 2 November 1939, p. 9., col. 7.

[301] 1940 U. S. Census, Whatcom County, Washington, population schedule, Delta, ED 37-39, p. 3B, household 45, Clara Henchenrenther.

[302] "Lynden Defendant in Damage Action," *The Bellingham Herald*, 27 January 1943, p. 7.

[303] Ibid.

[304] 1950 U.S. census, Duval County, Florida, population schedule, Other Places,, 16-61,

their grandmother Clara. The photo was taken in Brooklyn, New York.[305] On her return trip, Clara stopped in Webster City to visit her long-time friends the August Baumans. She then returned home to Lynden, Washington.[306]

In 1950 Clara continued her residency in Lyndon with her foster mother, now 88 years old. Neither had outside employment.[307] Charlotte J. Krohn died 11 May 1950 at her home of senile arteriosclerosis. [308]

After her mother's death, Clara moved to Seattle, probably to work as a practical nurse.

Clara Lavinia Kuchenreuther, age 94, died of cardiac arrest on 2 July 1978 at the Northshore Manor in Seattle, King County, Washington.[309] Clara was the last of the identified 1890 Hamilton County orphans to die.

Krohn is the surname of Clara's foster parents, not her birth parents. Mason was her birth surname. Either Clara or Lavina could possibly be her given name at birth. Lavinia is unusual and may reflect some aspect of her pre-Iowa family.

---

[305] Formal photograph of Clara Kuchenreuther and Joyce June Hoover, not dated, but location of photographer, and label indicates summer of 1944, photo taken at Portraits by Herbert, Brooklyn, New York. Label reads "Grandmother - age 60, Joyce June - age 3-7/12 months. Original in the family papers of Randall Kuchenreuther, Bellingham, Washington, and the Whatcom County Historical Society. Collected by Linda Lawson, 16 November 2023.

[306] "Other Lakota News," *Kossuth County Advance*, 9 November 1944, p. 1, col. 4.

[307] 1950 U.S. census, Whatcom County, Washington, population schedule, Lynden, ED 37-15, p. 14, household 161, Care Kuchenreuther.

[308] Washington State Department of Health, Public Health Statistics Division, Certificate of Death, no. 9557, Charlotte J. Krohn death certificate (11 May 1950).

[309] Washington, Death Index, 1940-2017, certificate of death (original), state file no. 15962, Clara Lavina Kuchenreuther death certificate (2 July 1978). Her daughter, Jewell Welsch was the informant. While the collection title is an index the original document is contained within the collection. Also, "27. Funerals: Kuchenreuther, Clara," *The Bellingham Herald*, 4 July 1978, p. 20, col. 6.

A letter confirms Mason as the family surname and the mother's name as Lavinia Mason. It also confirms that Clara (Krohn) Kuchenreuther was placed with the Christ Krohn family by CAS.[310]

                                            [partial corporate logo]
                              TH_____ID Society

                                              Founded 1853

                                                October 4, 1989

Ms. June Hoover
853 Ridgenmark Drive
Hollister, Ca. 95023

Dear Ms. Hoover :

       I am writing in reply to your request for information about your mother, Clara Mason. Unfortunately, we have very little information about her background; but I will give you the information we have. Or records state that your mother was "born in Nursery on January 16, 1884. Her mother, Lavinia Mason was Irish. After placing your mother with The Children's Aid Society she went to live with a Mrs. Baker of 696 East 165th Street, New York. Your mother was placed with the family of Christ Krohn. We have no further information about her background.

       I am sorry we do have more information about your mother, but I hope this information will be helpful.

                              Sincerely,

                         Helen Steinman [signature]

                          (Mrs.) Helen Steinman, CSW

HS:rab

---

[310] Helen Steinman, CSW, of The Children's Aid Society to June (Kuchenreuther) Hoover, daughter of Clara (Krohn) Kuchenreuther, dated 4 October 1998. Recounting the information in Clara Krohn's file at the Society. Original copy in the family papers of Randall Kuchenreuther, Bellingham, Washington, and the Whatcom County Historical Society. Collected by Linda Lawson, 16 November 2023. The second quote mark is not given.

The letter is a copy of a copy, typed with a handwritten signature at the closing salutation. The copying process cut off the logo at the top. Since Mrs. Steinman referred to the Children's Aid Society as receiving the child and the visible letters agree, the author wrote this letter while working for the CAS. Physical damage occurred in the form of a tear under the closing salutation of the original letter, but not the copy. The tear extended about half way across the page from left to right and was repaired with tape. The tear and its repair do not affect readability.

The CAS identified the connection between Lavinia Mason and Clara Krohn Kuchenreuther, as mother-daughter, but the letter raises a series of questions that deserve clarification:

1. Who is June Hoover, called daughter to Clara (Krohn) Kuchenreuther?
   June (Kuchenreuther) Hoover was the youngest daughter of Clara and Henry Kuchenreuther.[311]

2. What is "the Nursery?"
   The capitalization of the word Nursery implies that the birth might have occurred at the Nursery & Child's Hospital, 61st and Amsterdam, in Manhattan. Its mission was to care for poor mothers and children.[312]

3. Was Clara born on 16 January 1884?
   No parent or female child with a surname of Mason was recorded on birth certificates dated 16 January 1884 in Kings County or Manhattan. Only one child, born with both parents named, was born in a foundling hospital, but not at Nursery & Child's.[313]

4. Who was Lavinia Mason, Clara's mother?
   There could be more than one Lavinia Mason located in New York. See below for analysis.

---

[311] "Mason Kuchenreuther," obituary, *The Bellingham Herald*, 15 October 1997, p. 8. Col. 1.

[312] *Wikipedia*, "New York Nursery & Child's Hospital', https://en.wikipedia.org/wiki/New_York_Nursery_and_Child's_Hospital

[313] New York City Municipal Archives, "Historical Vital Records," a search of birth returns for female infants born on 16 January 1884 was conducted for Kings County (n=33) and Manhattan (n=43). On that day, no Masons gave birth and only eight remain candidates. Only one was born in a Foundling hospital.

5. Was Lavinia Irish?
   This is an identifier for the mother of Clara. See below.

6. Who is Mrs. Baker?
   Lavinia Mason may have boarded with Mrs. Baker. This has no bearing on the investigation of Clara's parents.

Lavinia, an unusual name, would have to fulfill three criteria: reside in New York City c. 1884, be born in Ireland, and be in her birthing years. The 1880, 1870, 1892, and 1900 censuses were reviewed for other same named candidates. Several Lavinia Masons resided in NYC, but were too old or too young, colored, or not yet born in 1884. None were born in Ireland. Only two Lavinia Masons matched the criteria—one candidate fulfilled two of the three criteria, and one candidate fulfilled one criteria.

Lavinia Mason I
Lavinia (Viele) Mason, widow of Charles P. Mason, was born in Ulster County, New York, but raised her family in Brooklyn. Lavinia I was born in 1824, making her 60 years old at the time of Clara's birth. Other than the name and the location of the family, no other criteria align with the identifiers needed to be the mother of Clara. Lavinia I is not a candidate for Clara's mother.

Lavinia Mason II
Sarah Lavinia Mason was born 6 March 1867 in Brooklyn and died 22 February 1914 at 89 Waverly Avenue, Brooklyn, New York. Her parents were Robert A. and Annie (Robinson) Mason, both born in New York. During her childhood she went by Lavinia.

Sarah Lavinia Mason married Joseph Foster Ellery Horton on 11 May 1887 in Brooklyn. Both were born in Brooklyn. Robert H. Mason and Charlotte Mason served as witnesses.[314]

By 1900 Sarah Lavinia had given birth to two children, neither of whom survived.[315] Sarah and Joseph resided with Joseph's parents from 1900 until her death. Sarah Lavinia died of chronic interstitial nephritis, contributed by cerebral hemorrhage on 22 February 1914. Lavinia

---

[314] New York City Municipal Archives, "Historical Vital Records," Marriage Returns, certificate 1588, Horton-Mason marriage(11 May 1887).

[315] 1900 US census, Kings County, New York, population schedule, Brooklyn, Ward 20, ED 311, household 167, dwelling 265, Sarah L. Horton in the household of John R. Horton.

predeceased her husband, Joseph Horton, and was buried in Greenwood Cemetery.[316]

Nothing in Sarah Lavinia Mason's timeline precludes her from being the mother of Clara Krohn.

Table 1-CLK
Timeline for Sarah Lavinia (Mason) Horton
(Birth Year included to identify the correct Lavinia
and to illustrate the use of the name Lavinia)

Event	Name Used	SLM's Birth year	Comments
Birth[a]	Sarah Lavinia Mason	6 March 1867	
1870 census[b]	Lavinia Mason	1864	In household of Robert A. Mason
1875 NY census[c]	Lavinia Mason	1865	F: Robert A Mason M: Ann Mason
1880 census			Neither Robert nor Sarah L can be found
1884 Clara born[d]			16 January 1884, Nursery & Childs Hospital
1887 Marriage to Joseph Horton[e]	Sarah Lavinia Mason	1867	M.. 11 May 1887; F: Robert A. Mason, M: Annie Robinson
1892 NY census[f]	Lavinia Horton	1869	In household of John Horton; 89 Waverly Ave.
1900 census[g]	Sarah L. Horton	March 1866	Wife of Joseph Horton; 89 Waverly Ave.
1910 NY census[h]	Sarah V. Horton	1867	Wife of Joseph Horton; 89 Waverly Ave.
1914 Obituary[i]	Sarah Levinia Horton		
22 Feb 1914 death certificate & obituary[j]	Sarah Lavinia (Mason) Horton	6 March 1867	F: Robert A Mason M: Annie Richardson [sic]; wife of Joseph Horton; 89 Waverly Ave.

---

[316] New York City Municipal Archives, "Historical Vital Records," Standard Certificate of Death, certificate no. 4096, Sarah Lavinia (Mason) Horton.

a. New York City Municipal Archives, "Historical Vital Records," Standard Certificate of Death, certificate no. 4096, Sarah Lavinia (Mason) Horton (22 February 1914).
b. 1870 US census, Kings County, New York, population schedule, Brooklyn, Ward 10, p. 735B, dwelling 2183, Lavinia Mason in the household of Robert A. Mason.
c. 1875 New York census, Kings County, New York, population schedule, Brooklyn, Ward 10, ED6, p. 20, dwelling 151, Lavinia Mason in the household of Robert Mason.
d. Helen Steinman, CSW, of The Children's Aid Society to June (Kuchenreuther) Hoover, daughter of Clara (Krohn) Kuchenreuther, dated 4 October 1998.
e. New York City Municipal Archives, "Historical Vital Records," Marriage Returns, certificate 1588, Horton-Mason marriage (11 May 1887).
f. 1892 New York State census, Kings county, Brooklyn, Ward 20, ED 11, p. 3 recto, household 89, John Horton.
g. 1900 US census, Kings County, New York, population schedule, Brooklyn, Ward 20, ED 311, household 167, dwelling 265, Sarah L. Horton in the household of John R. Horton.
h. 1910 US census, Kings County, New York, population schedule, Brooklyn, Ward 20, ED 82, household 139, dwelling 256, Sarah L. Horton in the household of John R. Horton.
i. New York City Municipal Archives, "Historical Vital Records," Standard Certificate of Death, certificate no. 4096, Sarah Lavinia (Mason) Horton (22 February 1914). Also, "Deaths," *The Brooklyn Daily Eagle*, 23 February 1914, p. 2, col 6.

Lavinia was the name used by Sarah in her younger years.

Summary of findings

- According to the CAS, the mother of Clara (Krohn) Kuchenreuther was Lavinia Mason, an Irish woman who gave birth "in Nursery" on 16 January 1884.
- Lavinia Mason, daughter of Robert A. and Annie (Robinson) Mason is within her birthing years and from the same geographic area as that proposed by CAS.
- In conflict with the CAS letter is that Sarah Lavinia was not Irish. This can only be explained by a simple error.
- Lavinia went by Lavinia in her earliest years and Sarah later.
- Clara's birth in 1884 preceded the marriage of Sarah to Joseph Horton in 1887.
- In 1910 Sarah declared she had given birth to three children but none survived.
- No other candidates for Clara's mother exist.
- The timeline of Sarah Lavinia (Mason) Horton's life identifies no exceptions that would conflict with the birth of Clara.

Clara traveled to New York City at least twice to visit her daughter June. Considering it was acoast-to-coast trip, this was an unusual occurrence during this time. She might also have visited the CAS headquarters and obtained information about the Mason/Horton families. If the CAS letter constitutes known information of her birth mother, Sarah Lavinia married and died before Clara's first visit in 1935.[317] There appears to be no credible birth certificate for Clara.[318] Sarah Lavinia Horton had no other children that survived infancy.[319]

The Horton family lived at 89 Waverly Avenue. The photographer of Clara with her granddaughter had his studio at 23 Flatbush Avenue, a distance of about 1.5 miles. Perhaps Clara passed the Hortons on the street.

CONCLUSION

Clara (Mason/Krohn) Kuckenreuther was born 16 January 1884 in New York City. Sarah Lavinia Mason was her mother, but the father is unknown. Clara was in the August delivery of children to Hamilton County in 1890 where she was fostered into the family of Christ Krohn and his wife Charlotte "Lottie" (Roseneau) Krohn. The family had recently moved to Hamilton County from Wisconsin; by 1895 they had moved to Kossuth County.

Clara married Henry J. Kuchenreuther on 27 February 1901 in Kossuth County. The couple made their home in Iowa until about 1908 when they moved to Whatcom County, Washington. Clara's foster parents moved to Whatcom County a few years later.

In 1935, Lottie Krohn told a Notary Public that Clara was an officially adopted daughter, but gave no credible information to substantiate her claim.

Henry died in 1938 after a lifetime of farming,. Shortly after his death, Clara moved in with her foster mother Charlotte Krohn. In 1935 and 1944, Clara visited her daughter in New York City. She probably did not visit her birth family, although she might have known she was from that area.

In 1953 Clara moved from Lynden to Seattle, probably to serve as a practical nurse. Clara Lavinia (Mason/Krohn) Kuchenreuther, age 94, died of cardiac arrest on 2 July 1978 at the Northshore Manor in Seattle, King

---

[317] New York City Municipal Archives, "Historical Vital Records," Marriage Returns, certificate 1588, Horton-Mason marriage (11 May 1887). For death: New York City Municipal Archives, "Historical Vital Records," Standard Certificate of Death, certificate no. 4096, Sarah Lavinia (Mason) Horton (22 February 1914).

[318] New York City Municipal Archives, "Historical Vital Records," Standard Certificate of births, A thorough investigation of birth records of a female white child born on 16 January 1884 yielded no child born to a Mason.

[319] 1910 U.S. census, Kings County, new York, population schedule, Brooklyn, Ward 20, ED 82, household 139, dwelling 256, Sarah V. Horton residing in the household of John Horton. Sarah has given birth to three children, none of which are still living.

County, Washington. She was the last of the Hamilton County orphans to die.

Although Sarah Lavinia Horton had no other children, she had siblings who did. With numerous Kuchenreuther children, DNA may confirm her mother and identify her father.

(*See* https://iawaorhans.wordpress.com for any additional information.)

James Wilfred (—?—) Lyons

B. 12 OR 19 JULY 1885 IN NEW YORK
D. 4 JULY 1953, SAN MATEO COUNTY, CALIFORNIA
BIRTH FAMILY: UNKNOWN
FOSTER FAMILY: KEARNES E. AND MARY LYONS

WWII Draft Registration Card

No direct evidence exists that James was an out-placed orphan who arrived in Hamilton County in 1890; but his birth location, his New York parent's birth locations; the contrast of those data points with those of his foster family, his age, identification as "adopted;" and living in Hamilton County all identified him as one of the out-placed orphans. It seems likely that with the birth of only a daughter, Kearnes Lyons needed help on the farm, and the young James provided it.

James assimilated into his foster family so completely as to obscure his origins. The first few documents are. examples of how complete the integration was, but later information provides evidence that James was an orphan who arrived in 1890.

In 1895 James Lyons resided with Kearnes and Mary Lyons. He was nine years old and born in Hamilton County, Iowa. An older female lived with the family, likely the daughter.[320]

In 1900 James continued living on the farm with the Lyons family in Cass Township. James was born July 1885 in Iowa and his parents were born in Ireland, reflecting the birth locations of his foster family. He attended school.[321]

---

[320] 1895 Iowa state census, Hamilton County, Iowa, population schedule, image 210 of 681, James Lyon in the household of Kerance Lyons.

[321] 1900 U.S. census, Hamilton County, Iowa, population Schedule, Cass Township, ED 103, household 54, dwelling 54, James Lyons in the household of Kearns Lyons.

On 8 February 1910 James Lyons, age 22, and Calla Bishop, age 17, filed for a marriage license in Dubuque, Iowa. Calla, being under-age required permission of a parent. The record is blank—lacking in parental names, residences, witnesses' names and the cleric's entry of date of marriage.[322] Other entries also lacked that information. It is possible the couple never married.

James W. Lyons and his wife were enumerated twice in 1910. In the first, the couple resided in the household of K. E. and Mary Lyons. James was born in Iowa but his parents were born in New York.[323] In the second enumeration, James W. Lyons and his wife resided in the household of Joseph A. and Sarah J. Bishop, the parents of his wife. James was 24 years old and born in New York; the birth location of his parents was unknown.[324] The differing locations of birth of the foster parents and the birth parents of James is the first evidence that James was an orphan.

In 1911 Kearns Lyons died. He was a lifelong member of the St. Thomas Aquinas Catholic Church. James was noted as a survivor who resided in Minneapolis and was described as "an adopted son."[325] No evidence of a court adoption exists. If James Wilfred Lyons was a birth son of Kearns Lyons he would have been baptized shortly after birth in St. Thomas Aquinas Church. No entry for James is recorded in the records of the church.[326]

James announced a series of moves first to Minneapolis, then back to Webster City, and in 1913 to Chicago.[327] Whether the move to Chicago occurred is questionable.

---

[322] "Iowa, U.S., Marriage Records, 1880-1947, 1909-1910, 435 (Adair-Dubuque), entry 69 for the year ending in 30 June 1910, James Lyons-Calla Bishop license entry (8 February 1910). Permission was noted as being attached, but was not.

[323] 1910 U.S. census, Hamilton County, Iowa, population schedule, Webster City, Ward 4, ED 112, household 35, dwelling 36, James W. Lyons in the household of K. E. Lyons.

[324] 1910 U.S. census, Hamilton County, Iowa, population schedule, Webster City, Ward 3, ED 111, household 109, dwelling 109, James W. Lyons in the household of Joseph A. Bishop.

[325] "Death of Long Time Resident," obituary of K.E. Lyons, *Daily Freeman Tribune*, 23 March 1911, p. 5, col. 3.

[326] Ruth Wolfgram, [(DBQ218SEC@DBQARCH.ORG),], Secretary/Bookkeeper, St. Thomas & St. Mary's Churches, Webster City, Iowa, to Jill Morelli, email, 23 June 2023, "Looking for a birth record for James W. Lyons," OTR folder, privately held by Morelli, [(E-ADDRESS), & STREET ADDRESS FOR PRIVATE USE], Seattle, Washington, 2023. There was no record for James W. Lyons.

[327] "Personal Briefs," *Daily Freeman Tribune*, 19 December 1913, p. 4, col. 3.

Why, when, and where the marriage of Calla and James dissolved, if it occurred, is not known. On 26 June 1915, James Wilfred Lyons married Florence Dorothy Bugbee in St. Croix, Wisconsin.[328]

By 1917 James and Florence lived in Minneapolis where James was a mechanic at the Anderson Hays Motor Company.[329] Between 1920 and 1930, the family moved from Minneapolis to San Francisco. James was a mechanic in a garage; the couple owned their own home; and Florence was a sales lady for a department store.[330] Whether James was aware that James Baldwin, another Hamilton County orphan, lived in San Fransisco is not known.

Between 1930 and 1935, the couple moved again, this time to Brisbane, an unincorporated town in San Mateo County, California, where James worked as the manager of garage. In 1939 he worked 52 weeks and had an income of $1650. The family had no other income.[331] In 1942 James Wilfred Lyons registered for the World War II draft.[332]

James Lyons, born 19 July 1885, filed a delayed birth certificate attesting that his parents were Kearns and Mary (Cassidy) Lyons and that he was born in Webster City, Hamilton County, Iowa. The evidence provided included his draft registration from 1918; a Policy Loan Agreement, dated 1932; his Social Security card; and his Old Age & Survivors Insurance Account document. The latter two had no date of issuance attached.[333] The assimilation of James into his Iowa life was now complete.

On 4 July 1953, James Wilfred Lyons of Brisbane, in San Mateo County, died at the Campbell's Sanitarium in Belmont after a long illness.[334] Neither of James's marriages produced children.

---

[328] "Wisconsin, U.S., Marriage Records, 1820-2004," index, St. Croix, Wisconsin, James Wilfred Lyons-Florence Dorothy Bugbee marriage entry (26 June 1915).

[329] "U.S. World War I Draft Registration Cards, 1917-1918," Minnesota > Minneapolis City > 12 > Draft Card L, serial number too faint to read, James Wilfred Lyons.

[330] 1920 U.S. census, Hennepin County, Minnesota, population schedule, Minneapolis, Ward 12, ED 227, household 51, dwelling 51, James Lyons.

[331] 1940 U.S. census, San Mateo County, California, population schedule, Other places (Brisbane), ED 41-23, household 237, James Lyons. James was the informant.

[332] "U.S., World War II Draft Registration Cards, 1942, California > all > Dini, Achille-Questoni, Mario, Serial number 2920, James Wilfred Lyons.

[333] "Iowa, U.S., births (series) 1880-1904, 1921-1944 and Delayed Births (series, 1856-1940," All > Delayed births, no. 125001-130000, 1884,1886, no. 127451, James Lyons.

[334] "James Wilfred Lyons," *The Times (San Mateo, California)*, 6 July 1953, p. 17, col. 3.

It was clear that Kearnes and Mary were not the NYC parents of James. One would not randomly say a person was adopted, nor would one say they were born in New York when they weren't. There would be social reasons, however, to declare one was born in the location where one lived with loving family members. This information coupled with the declaration in the 1910 census enumerations, leads to the conclusion that James was an orphan who was born in New York and did not know the names of his NY parents.

His age and residence in 1895 also support that he arrived in the 1890 delivery of children to Hamilton County.

The documentary evidence is plentiful, and the birth date is consistent, but the integration of James into the Lyons family was so complete that many records obscure his origins.

Table 1-JL
Name, location and date of birth, foster and birth parents
of James Wilfred (—?—) Lyons

Year	Name	Birth date	Birth location	Birth parents	Foster parents
1895	James Lyons[a]	1885	Iowa		Kereance & Mary Lyons
1900	James Lyons[b]	July 1885	Iowa	b. Ireland	
1910	James Lyons[c]	1888			
1910	James W. Lyons[d]	1885	Iowa	b. New York	K. E. Lyons
1910	James W. Lyons[e]	1886	New York	b. Unknown	
1917	James Wilfred Lyons[f]	19 July 1885			
1920	James W. Lyons[g]	1886	Iowa	b. Iowa	
1930	James W. Lyons[h]	1886	Iowa	b. Iowa	
1940	James Lyons[i]	1886	Iowa		
1942	James Wilfred Lyons[j]	19 July 1885	Webster City, Iowa		
1944	James Lyons[k]	12 July 1885	Hamilton County, Iowa	Kearns & Mary (Cassidy) Lyons, b. Ireland [sic]	
1950	James Lyons[l]	1886	Iowa		

a. 1895 Iowa state census, Hamilton County, Iowa, population schedule, image 210 of 681, James Lyon in the household of Kerance Lyons.
b. 1900 U.S. census, Hamilton County, Iowa, population Schedule, Cass Township, ED 103, household 54, dwelling 54, James Lyons in the household of Kearns Lyons.
c. "Iowa, U.S., Marriage Records, 1880-1947, 1909-1910, 435 (Adair-Dubuque), entry 69 for the year ending in 30 June 1910, James Lyons-Calla Bishop license entry (8 February 1910).
d. 1910 U.S. census, Hamilton County, Iowa, population schedule, Webster City, Ward 4, ED 112, household 35, dwelling 36, James W. Lyons in the household of K. E. Lyons.
e. 1910 U.S. census, Hamilton County, Iowa, population schedule, Webster City, Ward 3, ED 111, household 109, dwelling 109, James W. Lyons in the household of Joseph A. Bishop.
f. "U.S. World War I Draft Registration Cards, 1917-1918," Minnesota > Minneapolis City > 12 > Draft Card L, serial number too faint to read, James Wilfred Lyons.
g. 1920 U.S. census, Hennepin County, Minnesota, population schedule, Minneapolis, Ward 12, ED 227, household 51, dwelling 51, James Lyons.
h. 1930 U.S. census, San Francisco County, California, population schedule, San Francisco, Ward 24, ED 108, household 42, dwelling 43, James Lyons.
i. 1940 U.S. census, San Mateo County, California, population schedule, Other places (Brisbane), ED 41-23, household 237, James Lyons.
j. "U.S., World War II Draft Registration Cards, 1942, California > all > Dini, Achille-Questoni, Mario, Serial number 2920, James Wilfred Lyons.
k. "Iowa, U.S., births (series) 1880-1904, 1921-1944 and Delayed Births (series, 1856-1940," All > Delayed births, no. 125001-130000, 1884,1886, no. 127451, James Lyons.
l. 1950 U.S. census, San Mateo County, California, population schedule, Other places (Brisbane), ED 41-98, household 84, James Lyons.

James Wilfred or some variation could be his birth name; Lyons is not. The birth date is consistent for July 1885, but differing dates of the birth were recorded later in life.

The databases for MyHeritage, the Italian Genealogical Group and the New York Historic Vital Records were searched for a James born in July 1885. No candidates revealed themselves. Surname searches were also conducted for Wilfred/Wilford/Wolford with no findings. Not enough data exist to piece together candidate parents for James Lyons.

CONCLUSION

James Wilfred (—?—) Lyons was born either 12th or the 19th of July 1885 in New York. He was fostered into the family of Kearnes and Mary (Cassidy) Lyons.

On 8 February of 1910, James and Calla Bishop took out a license to marry in Dubuque, Iowa. No record of the marriage exists; however, they indicated they were married in the 1910 census enumeration. On 26 June 1915 James married second Florence Dorothy Bugbee in St. Croix, Wisconsin. He lived in Minneapolis at the time. Between 1930 and 1935, James and Florence moved to Brisbane, San Mateo County, California. James died of a prolonged illness in the sanitarium in Belmont, California, on 4 July 1953.

No children were born of either marriage. DNA will not assist in identifying his parents.

(*See* https://iowaorphans.wordpress.com for the effort invested in finding candidate parents for James.)

Anna (Crane) McIntyre

B. March 1887 in New York
D. 14 December 1959, Hospital for the Insane, Yankton, South Dakota
Birth Family: —?— McIntyre
Foster Family: Robert and Mary A. Crane

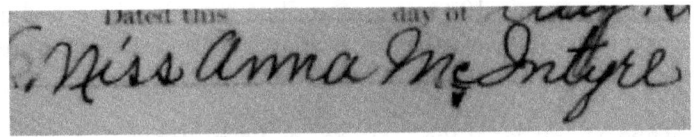

Receipt of allocation, Robert Crane's probate packet

Anne McIntyre, probably age 3, arrived in Hamilton County in 1890. In 1895 Anna Crane, now age 8 and born in New York, resided with Robert and Mary Crane and adult Frances E. Crane. Robert and Mary, both age 66, were born in England and Canada respectively.[335] Anne was one of the youngest orphans who came to Hamilton County.

No direct evidence indicates Anne was an out-placed orphan from New York City, but the location of her birth, her age, the advanced age of her foster parents, and living in Hamilton County identifies her as one. Her later actions and those of Robert Crane confirm she was an orphan that came into the family.

Anna Crane attended country school with 18 other students in Marion Township. Teacher Clara Carlson reported that Anna had perfect attendance in the month of November 1894, even if she wasn't on time every school day.[336]

---

[335] 1895 State of Iowa census, Hamilton County, Iowa, population schedule, Marion Township, p. 590, image 520 of 681, Anna Crane in the household of Robert Crane.

[336] "Report of school taught…," *Stratford Courier*, 19 December 1894, p. 4, col. 2.

School records are in conflict. In 1940 Anne was enumerated as attending school through the 4th grade.[337] Previously, she was reported as attending school when she was age 15.[338]

In 1897 Annie Crane, described as the 12 year-old "adopted daughter" of Robert Crane, broke her leg after slipping on a step inside the home. The Cranes were not at home and Annie spent several hours on the floor waiting for their return. She received medical care and was reported as "getting along nicely."[339]

In 1900 Annie Crane, age 15, still lived with Robert Crane, his wife Mary and their grandson, age 10. Annie, described as a daughter, had attended school seven and a half months this past year.[340] It is unclear whose child the grandson was, but it was not Annie's.

In 1905 Anne McIntyre, of the same age and birth location as Anne Crane, lived in the Stratford area.[341] The name change probably reflects a return to her New York City name.

Robert Crane, Anne Crane's foster father, died 16 November 1905 in Stratford, Hamilton County. In a codicil to his will added in October 1905, Robert wrote:

> I give to Anna McIntire the sum of Two hundred dollars, to be paid to her at the same time as the legacies are paid to my children, i.e. after the death of myself and wife. *This bequest being made on condition that said Anna McIntire will file no further claims or demands against the estate of myself or wife.* If any such claims are filed by said Anna McIntire this bequest will be withdrawn and of no effect.[342]

---

[337] 1940 U.S. census, Yankton County, South Dakota, population schedule, Utica, ED 68-14, p. 15B, line 78, Anna McIntyre.

[338] 1900 U.S. census, Hamilton County, Iowa, population schedule, Marion Township, ED 112, p. 6 & 7, household 144, dwelling 146, Anne Crane residing in the household of Robert Crane.

[339] "Broken Limb," *Stratford Courier*, 4 November 1897, p. 4, col 2.

[340] 1900 U.S. census, Hamilton County, Iowa, population schedule, Marion Township, ED 112, p. 6 & 7, household 144, dwelling 146, Anne Crane residing in the household of Robert Crane.

[341] 1905 State of Iowa census, Hamilton County, Iowa, population schedule, Stratford, image 3633 of 5304, card no. 95, Anne McIntire. Also, 1905 State of Iowa census, Hamilton County, Iowa, population schedule, Stratford, image 2 of 9, lines 93 and 94, Robert Crane.

[342] Hamilton County, Iowa, probate file number #1178, final report, Robert Crane, codicil (19 October 1906); Office of the Court Clerk, Hamilton County Courthouse, Webster City, Iowa. Text is enhanced by the author.

A tone of irritation is apparent in the codicil, as if Anna McIntyre was repeatedly asking for money from the family. Robert wanted it to stop, and it worked.

Anna had to wait for her money from the Cranes. With the death of Mary Crane on 3 November 1911 in Hamilton County, Iowa, the codicil was activated.[343] On 13 October 1913, Anna McIntyre of Woonsocket, South Dakota, signed the waiver acknowledging receipt of the $200.[344] This codicil linked the Crane family with the out-placed orphan Annie McIntyre.

Between 1905 and 1910, Anne moved to South Dakota. In 1910 Anne McIntyre, age 23 and born in New York, was a servant in the household of Harry M. Lucas, his wife, and their two children in Woonsocket, Sanborn County, South Dakota.[345] The lack of presence of Anne Crane/McIntyre in Hamilton County coincides with the appearance of Anna McIntyre in Stratford and South Dakota. Coupled with the reference in Robert Crane's will, Anna McIntyre is the same person as Anne Crane.

Also residing in Woonsocket at the same time was another Hamilton County orphan. Iris Doutrich, alias Harry Dawson, had recently been released from Leavenworth prison. Harry, single, age 26 (b. 1884, New York) was a clerk for a hotel.[346] It is unlikely this was a coincidence.

In 1915 Anna still resided in Woonsocket, working as a domestic.[347] Harry Dawson had left the area.

The remaining story of Anna's life provides the basis for the Crane family severing their relationship with Anna (Crane) McIntyre.

---

[343] "Highly Respected Pioneer Called Home" obituary of Mrs. Robert Crane, *Stratford Courier*, 9 November 1911, p. 8, col. 4.

[344] Hamilton County, Iowa, probate file number #1178, final report, Robert Crane, acknowledgement of receipt by Anna McIntyre (6 August 1913); Office of the Court Clerk, Hamilton County Courthouse, Webster City, Iowa.

[345] 1910 U.S. census, Sanborn County, South Dakota, population schedule, Woonsocket, Ward 1, ED 386, p. 2A, household 37, dwelling 38, Anne McIntyre in the household of Harry Lucas.

[346] 1910 U.S. census, Sanborn County, South Dakota, Woonsocket, Ward 1, ED 386, p. 4B, household 92, dwelling 96, Harry Dawson in the employment of Fredrick H. Davis, proprietor. See Bio of Iris (McFarland) Doutrich/Harry Dawson for alias.

[347] 1915 South Dakota state census, Sanborn County, South Dakota, population schedule, Woonsocket, Ward 1, card no. 214, Anna McIntire.

Between 1915 and 1920, Anna McIntyre became an "inmate" in the South Dakota Hospital for the Insane.[348]

The Dakota Hospital for the Insane, as it was then called, was established in 1880, but quickly suffered from overcrowding and under-funding. In 1899 a devastating fire killed seventeen women patients, which encouraged the legislature to fund new buildings and greater staffing levels. In 1918 about the time Anna became a resident, the name changed officially to Yankton State Hospital. During the 1920s and the 1930s, the facility went through a difficult time with few funds and low levels and expertise of staffing. When the war broke out, the available staff were generally too young or too old to be drafted or serve. After the war with advances in therapeutic care, the population started to decrease.[349]

Anna resided in the state facility in Yankton until her death on 14 December 1959.[350] She is probably buried at the hospital cemetery. Unless a family member paid for a stone, most markers provide only the patient's number.[351] An historical inventory of the occupants of the cemetery and their patient number was created in 1941. This predates Anna's death.

The documents generated during the life of Anna (Crane) McIntyre provide identifiers of her New York birth.

---

[348] 1920 U.S. census, Yankton County, South Dakota, population schedule, Utica, ED 262, p. 9B, line 58, Anna McIntyre.

[349] "Yankton State Hospital," *Asylum Projects*, https://www.asylumprojects.org/index.php/Yankton_State_Hospital

[350] South Dakota Death Index, 1879-1955, no. 315438, Anna McIntyre death entry (14 December 1959). As a resident: 1930 U.S. census, ED 14, p. 16B, line 58, Anna McIntyre. Also, 1940 U.S. census,, ED 68-14, p. 15B, line 78, Anna McIntyre. 1950 U.S. census, ED 67-14, p. 33, line 29, Anna McIntyre. All in the populations schedule for Utica, Yankton County, South Dakota.

[351] *Asylum Project*, "Yankton State Hospital: Cemetery," (https://www.asylumprojects.org/index.php/Yankton_State_Hospital).

Figure 1-AMc
Name, location and date of birth, foster and birth parents of Anna McIntyre

Year	Name	Birth date	Birth location	Birth parents	Foster parents
1895	Anna Crane[a]	1887	New York		Robert Crane
1900	Annie Crane[b]	March 1885	New York	b. Unknown	Robert Crane
1905	Anne McIntire[c]	1885	Unknown	b. Unknown	
1906	Anna McIntyre[d]				Robert Crane
1910	Anna McIntyre[e]	1887	New York	b. New York	
1915	Anna McIntyre[f]	1890	US	b. US	
1920	Anne McIntyre[g]	1890	New York	b. Unknown	
1930	Ana McIntyre[h]	1890	New York	b. Unknown	
1940	Anna McIntyre[i]	1889	New York	b. Unknown	
1950	Anna McIntyre[j]	1889	New York	b. Unknown	

a. 1895 State of Iowa census, Hamilton County, Iowa, population schedule, Marion Township, p. 590, image 520 of 681, Anna Crane in the household of Robert Crane.
b. 1900 U.S. census, Hamilton County, Iowa, population schedule, Marion Township, ED 112, p. 6 & 7, household 144, dwelling 146, Anne Crane in the household of Robert Crane.
c. 1905 State of Iowa census, Hamilton County, Iowa, population schedule, Stratford, image 3633 of 5304, card no. 95, Anne McIntire.
d. Hamilton County, Iowa, probate file number #1178, final report, Robert Crane, acknowledgement of receipt by Anna McIntyre (6 August 1913); Office of the Court Clerk, Hamilton County Courthouse, Webster City, Iowa.
e. 1910 U.S. census, Sanborn County, South Dakota, population schedule, Woonsocket, Ward 1, ED 386, p. 2A, household 37, dwelling 38, Anne McIntyre in the household of Harry Lucas.
f. 1915 South Dakota state census, Sanborn County, South Dakota, population schedule, Woonsocket, Ward 1, card no. 214, Anna McIntire.
g. 1920 U.S. census, Yankton County, South Dakota, population schedule, Utica, ED 262, p. 9B, line 58, Anna McIntyre.
h. 1930 U.S. census, Yankton County, South Dakota, population schedule, Utica, ED 14, p. 16A, line 53, Anna McIntyre.
i. 1940 U.S. census, Yankton County, South Dakota, population schedule, Utica, ED 68-14, p. 15B, line 78, Anna McIntyre.
j. 1950 U.S. census, Yankton County, South Dakota, population schedule, Utica, ED 67-14, p. 33, line 29, Anna McIntyre. Anna was selected for more information.

Anna McIntyre used her foster father's name while growing up and switched to her New York name when she reached adulthood. She was probably born in March 1885 or 1887 in New York City.

The identification of the birth parents of Anna McIntyre is inconclusive. Too many candidates make it difficult to identify the orphan.

CONCLUSION

Anna (Crane) McIntyre was probably born March 1885-1887 in New York City. She was one of the youngest orphans to travel to Hamilton County in 1890. Anna lived with Robert and Mary Crane until early adulthood at which time she moved to Woonsocket, South Dakota, and worked as a domestic. Between 1915 and 1920, she was confined to the South Dakota Hospital for the Insane in Yankton until her death on 14 December 1959.

Privacy rules in the state of South Dakota allow only descendants to access the records. Anna McIntyre had no known descendants; DNA would not assist in identifying her New York parents.

(*See* https://iowaorphans.wordpress.com for future information as it is acquired.)

Harry Guseka Moore

B. 7 October 1884, New York City
D. 25 February 1951, Webster City, Iowa
Birth Family: —?— Guseka
Foster Family: Alfred and Sarah E. Moore

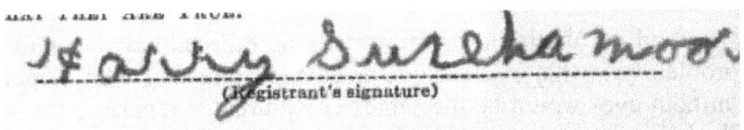

WWII Draft Registration Card

Harry Moore was an orphan train rider to Hamilton County in the fall of 1890.

> ...Harry Guseka Moore was born Oct. 2, 1884 in New York City. When he was six years old he came to Webster City to make his home with Mr. and Mrs. Alfred Moore, his foster parents....[352]

In 1895 Harry Moore, age 10 and born in New York, resided with Alfred and Sarah E. Moore, with two boarders, and Cora Kraft and her apparent husband Adam.[353] In 1900 Harry Moore, age 15 and born in New York state, continued his residency with Alfred and Sarah E. Moore in Webster City and was identified as their adopted son. The Moores had been married 29 years and had three children, two still living. Harry attended school. The location of Harry's birth parents was not known.[354]

The earliest recorded use of the name Guseka by Harry, a possible birth surname, was in 1905 when Harry Moore Guseka was party to a land transaction from M. M. B. Woodall and husband.[355]

---

[352] "Harry Moore Dies in City," *Daily Freeman Journal*, 26 February 1951, p. 1, col. 8.

[353] 1895 Iowa state census, Hamilton County, Iowa, population schedule, Webster City, p. 85, household 224, dwelling 244, Alf. Moore.

[354] 1900 U. S. census, Hamilton County, Iowa, population schedule, Webster City, ED 100, p. 4, household 75, dwelling 78, Harry Moore in the household of Alfred Moore.

[355] "Warranty Deed" town lot, M.M.B. Woodall and M. L. Woodall, husband, to Harry Moore Guseka, signed and filed 18 July 1905; Hamilton County Recorder's Office. Also, "Real Estate Transfers," *Webster City Journal*, 20 July 1905, p. 8, col. 2, from M.M.B. Woodall and husband to Harry Moore Guseka for "lot 2-blk 57 W C."

In 1910 Harry worked for the railroad as a bridge builder and continued his residency with the Moore family in Webster City. Also living with the family was a granddaughter.[356] In 1920 Harry continued to work for the railroad as a section foreman for construction. Harry's parents were noted as being born in Ohio and Kentucky, the birth location of his foster parents.[357]

In 1917 Harry, an employee of the Illinois Central Railway, received a promotion to Section Foreman of the Parkersburg section of the railroad.[358] Harry and his foster parents moved to Parkersburg for six years before returning to Hamilton County.[359]

Harry applied for another promotion with the railroad but was denied due to a problem with his eyes. A doctor advised him that with surgery, his sight in both eyes would be the same. The journalist reporting the surgery described Harry as a "very faithful and a good, honest man, and it is to be hoped that he can pass the required examination by reason of this operation."[360] The outcome of the surgery is not known, but no promotion occurred.

In 1925 the family was enumerated twice. In the first, Sarah Moore, now widowed, was head of household. Also living in the home was daughter Cora M. Kraft and her husband Adam Kraft. Harry was mistakenly enumerated as Harry Kraft. The birth location of Harry and his parents and the names of his parents were those of his foster parents.[361] In the second enumeration, probably more accurate, Adam Kraft was enumerated as the head of household with his wife Cora and Sarah E. Moore. Harry Guseka completed the family group. The names and birth locations of Harry's parents were unknown.[362]

In 1930 Harry was the head of the household occupied by widow Cora Kraft and Sarah E. Moore, the widowed wife of Alfred. Harry now 45 and

---

[356] 1910 U. S. census, Hamilton County, Iowa, population schedule, Webster City, ED 110, p. 13A, household check mark, dwelling check mark, Harry Moore in the household of Alfred Moore.

[357] 1920 U. S. census, Hamilton County, Iowa, population schedule, Webster City, ED 79, p. 4B, household 103, dwelling 106 Harry Moore in the household of Alfred Moore.

[358] "Gets Deserved promotion," *Webster City Freeman*, 19 June 1917, p. 1, col 2.

[359] "Obituary: Alfred Moore," *Webster City Journal*, 27 December 1923, p. 10, col 4.

[360] "About Former Local Man," *Webster City Daily News*, 7 March 1924, p. 8, col. 2.

[361] 1925 Iowa state census, Hamilton County, Iowa, population schedule, Webster City, lines 136 and 139, Harry Moore in the household of Sarah Moore.

[362] 1925 Iowa state census, Hamilton County, Iowa, population schedule, Williams Township, lines 27-30, Harry Guseka in the household of Adam Kraft.

single, was born in New York, and his parents were born in the United States. He was a laborer on a railroad section. He owned the home valued at $3000.³⁶³

Coming out of the Depression in 1940, the composition of the family remained the same. Harry, age 55, worked for the railroad as a trackman, but was unable to work. He had earned no money in the previous year. All three had income from other sources, but no payments from employment. The house was now valued at $1000.³⁶⁴

Harry Guseka Moore registered for the "old man's draft" on 27 April 1942 in Webster City, declaring that he was born 7 October 1884 in New York. He was 5'9" tall, weighed 137 pounds, had gray hair and blue eyes, and had a medium complexion. Mrs. Cora Kraft was the person who would always know his address. He was unemployed.³⁶⁵

Harry died at his home at 522 Bank Street in Webster City on 25 February 1952 at the age of 66. He willed to his "foster sister, Cora May Kraft of Webster City all property." His total estate was valued at $2500.³⁶⁶ this is a rare instance of personal or real property being willed to a foster family member, indicating close familial ties.

At the time of his death, Harry was a trackman for the Illinois Central Railroad. His parents' names were unknown, but he was born in New York City. ³⁶⁷ He never married; and had no descendants.

Possible spelling variations for Guseka include Geeseeka, Geseka, Cusick, Cusic, and Cusack.

---

³⁶³ 1930 U. S. census, Hamilton County, Iowa, population schedule, Webster City, ED 4, p. 2B, household 42, dwelling 54, Harry Moore.
³⁶⁴ 1940 U. S. census, Hamilton County, Iowa, population schedule, Webster City, ED 40-4, p. 8B, household 183, Harry Moore. Cora, Harry's "sister" was the informant.
³⁶⁵ U.S., World War II draft Registration Cards, 1942, Iowa, serial number U1791for Harry Guseka Moore.
³⁶⁶ Hamilton County, Iowa, probate file number #5916, will, Harry G. Moore; Office of the Court Clerk.
³⁶⁷ State of Iowa, Certificate of Death, certificate 02860, Hamilton County, Harry Guseka Moore death certificate (25 February 1951).

Table 1-HGM
Name, location and date of birth, foster and birth parents of Harry Guseka Moore

Year	Name	Birth date	Birth location	Birth parents	Foster parents
1895	Harry Moore[a]	1885	New York		Alf. Moore
1900	Harry Moore (adopted)[b]	Oct 1884	New York	b. Unknown	Alfred Moore
1905	Harry Moore Guseka[c]				
1910	Harry Moore[d]	1884	New York	b. Unknown	Alfred Moore
1920	Harry Moore[e]	1885	New York	b. Ohio & KY, (locations of birth of foster parents)	Alfred Moore
1925	Harry Kraft[f]	1885	Iowa	Lists foster parents	Alfred Moore
1925	Harry Guseka[g]	1884	New York	"No knowledge of parents"	
1930	Harry Moore	1885	NY	b. United States	Moore household
1940	Harry G. Moore[i]	1885	New York		Sarah Moore
1942	Harry Guseka Moore[j]	7 Oct. 1884	New York City, NY		Living with Mrs. Cora Kraft
1950	Harry G. Moore[k]	1885	New York		
1951	Harry Moore[l]	7 Oct. 1884	New York	Unknown	

a. 1895 Iowa state census, Hamilton County, Iowa, population schedule, Webster City, p. 85, household 224, dwelling 244, Alf. Moore.
   b. 1900 U. S. census, Hamilton County, Iowa, population schedule, Webster City, ED 100, p. 4, household 75, dwelling 78, Harry Moore in the household of Alfred Moore.
   c. "Warranty Deed" town lot, M.M.B. Woodall and M. L. Woodall, husband, to Harry Moore Guseka, signed and filed 18 July 1905; Hamilton County Recorder's Office.
   d. 1910 U. S. census, Hamilton County, Iowa, population schedule, Webster City, ED 110, p. 13A, household check mark, dwelling check mark, Harry Moore in the household of Alfred Moore.
   e. 1920 U. S. census, Hamilton County, Iowa, population schedule, Webster City, ED 79, p. 4B, household 103, dwelling 106 Harry Moore in the household of Alfred Moore.
   f. 1925 Iowa state census, Hamilton County, Iowa, population schedule, Webster City, lines 136 and 139, Harry Moore in the household of Sarah Moore.
   g. 1925 Iowa state census, Hamilton County, Iowa, population schedule, Williams Township, lines 27-30, Harry Guseka in the household of Adam Kraft.
   h. 1930 U. S. census, Hamilton County, Iowa, population schedule, Webster City, ED 4, p. 2B, household 42, dwelling 54, Harry Moore.
   i. 1940 U. S. census, Hamilton County, Iowa, population schedule, Webster City, ED 40-4, p. 8B, household 183, Harry Moore. Cora, Harry's "sister" was the informant.
   j. U.S., World War II draft Registration Cards, 1942," Iowa, Molsberry, Arthur-Moore, Perry, serial number U1791 for Harry Guseka Moore; Records of the Selective Service System.
   k. 1950 U.S. census, Hamilton County, Iowa, population schedule, Webster Township, ED 40-6, p. 17, household 178, Harry G. Moore.
   l. State of Iowa, Certificate of Death, certificate 02860, Hamilton County, Harry Guseka Moore death certificate (25 February 1951).

Based on the variety of sources, Harry Guseka Moore most likely was born 7 October 1884 in New York City. His birth parents are unknown but may have the surname of Guseka or one of its many variations.

In 1880 no likely families of the name Guseka resided in New York City.[368] This investigation revealed no additional evidence of the birth parents of Harry Guseka Moore.

CONCLUSION

Harry Moore, possibly Guseka, arrived in Hamilton County, Iowa, as an out-placed orphan in either August or November 1890. His foster parents were Alfred and Sarah Moore. He lived continuously in Hamilton County, Iowa, with the Moore family or their daughter until his death in 1951. He was born 7 October 1884 in New York, but the names and the locations of his birth parents are unknown.

---

[368] Searched 1880 U.S. census, New York, population schedule, New York City and its boroughs. No matches for G*s*ka, born 1850+/- 10 years.

Harry Guseka Moore never married and had no children; DNA cannot be used to identify his parents.

(*See* https://iowaorphans.wordpress.com for new and additional information.)

Nelson Morris

B. May 1883 in New York
D. Unknown
Birth Family: —?— Morris
Foster Family: Luther & Eva Boozel

In 1895 Nelson Morris, 10 years old and born in New York, resided with the Luther Boozel family. Luther was 42 years old and born in Illinois. His apparent wife, Eva, was 32 and born in Ohio. No other children lived in the household.[369] It seems likely that with no Boozel children, Luther needed help on the farm, and the young Nelson provided it.

In 1900 Nelson continued his residency with Luther and Eva. Nelson was described as an "adopted son." Nelson was born May 1883 in New York. The birth place of his parents was not known.[370] In 1905 Nelson Morris, age 22 and born in New York, had resided in Iowa for 15 years.[371] That makes his arrival in Iowa in 1890. There is no evidence of a formal adoption.

It appeared that Nelson had the usual childhood events. In 1896 he fell on the way to school and broke his collar bone.[372] Nelson attended an evening party in 1904.[373]

In 1911 Luther worked at the Little Chicago Cafe.[374] In 1912 he had a run-in with the law, was charged with selling liquor to minors, and had to appear in court.[375] He was acquitted of the charge.[376]

---

[369] 1895 Iowa state census, Hamilton County, Iowa, population schedule,, p. 57 (stamped), household 132, dwelling 139, Nelson Morris in the household of Luther Boozel.

[370] 1900 U.S. census, Hamilton County, Iowa, population schedule, Webster City, ED 99, p. 12, household 277, dwelling 287, Nelson Morris in the household of Luther Bozell.

[371] 1905 Iowa census, Hamilton County, Iowa, population schedule, Webster City, image no. 4030 of 5304, card no. 173, Nelson Morris.

[372] "Nelson Morris, a pupil….," *Hamilton County Journal*, 3 October 1896, p. 5, col3.

[373] "Society Events-Evening Party," *Daily Freeman-Tribune*, 18 February 1904, p. 4, col. 3.

[374] "Personal Items," *Webster City Journal*, 7 September 1911, p. 4, col 4.

[375] "In the District Court," *Webster City Journal*, 9 May 1912, p. 5, col 5.

[376] "In the District Court," *Webster City Journal*, 16 May 1912, p. 1, col. 4.

Nelson is not found in the 1910 census. It is possible that he boarded with the Alonzo Fuller family in Minneapolis, Minnesota, in 1910. The enumerator left many of the significant identifiers blank, but Minneapolis would have been a reasonable place for a young, single man to find work.377

Tragedy struck on 4 July 1912. Henry [sic] Reinhardt and his brother-in-law were riding in their car, when Henry was shot in a random act of holiday jubilation. Henry died within 30 minutes. Witnesses identified Nelson Morris as the probable perpetrator; but by the time the police mobilized, Nelson had left the county. The police thought he left for Des Moines.378 A credible unnamed witness informed them that Nelson had fled to "old Mexico."379 Henry Reinhardt's wife had died the year before in childbirth. With Henry's death, six children between the ages of one and twelve became orphans.380

The coroner's investigation ruled the death accidental.381 Manslaughter was the probable charge, but Nelson was never apprehended.

No additional information is available for Nelson Morris.

Few sources provide clues to the parentage and birth of Nelson Morris.

---

377 1910 U.S. census, Hennipin County, Minnesota, population schedule, Ward 4, Minneapolis, ED 65, p. 10B, household 80, dwelling 80, Nelson Morris in the household of Alonzo Fuller.

378 "Suspected man is Traced to Des Moines," *Webster City Herald*, 11 July 1912, p. 8, col 2. The newspaper report the name wrong. The victim was named William but for brevity and readability, the name is kept consistent with the initial reporting.

379 "In Old Mexico," *Webster City Herald*, 8 August 1912, p. 5, col 3.

380 Ancestry Public Tree, Nancy Mick-Holstrom, "Holstrom Family Tree," William Frederick Reinhardt, https://www.ancestry.com/family-tree/person/tree/161850861/person/252119792919/facts

381 "Corner's [sic] Record of Deaths, 1911-12," William A Reinhardt death entry (4 July 1912), unpaginated; Hamilton County (Iowa) Recorder's office, County Courthouse.

Figure 1-NM
Name, location and date of birth, foster and birth parents
of Nelson Morris

Year	Name	Birth date	Birth location	Birth parents	Foster parents
1895	Nelson Morris[a]	1885	New York		Luther Boozel
1900	Nelson Morris[b]	May 1883	New York	b. New York	Luther Bozel
1905	Nelson Morris[c]	1883	New York		

a. 1895 Iowa state census, Hamilton County, Iowa, population schedule,, p. 57 (stamped), household 132, dwelling 139, Nelson Morris in the household of Luther Boozel.
b. 1900 U.S. census, Hamilton County, Iowa, population schedule, Webster City, ED 99, p. 12, household 277, dwelling 287, Nelson Morris in the household of Luther Bozell.
c. 1905 Iowa census, Hamilton County, Iowa, population schedule, Webster City, image no. 4030 of 5304, card no. 173, Nelson Morris.

Nelson Morris was probably his birth name. No entries for a Nelson Morris exist in the IGG index or in NYC Historical Vital Records. A search for Nelson Morris, born May 1883 in New York City, yielded no likely candidates in the World War I draft registration.

Nelson may have fled to "Old Mexico" and then returned to a southwestern state. A common name with no geographic placement makes identification of Nelson impossible.

CONCLUSION
Nelson Morris was born May 1883 or 1885 in New York. The birth location of his parents may be New York. Perhaps Nelson worked in Minneapolis or Des Moines for a while before returning to Hamilton County to work or for the July 4th celebration. Nelson Morris quickly left Hamilton County after fatally shooting a William A. Reinhardt at a July 4th celebration in 1912.

With few documents, no geographic placement and no known descendants, Nelson's identification is unlikely.

(*See* https://iowaorphans.wordpress.com for any new information since the publication of the book.)

118

GEORGE JENSEN MYERS

B. 18 JUNE 1882 IN NEW YORK
D. 4 JUNE, 1963, HAMILTON COUNTY HOSPITAL, WEBSTER CITY, IOWA
BIRTH FAMILY: —?— MYERS[382]
FOSTER FAMILY: NELS AND NELLIE JENSEN

WWI Draft Registration Card

George Jensen Myers was an out-placed orphan who came to Hamilton County, Iowa in 1890.

George J. Myers was born 18 June 1882 in New York. At the age of 8 he came to Iowa to make his home with his foster parents, Mr. and Mrs. Nels Jensen…[383]

In 1895 George Jensen, age 11 and born in New York, was the only child living with Nels and Nellie Jensen. Nels was 39 years old, Nellie was 32, and both were born in Denmark.[384]

By 1900 the family of Nels and Nellie Jensen included an adopted girl named Carrie B., birth surname unknown, born May 1895 in Iowa. George Jensen worked one household away as a farm laborer for the Charles Courter family. George was 17 years old and born in New York in June 1882. His parents were born in Denmark, reflecting the birth locations of his foster parents and probably not his birth parents.[385]

George was responsible for the farm chores which varied by season.

---

[382] Madonna Harm, "Orphan Train Riders to Iowa," IAGenWeb, Special Project, database (http://iagenweb.org/history/orphans/riders/MH_IAOTR.htm) last updated 2003.

[383] "George Meyers Dies at 80," *Daily Freeman Journal*, 4 June 1963, p. 1, col. 1.

[384] 1895 State of Iowa census, Hamilton County, Iowa, population schedule, image 329 of 681, George Jensen in the household of Nels Jensen.

[385] 1900 U.S. census, Hamilton County, Iowa, population schedule, Fremont, ED 103, p. 1, household 8, dwelling 8, Nels Jensen and household 9, dwelling 9, George Jensen in the household of Charles Courter.

When [George] was 16 years old he helped thresh oats with a horse powered machine. His job was to cut the twine bands on the bundles and he had to stand on a box to reach them. Another man pushed the loosened bundles in the machine.[386]

Shortly after 1900 Nels and Nellie Jensen moved to Newaygo County, Michigan. George stayed in the Hamilton County area at the boarding house of S. A. Christenson for the next nine years. During this time, he assumed the surname Myers, probably the surname of his NYC parents.

In 1905 George Myers, age 22 and born in New York, declared he had been in Iowa for 15 years, making his arrival year 1890, and further confirming his status as an out-placed orphan from New York.[387]

As a young man he held a variety of jobs. He worked as a laborer for the Closz & Howard Sieve Manufacturing company and as a switchman on the Illinois Central Railroad.[388]

George J. Myers, age 33, married Anna Rabe, age 24, of Ackley, Iowa, on 17 June 1916. The entry is devoid of any other identifying information.
   [George] is a young man of exemplary habits and well worthy the bride he has chosen.[389]

After their marriage, George worked for Arthur Fink as a cement worker.[390]

In 1920 the couple moved to Webster City where George was a laborer working out and Anna was a teacher. They owned their home with a mortgage; their home was valued at $3500, a value higher than their

---

[386] Clara Madsen & Leta Seaman, R.N., "Along Friendship Lane," *Daily Freeman Journal*, 16 March 1963, p. 8, col 4.

[387] 1905 Iowa state census, Hamilton County, Iowa, population schedule, Fremont Township, image 3802 of 5304, card no. 17, George Myers.

[388] 1910 U.S. census, Hamilton County, Iowa, population schedule, Webster City, Ward 4, ED 112, p. 7B, household 156, dwelling 158, George Myers in the household of S.A. Christenson. Also, "Local Young Man Weds," *Webster City Freeman*, 20 June 1916, p. 5, col. 6.

[389] "Iowa, U.S., Marriage Records, 1880-1945, 1915-1916 > 463 (Payette-Lee), Return of Marriages in the County of Hardin, fiscal year ending, 30 Jun 1916, p. 123, Myers-Robe marriage entry (no date given.). Also, "Local Young Man Weds," *Webster City Freeman*, 20 June 1916, p. 5, col. 6.

[390] "U.S. World War I Draft Registration Cards, 1917-1918," serial number 7216; George Jensen Myers,

neighbors. They also had a $600 mortgage debt remaining and $2000 worth of insurance.[391]

In 1921 Goerge and Anna had a daughter, Dorothy Lorraine.[392]

In 1925 George was 42 years old and had spent 35 of them in Iowa, consistent with previous records. George had 8 years of schooling and Anna had 12 years of schooling. The family belonged to the Methodist church.[393]

Going into the Depression years, George worked at the Monarch factory as a pressman. The couple owned their home, now valued at $3000.[394] The Depression must have hit the family hard; by 1940 George was seeking employment. He no longer worked at the Monarch Factory and had worked just 20 weeks the past year as a general laborer, earning $300. He had other income, but the source was not named. Daughter Dorothy was a stenographer for a printing plant, working 50 weeks in the past year, and earning $520.[395]

After the war years, George was employed again as a pressman, but now for McCollough Inc., a livestock equipment company. In spite of their difficulties in the 1930s, the couple retained their home at 1027 3rd Street in Webster City.[396]

George died 4 June 1963 in the Hamilton County Hospital where he had been convalescing for a month.[397] Anna (Rabe) Myers died in February

---

[391] 1920 U.S. census, Hamilton County, population schedule, Webster City, Ward 4, ED 124, p. 12B, George Myers.

[392] Iowa, U.S., births (series) 1880-1904, 1921-1944 and Delayed Births (series, 1856-1940, Birth records, Polk County, 1921-1923, Standard Certificate of Birth, Dorothy Lorraine Myers birth certificate (29 June 1921).

[393] 1925, Iowa state census, Hamilton, county, Iowa, population schedule, Webster City, 1027 third Street. George Myers.

[394] 1930 U.S. census, Hamilton County, Iowa, population schedule, Webster City, ED 6, p. 6B, household 133, dwelling 140, George J. Myers.

[395] 1940 U.S. census, Hamilton County, Iowa, population schedule, Webster City, ED 40-6, p. 20A, household 434, George J. Myers. Social Security began collecting taxes in 1937 and making monthly payments in January 1940.

[396] 1950 U. S. Census, Hamilton County, Iowa, population scheduled, Webster City, ED 40-10, p. 8, George J. Myers.

[397] "George Meyers Dies at 80," *Daily Freeman Journal*, 4 June 1963, p. 1, col. 1.

1986, in Lake Wilson, Minnesota. Both are buried in Oakwood Cemetery in Ackley, Iowa.[398]

The known information about George Jensen Myers:

Figure 2-GJM
Name, location and date of birth, foster and birth parents
of George Jensen Myers

Year	Name	Birth date	Birth location	Birth parents	Foster parents
1895	George Jensen[a]	1884	New York		Nels Jensen
1900	George Jensen[b]	June 1882	New York	b. Denmark	Nels Jensen
1905	George Myers[c]	1883	New York	b. Don't know	
1910	George Myers[d]	1883	New York	b. New York	
1917	George Jensen Myers[e]	18 June 1882			
1920	George Myers[f]	1884	New York	b. US	
1925	George Myers[g]		New York	names: don't know	
1930	George J. Myers[h]	1883	New York	b. don't know	
1940	George J. Myers[i]	1883	New York	b. U.S.	
1942	George J. Myers[j]	18 June 1882	New York City, NY		
1950	George J. Myers[k]	1883	New York		
1963	George Myer[l]	1882			

---

[398] Find a Grave, database and images (https://www.findagrave.com/memorial/146286599/george_jensen-myers: accessed July 11, 2024), memorial page for George Jensen Myers (18 Jun 1882–1963), Find a Grave Memorial ID 146286599, citing Oak Wood Cemetery, Ackley, Franklin County, Iowa, USA; Maintained by Jacki Bierma (contributor 47657130).

a. 1895 State of Iowa census, Hamilton County, Iowa, population schedule, image 329 of 681, George Jensen in the household of Nels Jensen.
b. 1900 U.S. census, Hamilton County, Iowa, population schedule, Fremont, ED 103, p. 1, household 8, dwelling 8, Nels Jensen and household 9, dwelling 9, George Jensen in the household of Charles Courter.
c. 1905 Iowa state census, Hamilton County, Iowa, population schedule, Fremont Township, image 3802 of 5304, card no. 17, George Myers.
d. 1910 U.S. census, Hamilton County, Iowa, population schedule, Webster City, Ward 4, ED 112, p. 7B, household 156, dwelling 158, George Myers in the household of S.A. Christenson.
e. "U.S. World War I Draft Registration Cards, 1917-1918," Hamilton County, Iowa > All < Draft Card M, George Jensen Myers.
f. 1920 U.S. census, Hamilton County, population schedule, Webster City, Ward 4, ED 124, p. 12B, George Myers.
g. 1925, Iowa state census, Hamilton, county, Iowa, population schedule, Webster City, 1027 third Street. George Myers.
h. 1930 U.S. census, Hamilton County, Iowa, population schedule, Webster City, ED 6, p. 6B, household 133, dwelling 140, George J. Myers.
i. 1940 U.S. census, Hamilton County, Iowa, population schedule, Webster City, ED 40-6, p. 20A, household 434, George J. Myers.
j. U.S., World War II draft Registration Cards, 1942, Iowa > All > Munson, severe-myers, John, serial number U655, George J. Myers.
k. 1950 U. S. Census, Hamilton County, Iowa, population scheduled, Webster City, ED 40-10, p. 8, George J. Myers.
l. Find a Grave, database and images (https://www.findagrave.com/memorial/146286599/george-jensen-myers), memorial page for George Jensen Myers (1882–1963), Find a Grave Memorial ID 146286599, citing Oak Wood Cemetery, Ackley, Franklin County, Iowa, USA.

Based on the accumulated information, George Jensen Myers was probably born 18 June 1882 in New York City, but 1883 and 1884 are also possible. Myers may be his birth name.

CONCLUSION

Based on the documentary evidence, George Jensen Myers was born 18 June 1882 in New York City. His parents are unknown. George was fostered into the Nels Jensen family; but when they moved to Michigan, he stayed in Hamilton County. On 17 June 1916, George married Anna Rabe, a school teacher. George held a series of jobs, but his job prospects decreased during the Depression. George died 4 June 1963 in Webster City.

George and Anna had a daughter Dorothy. DNA may assist in identifying George's NYC parents.

(*See* https://iowaorphans.wordpress.com for efforts to identify George's NYC parents.)

Edward Graham "Shorty" Pruismann

B. 15 July 1884 in Staten Island, New York
D. 5 April 1946, Webster City, Hamilton County, Iowa
Birth family: —?— Graham
Foster family: Frank and Henrietta Pruismann

(Signature or mark)

WWI Draft Registration Card

Superintendent Trott recorded F. Pruismann as the recipient of a male child in the 29 August 1890 delivery of children to Hamilton County.[399] The obituary of Ed Pruismann confirms that he was the child selected by Frank Pruismann.

    As a lad of about 5 years, Edward Graham was adopted by Frank and Henrietta Pruismann. He was raised and educated in this community.[400]
Edward's age at time of "adoption" aligns with the fall of 1890.

No child was enumerated in the Pruismann home in 1895. Frank, age 36, and Henrietta, age 24, were both born in Germany.[401]

In 1900 Edward Graham worked for George and Mary Klaus as a farm laborer. Edward was born in New York in 1884, possibly June or July. His parents were also born in New York.[402]

---

[399] "E. Trott of the children's aid society...," *The Freeman (Webster City, Iowa),* 3 September 1890, p. 5, col. 3.

[400] "Ed Pruisman Died at Home," *Webster City Freeman,* 8 April 1946, p. 5, col. 4. Formal adoption records in Hamilton County are not extant for Edward.

[401] 1895 State of Iowa census, Hamilton County, Iowa, population schedule, Independence Township, p. 425, image 381 of 681, Frank Pruismann.

[402] 1900 U.S. census, Hamilton County, Iowa, population schedule, Rose Grove Township, ED 109, p. 1, household 2, dwelling 3, Edward Graham residing in the household of Geo. Class. Month of birth is indexed as June, but the digital copy is too light to read.

In 1914, Edward was involved in an accident when he leaped out of a moving car to retrieve his hat. He became unconscious and was taken to the hospital; he fully recovered.[403]

By 1915 E. G. Pruismann, 29 years old and born in New York, resided in Hamilton County. The birth location of his parents was unknown. He stated that he had been in Iowa for 20 years (arrived in 1895). He was a barber and earned $400 in 1914. He had eight years of common school.[404]

Edward held a variety of jobs in Hamilton County. In 1915 he advertised
> If you are looking for a place to sleep while in Kamrar don't forget the City Restaurant. We are always ready with the best accommodations and a price that will suit your purse. Board and lodging by the day or week. Lunches at all hours. E.G. Pruisman, proprietor.[405]

That same year, E.G. Pruismann sold his barber shop.[406]

Edward participated in the Jewell and Webster City communities throughout his life. For example, in 1915 he was in charge of the merry-go-round for the Harvest Home Festival held in Webster City.[407] When the same event was held in 1917, he headed the Soliciting Committee.[408]

The Pruismann family included Edward in their many events. Edward, described as a cousin, attended a funeral of a relative killed in World War II.[409] In his obituary, the children of the Pruismanns were described as siblings.[410] This appears to be a close and supportive family throughout Edward's life.

In answering the call for young men to fight in Europe in 1917, Edward G. Pruismann registered for the draft. He declared he was born 15 July 1885 on Staten Island, New York, and described himself as short in height with a short build. He was blind in one eye and managed a restaurant.[411] Given

---

[403] "Badly Bruised in Auto Accident," *Webster City Freeman*, 25 August 1914, col. 2, p. 1

[404] 1915 State of Iowa census, Hamilton County, Iowa, population schedule, Kamrar, card no. 35, E. G. Pruismann.

[405] "City Restaurant," *Jewell Record*, 5 August 1915, p. 6, col 3.

[406] "George Carson....," *Jewell Record*, 5 August 1915, p. 6, col 1.

[407] "Harvest Home September 25," *Jewell Record (/Webster City)*, 15 September 1915, p. 1, col 3.

[408] "Harvest Home Next Tuesday," *Jewell Record (/Webster City)*, 16 August 1917, p. 6, col 4.

[409] "Held Service for Soldier," *Daily Freeman Journal*, 4 August 1944, p. 2, col. 3.

[410] "Ed Pruismann Died at Home," *Webster City Freeman*, 8 April 1946, p. 5, col. 4.

[411] "U.S., World War I Draft Registration cards, 1917-1918, Iowa, Hamilton County, Edward G. Prusmann.

his physical description, it is understandable why his nickname was "Shorty."[412] He did not serve in the war.[413]

Edward Pruismann, age 36 (b. 1889) was a roomer in the Eveline Baker household in 1925 in Webster City. He was born in New York.[414]

On 5 December 1927 in Ft. Dodge, Iowa, a Lutheran minister married E. G. Pruismann and Emma Rathman. Edward stated he was born in New York and identified his foster parents as his parents. Edward had returned to barbering.[415]

Heading into the Great Depression of the 1930's, Edward, his wife and their four-month-old daughter, Anna, resided in Webster City where Edward was a barber with his own shop. They owned their own home at 1414 Division Street, valued at $780; they did not own a radio. The informant declared Edward was born in Iowa, his father in the United States, and his mother in Iowa.[416] It is unlikely that Edward was the informant.

Coming out of the Depression in 1940, Edward Pruismann was a a laborer in a hog trough manufacturing plant and earned $748 the previous year. Edward, his wife, and their three daughters resided in the same house on Division Street. No other individual in the family had income.[417]

In 1942 the draft was again reinstated and Edward registered, declaring that he was born 15 July 1888 on Staten Island, New York. His closest kin was Mrs. Emma Pruismann. Edward worked for the McCollough Factory in Webster City.[418]

---

[412] "Ed Pruismann Died at Home," *Webster City Freeman*, 8 April 1946, p. 5, col. 4.

[413] 1930 U.S. census, Hamilton County, Iowa, population schedule, Webster City, ED 5, p. 1A, household 4, dwelling 4, Edward G. Pruismann.

[414] 1925 Iowa state census, Hamilton County, Iowa, population schedule, Scott-Webster City, line 19, Edward Pruisman in the household of Eveline Baker.

[415] "Iowa, U.S. Marriage Records, 1880-1945," marriage certificate, no. 94-019755, Pruismann-Rathman marriage entry (5 December 1927).

[416] 1930 U.S. census, Hamilton County, Iowa, population schedule, Webster City, ED 5, p. 1A, household 4, dwelling 4, Edward G. Pruismann.

[417] 1940 U.S. census, Hamilton County, Iowa, population schedule, Webster City, ED 40-5, p. 5A, household 102, Edward Pruismannn. Emma was the informant.

[418] "U.S., World War II Draft Registration Cards, 1942," Iowa, Price, Koehler-Pruseck, Frank, Edward Graham Pruismann.

In 1946, Edward applied for Social Security, declaring his birthdate as 15 July 1890.[419]

Edward Graham "Shorty" Pruismann died 5 April 1946 at his home in Webster City, Iowa. His birth place was unknown, and his foster parents were identified as his parents.[420]

Multiple sources provide inconsistent information concerning the birth of Edward Graham Pruismann.

Figure 1-EGP
Name, location and date of birth, foster and birth parents of Ed Graham Pruismann

Year	Name	Birth date	Birth location	Birth parents	Foster parents
1900	Edward Graham[a]	June 1884	New York	B. New York	
1915	Edward Pruismann[b]	1886	New York	b. Unknown	
1917	Edward G. Pruismann[c]	15 July 1885	Staten Island, New York	b. New York	
1925	Edward Pruiseman[d]	1889	New York	Unknown	
1927	E.G. Pruismann[e]	1888	New York	Frank & Henretta (Tapper) Pruisman	
1930	Edward G. Pruismann[f]	1892	Iowa	b. United States	
1940	Edward Pruismann[g]	1891	New York		
1942	Edward Graham Pruismann[h]	15 July 1888	Staten Island, New York		
	Edward Pruisman[i]	15 July 1890			
1946	Ed "Shorty" Prussian[j]	1889			Frank Pruisman

---

[419] U.S., Social Security Applications and Claims Index, 1936-2007," social security no. 484073433, Edward G. Pruisman.

[420] "Iowa Death Records, 1880-1904, 1921-1952," Iowa State Department of Health, State Office Number 40 4/5 45, Edward G. Pruisan death certificate (5 April 1946); digital image, *Ancestry*. Emma, his wife was the informant.

a. 1900 U.S. census, Hamilton County, Iowa, population schedule, Rose Grove Township, ED 109, p. 1, household 2, dwelling 3, Edward Graham residing in the household of Geo. Class.
b. 1915 State of Iowa census, Hamilton County, Iowa, population schedule, Kamrar, card no. 35, E. G. Pruismann.
c. "U.S., World War I Draft Registration cards, 1917-1918, Iowa, Hamilton County, Edward G. Prusmann.
d. 1925 Iowa state census, Hamilton County, Iowa, population schedule, Scott-Webster City, line 19, Edward Pruisman in the household of Eveline Baker.
e. "Iowa, U.S. Marriage Records, 1880-1945," marriage certificate, no. 94-019755, Pruismann-Rathman marriage entry (5 December 1927).
f. 1930 U.S. census, Hamilton County, Iowa, population schedule, Webster City, ED 5, p. 1A, household 4, dwelling 4, Edward G. Pruismann.
g. 1940 U.S. census, Hamilton County, Iowa, population schedule, Webster City, ED 40-5, p. 5A, household 102, Edward Pruismannn.
h. "U.S., World War II Draft Registration Cards, 1942," Iowa, Price, Koehler-Pruseck, Frank, Edward Graham Pruismann.
i. U.S., Social Security Applications and Claims Index, 1936-2007," social security no. 484073433, Edward G. Pruisman.
j. "Ed Pruisman Died at Home," *Webster City Freeman*, 8 April 1946, p. 5, col. 4.

A variety of sources indicate that Edward Graham Pruismann was born 15 June or July in 1884 or 1885 on Staten Island. Graham was possibly the surname of his New York parents; Pruismann was the name of his foster parents.

The birth records for Richmond County (Staten Island) start in 1898. If Edward Graham was born in Staten Island there are no online records of his birth.

CONCLUSION

Edward Graham was born June or July 1884 or 1885 on Staten Island, New York, and was fostered into the Frank Pruismann family. On 5 December 1927, in Ft. Dodge, Iowa, a Lutheran minister married E. G. Pruismann and Emma Rathman. Edward Graham Pruismann lived his whole life in Hamilton County, and died 5 April 1946 at his home in Webster City, Iowa.

Three daughters, Anna (b. 1930), Darlene (b. 1933), Henrietta (b. 1935), and a son still living at the time of the writing of this book, were born in Iowa. DNA may help identify Edward's parents.

(See https://iowaorphans.wordpress.com for more information about Edward acquired since publication.)

LILLIAN FLORENCE LINGREEN ROOP

B. FEBRUARY 1886 IN NEW YORK
D. 26 SEPTEMBER 1937, CALIFORNIA
BIRTH FAMILY: —?— LINGREEN
ADOPTING FAMILY: Charles H. and Sophronia Roop

Lilly Lingreen, age 5, arrived in Hamilton County in the October delivery of children. She was placed with the C. H. Rook [sic] family of Webster City.[421] Henry & Sophronia Roop selected Lillian and formally adopted her in late November 1890.

> Mr. and Mrs. H.C. Roop are so well pleased with the little girl, Lillian Lengren, that they took recently from the Children's Aid Society of New York, that they last week took out adoption papers according to law and the little Miss is now Lillian L. Roop.[422]

Lillian is the only known adoption of any of the identified orphans.

Lillian Roop, age 9 and born in New York, appeared in the household of Charles H. And Flora S. Roop in 1895. No other children lived with the family.[423]

Lillian participated in the activities offered a young girl in her community. In March 1899 she entered a biscuit making contest, hoping to win the Buck Range offered by the Buck Steel Range Company. Her biscuits were not the winner.[424] In 1901 she and many other "pretty girls" went to Fort Dodge to cheer for the boys in the inter-high school debate.[425] She attended a surprise party for a friend where there was a candy pull and other entertainment.[426] No other orphans attended these events.

---

[421] Kialy Carson, Kansas, [(CURATOR@ORPHANTRAINDEPOT.COM),] to Jill Morelli, email, 7 March 2023, "Info from the CAS," OTR folder.

[422] "Mr. and Mrs. H.C. Roop...," *Webster City Tribune,* 28 November 1890, p. 5, col. 4. Adoption records are closed in the state of Iowa unless under a court order.

[423] 1895 State of Iowa census, Hamilton County, Iowa, population schedule, image 106 of 681, Lillian Rook in the household of Chas. H. Rook.

[424] "The Baking Contest," *Hamilton County Journal,* 11 March 1899, p. 7, col. 6.

[425] "Off For Fort Dodge," *Daily Freeman Tribune,* 26 April 1901, p. 8, col. 2.

[426] "Society Events," *Daily Freeman Tribune,* 12 February 1902, p. 8, col. 2.

In 1900 the enumerator recorded that Lillian L. Roop was born February 1886 in New York.[427] Although Sophronia was born in New York, she migrated to Iowa prior to 1874, reducing the chance of a familial relationship with Lilian prior to 1890.

In 1903 Lillian and seven other Hamilton County residents attended a Royal Neighbors Camp in Eagle Grove, Iowa, for a day of entertainment and a box supper.[428] The Royal Neighbors organization, founded in 1895 by six women, provided insurance for women which they marketed by holding all day camp meetings.[429]

Lillian married John Bennett Gray of Eagle Grove, Wright County, Iowa, on 26 November 1903 in Webster City, Iowa. She declared her parents were Charles H. Roop and Sophronia (Stone) Roop.[430] Lillian and John resided in Eagle Grove, a community located north of Hamilton County. Mrs. Lillian Gray and her two sons visited the Roop family and Hamilton County area frequently.[431] By February 1908, Lillian and John had moved to Ames, Story County, Iowa.[432]

Lillian's adopted mother, Sophronia Roop, died prior to 3 March 1908.[433]

John and Lillian then began a series of moves, which continued throughout their married life. After a brief stay in Ames and before 1910, John and Lillian moved to Arkansas City, Cowley County, Kansas. John was a dairyman and the family rented their home.[434] By 1920 the family moved to Craig, Moffat County, Colorado, where John and Lillian owned a farm with a mortgage. The family had increased to three sons. Based on the age of the youngest son and his birth location, the family moved to Colorado prior to 1914.[435] Based on the year and location of death of their youngest

---

[427] 1900 U.S. census, Hamilton County, Iowa, population schedule, Webster City, ED 102, p. 8B, household 181, dwelling 182, Henry C. Roop.

[428] "Visited Eagle Grove," *Daily Freeman Tribune*, 13 March 1903, p. 8, col. 4.

[429] "About Us," *Royal Neighbors of America*, https://www.royalneighbors.org.

[430] "Iowa, U.S., Marriage Records, 1880-1951," Hamilton County, vol 416, Gray-Roop marriage entry (26 November 1903); digital image, *Ancestry*.

[431] "Personal Gossip," *Daily Freeman Tribune* (Webster City), 8 September 1906, 15 October 1906, 31 December 1906, 1 January 1907, 20 February 1907, 26 February 1907.

[432] "Mrs. H.C. Roop Passes Away at Ames," *Daily Freeman Tribune*, 28 February 1908, p. 8, col. 1.

[433] "Obituary," *Webster City Freeman*, 3 March 1908, p. 3, col. 5.

[434] "Personal Gossip," *Daily Freeman Tribune*, 16 March 1907, p. 4, co l5. Also, 1910 U.S. census, Cowley County, Kansas, population schedule, Arkansas City, ED 45, p. 1B, household 25, dwelling 28, John B. Grey.

[435] 1920 U.S. census, Moffat County, Colorado, population schedule, Craig, ED 170, p. 1B, household 19, dwelling 19, John B. Gray.

son in 1927, the Grays had moved again to Stanislaus County, California.[436] The family rented their home for $20 per month, and they owned a radio. They did not live on a farm, but John and their son were farm laborers.[437] The fortunes of the family were on a downward trajectory going into the Depression years.

Lillian died on 26 September 1937 in California, survived by her husband John and two sons, Gilford and Paul.[438] After Lillian's death, John moved back to Colorado and resided in Loveland, Larimer County. John remarried. He was unemployed in 1942.[439]

John B. Gray died in 1964.[440] Lillian, John, and their youngest child were buried in Jefferson County, Colorado.[441]

---

[436] Find a Grave, database and images (https://www.findagrave.com), memorial page for Howard B. Gray (1913–1927), Find a Grave Memorial ID 1.

[437] 1930 U.S. census, Stanislaus County, California, population schedule, Ceres, ED 3, p. 17A, household 388, dwelling 396, John B. Gray.

[438] California Death Index, 1905-1939," > 1930-1939 > F-H, Lillian Gray death entry 26 September 1937. Three Lillian Grays were noted; she is number 3. Also, "Mrs. Lillian Gray Passes Away Here," *The Modesto Bee (California)*, 27 September 1937, p. 7, col 4.

[439] "U.S., World War II Draft Registration Cards, 1942," Colorado, Graves, Joseph-Grieves, Wallace, serial number U1821, John Bennett Gray.

[440] "California, U.S. Death Index, 1940-1997," John B Gray death entry (22 November 1971).

[441] *FindAGrave*, database with images, (https://findagrave.com), memorial number 144962748, Lillian F. Gray (1885-1937) and John Bennett Gray (1880-1964) Crown Hill Cemetery, Wheat Ridge, Jefferson County, Colorado, block 14; gravestone photograph only available for Lillian.

Documents produced during her life provide clues to the Lillian's parentage.

Figure 1-LLR
Name, location and date of birth, foster and birth parents
of Lillian Lingreen Roop

Year	Name	Birth date	Birth location	Birth parents	Foster parents
1890	Lillian Lingreen[a]	1885			C. H. Roop
1895	Lillian Roop[b]	1886	New York		Chas. Roop
1900	Lillian L. Roop[c]	Feb 1885	New York	b. Unknown	Henry C. Roop
1903	Lillian F. Roop[d]	1884	New ork	C.H. Roop Sophronia Stone	
1905	Lillian Gray[e]	1885	Native born	don't know.	
1910	Lillian Grey[f]	1886	New York	b. Vermont & NY	
1920	Lillian L. Gray[g]	1887	Unknown	b. Unknown	
1930	Lillian L. Gray[h]	1885	New York	b. New York & New York	
1937	Lillian F. Gray[i]	1885			
1937	Lillian Florence Gray[j]		New York		

a. Kialy Carson, Kansas, [(CURATOR@ORPHANTRAINDEPOT.COM),] to Jill Morelli, email, 7 March 2023, "Info from the CAS," OTR folder.
b. 1895 State of Iowa census, Hamilton County, Iowa, population schedule, image 106 of 681, Lillian Rook in the household of Chas. H. Rook.
c. 1900 U.S. census, Hamilton County, Iowa, population schedule, Webster City, ED 102, p. 8B, household 181, dwelling 182, Henry C. Roop.
d. "Iowa, U.S., Marriage Records, 1880-1951," Hamilton County, vol 416, Gray-Roop marriage entry (26 November 1903).
e. 1905 State of Iowa census, Wright County, Iowa, population schedule, image 5312 of 6305, card no. 520, Lillian Gray.
f. 1910 U.S. census, Cowley County, Kansas, population schedule, Arkansas City, ED 45, p. 1B, household 25, dwelling 28, John B. Grey.
g. 1920 U.S. census, Moffat County, Colorado, population schedule, Craig, ED 170, p. 1B, household 19, dwelling 19, John B. Gray.
h. 1930 U.S. census, Stanislaus County, California, population schedule, Ceres, ED 3, p. 17A, household 388, dwelling 396, John B. Gray.
i. *FindAGrave*, database with images, memorial number 144962748, Lillian F. Gray (1885-1937), Crown Hill Cemetery, Wheat Ridge, Jefferson County, Colorado, block 14.
j. "Mrs. Lillian Gray Passes Away Here," *The Modesto Bee (California)*, 27 September 1937, p. 7, col 4.

Based on the documentary evidence, Lillian Lingreen Roop was probably born in February 1885 in New York. Her New York City parents and their birth places are unknown. Lingreen and its variations was probably the surname of Lillian's New York parents. Based on a survey of possible candidates, no conclusion can be drawn about the birth parents of Lillian.

CONCLUSION

Lillian Lingreen Roop was probably born February 1885 in New York. She was in the October delivery of children to Hamilton County, Iowa, and was formally adopted by Charles Henry and Sophronia Roop family. In 1903 Lillian married John Gray, and they had four children.

The family moved frequently: From Hamilton County to Story County, Iowa; to Cowley County, Kansas; to Moffat County, Colorado; and to Stanislaus County, California. Lillian (Roop) Gray died 26 September 1937 in California.

This investigation revealed no evidence of the identification of Lillian Lingreen Roop's New York parents.

The children include Gilford (b. 1904), Paul (b. 1906), and Howard (b. 1914).[442] There was at least one grandchild, Geraldine "Ina" Gray.[443] DNA of descendants could reveal the parents' names.

(*See* https://iowaorphans.wordpress.com for efforts to identify Lillian's NYC parents.)

---

[442] 1920 U.S. census, Moffat County, Colorado, population schedule, Craig, ED 170, p. 1B, household 19, dwelling 19, John B. Gray.

[443] "Paul Harvey Gray, 41 is Called by Death," *Modesto (California) Bee*, 7 January 1848, p. 4, col. 3. 1940 U.S. census, Stanislaus County, California, population schedule, Modesto, household 417, Paul Gray. Ina was the informant.

WILLIAM SCHLOSSHAUER

B. 1883/1884 IN NEW YORK
D. UNKNOWN
BIRTH FAMILY: JACOB DUBERT & KATHARINA "CARRIE" SCHLOSSHAUER
FOSTER FAMILY: BENJAMIN & MARIA SEGAR

William Schlosshauer, age 7, arrived in Hamilton County in 1890 in the October delivery of children, and fostered into the Benjamin Seger family of Blairsburg.[444] Five years later, Willie Schlosshauer, age 11 and born in New York, resided with Benjamin E. Segar, his wife Maria, and their apparent children.[445]

Horace Segar, Benjamin's father, received an unidentified child in the August delivery of children. Benjamin Segar received William Schlosshauer in October—two different children.

The Segars settled early in Iowa and Hamilton County. Benjamin was one of eight children. Emmert, Benjamin's younger brother, remembered when only three houses separated their farm and Blairsburg. The family lived a pioneer life on the farm.[446]

By 1900 William was not living with the Segar family.[447] Willie Schlosshauer is not found in the 1900 or 1910 census.[448]

William disappears from the records after 1895.

---

[444] Kialy Carson, Kansas, [(CURATOR@ORPHANTRAINDEPOT.COM),] to Jill Morelli, email, 7 March 2023, "Info from the CAS," OTR folder.

[445] 1895 State of Iowa census, Hamilton County, Iowa, population schedule, image 13 of 681, Willie Schlorhauer in the household of Benj. E. Segar.

[446] *History of Hamilton County, Iowa, vol II* (Chicago: S.J. Clarke Publishing Company, 1912) 135-136.

[447] 1900 U.S. census, Hamilton County, Iowa, population schedule, Blairsburg, ED 98, household 217, dwelling 217, Benjamin E. Sugar.

[448] Negative findings: 1900 & 1910 U.S. census, population schedules, *Ancestry*. Searched for W* Schl*h*r, born 1884 in New York at the lowest surety level.

William is not fmentioned in the local newspapers or any Ancestry public tree or FamilySearch World Tree. Schlosshauer or some variation was probably his birth name, but the given name could have been changed. Name variations include Schlothauer, Schlorhauer, Schloshauer, Schlorhaufer, Schlossbauer and Sch*hau*r. The most common variation in Germany is Schlothauer or Schlosser.

It is unlikely that he adopted the name of his foster parents as an adult.

Figure 1-WS
Name, location and date of birth, foster and birth parents of Willie Schlosshauer

Year	Name	Birth date	Birth location	Birth parents	Foster parents
1890	Willie Schlosshauer[a]	1883			Benjamin Seger
1895	Willie Schlorhauer[b]	1884	New York		Benjamin Segar

a. Kialy Carson, Kansas, [(CURATOR@ORPHANTRAINDEPOT.COM),] to Jill Morelli, email, 7 March 2023, "Info from the CAS," OTR folder.
b. 1895 State of Iowa census, Hamilton County, Iowa, population schedule, image 13 of 681, Willie Schlorhauer in the household of Benj. E. Segar.

Two candidates appear in the NYC Historic Vital Records database.

Figure 2-WS
Male Schl*h*ers/Schl* born in New York City in 1882-1884

No	Name	Date of birth	Cert #	Parent's names
1	Edward Schlosshauer (out of wedlock)	23 June 1883	371007	Jacob Dubert & Carrie Schlosshauer; 30, US; 16, Germany
2	William Schloss	23 July 1883	372462	Benjamin & Fann (Belz) Schloss; 27, Germany; 22, Germany

a. New York City Municipal Archives, "Historical Vital Records," Birth Return.

An analysis of the candidates revealed:
1. Neither Edward, Jacob, nor Carrie were found in the 1892, or 1900 censuses. The couple was not married. Edward remains a viable candidate.

2. The Benjamin and Fann (Belz) Schloss family is found in the 1900 census with a child William born in July 1883.[449] William Schloss is not a candidate for William Schlosshauer.

Examination of Edward's Birth Return reveals a typical NY family that would release a child.

Figure 3-WS
Birth return for Edward Schlosshauer, 23 June 1883[450]

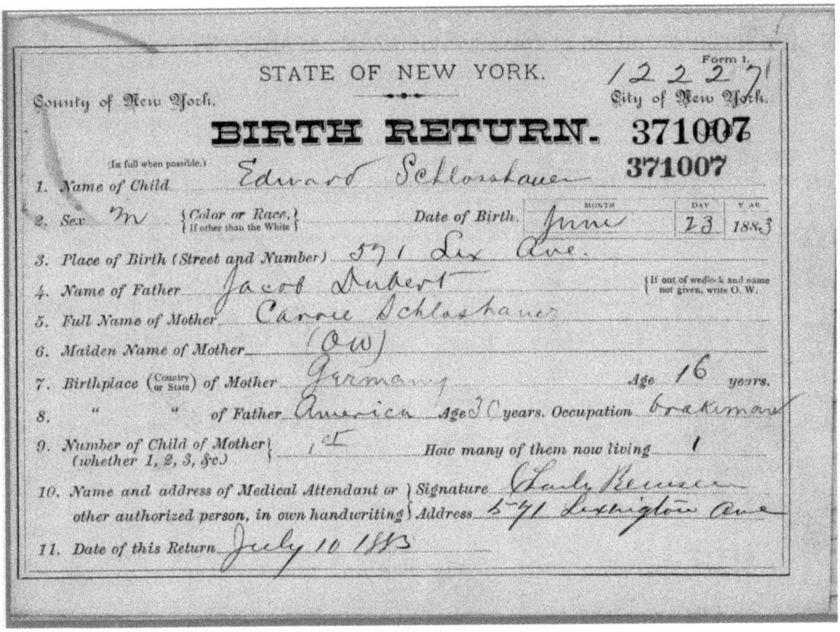

[Birth Return form image: State of New York, City of New York, Birth Return 371007. Name of Child: Edward Schlosshauer; Sex: m; Date of Birth: June 23 1883; Place of Birth: 571 Lex Ave.; Name of Father: Jacob Aubert; Full Name of Mother: Carrie Schloshauer; Maiden Name of Mother: (ow); Birthplace of Mother: Germany, Age 16 years; of Father: America, Aged 0 years, Occupation: brakeman; Number of Child of Mother: 1st; How many of them now living: 1; Name and address of Medical Attendant: Charly Benner, 571 Lexington Ave; Date of this Return: July 10 1883.]

The given name on the birth return of "Edward" is in conflict with the CAS name on the 1890 manifest of "William."

This is the first child of the unmarried 16 year-old Carrie Schloshauer. The child did not assume the surname of the father, but rather that of the mother. It is likely that economic conditions forced Carrie to place this child in the orphanage and subsequently be released by her. Corroborating evidence moves this candidate from certainty to proven.

---

[449] 1900 U.S. census, New York, New York County, population schedule, Manhattan, ED 609, p. 4, household 26, dwelling 90, Beng. Schloss.
[450] New York City Municipal Archives, "Historical Vital Records," Birth Return, certificate 371007, Edward Schlosshauer birth entry (23 June 1883).

Carrie (or any variation) Schlosshauer is not found after the birth of Edward.

CONCLUSION

William "Willie" Schlosshauer was born in 1883 in New York City. His parents were probably the unwed couple Jacob Dubert and Carrie Schlosshauer. Carrie was 16 at the time of William's birth. William came to Hamilton County in 1890 in the October delivery of children and was assigned to Benjamin Seagar.

No further information is known about William after 1895.

Mary "MAYME/MAE" (—?—) SMITH

B. 10 APRIL 1886 IN NEW YORK
D. 26 JULY 1958, EVANSTON, COOK COUNTY, ILLINOIS
BIRTH FAMILY: UNKNOWN
FOSTER FAMILY: ANDREW AND MARY SMITH

Mary —?—, age 4, was an out-placed orphan in the August or November delivery of children in 1890 to Hamilton County, Iowa. No direct evidence exists that Mayme was a an out-placed orphan, but the location of her birth, her age, the advanced age of her foster parents, and living in Hamilton County identifies her as a member of this cohort.

In 1895 Mayme resided with the Andrew Smith family, composed of Andrew, age 64, his apparent wife Mary, age 66, and a son Peter with his wife and one year old infant. Andrew and Mary were born in Ireland. Mayme was nine years old and born in New York.[451] Mayme was too old to be child of the younger couple and too young to be the child of Andrew and Mary.

After accepting Mayme into the family, the Smiths were beset with problems. In the early morning of 15 January 1898, a fire broke out in the barn. The barn, 15 head of cattle, 17 horses, and 20 tons of hay were destroyed. Insurance covered only a portion of the loss.[452] To add to this tragedy, Andrew Smith died on 4 January 1900.[453]

Andrew wrote a will and signed with his mark on 20 December 1899, giving his wife $300 per year to be paid by his two sons, Peter and Andrew. Peter, the executor, received 124 acres of land; Andrew received 153 acres. Each son received half of the personal property. Daughter Agnes O'Neill received $1700. No probate document mentioned Mayme.[454]

---

[451] 1895 State of Iowa census, Hamilton County, Iowa, population schedule, image 649 of 681, Marnie Smith in the household of Andrew Smith.
[452] "A Bad Fire at Blairsburg," *Hamilton County Journal,* 22 January 1898, p. 7, col. 3.
[453] "Williams," *Daily Freeman Tribune,* 9 January 1900. p. 8, col. 2.
[454] "Iowa, Wills and Probate Records, 1758-1997," Hamilton County, Iowa, probate records, vol 4-7, 1901-1933, p. 356-357, Andrew Smith, will proven 12 May 1902.

In 1900 neither widow Mary Smith nor Mayme resided with the Peter C. Smith family nor were they identified as residing in Hamilton County.[455] although no enumerated, Mary probably stayed the area; in 1902, widow Mary Smith and the heirs of Andrew Smith transferred Peter's inheritance of 124 acres to him for $5.[456]

In August of 1904, Mayme Smith, recording her name as Mary, married W. J. Schmitz, a "traveling man," from Dixon, Lee County, Illinois, in Hamilton County. Mayme stated she was 19 years old and resided in Williams, Iowa; her parents were Andrew Smith and Mary Smith.[457] Although this is the orphan Mayme Smith, Andrew and Mary Smith were her foster parents, and she was not born in Iowa. Mayme had clearly assimilated into her foster family.

In 1910 William J. and Mayme Smith resided in Dixon, Illinois, with their daughter, Blanche, age five. The couple had been married for six years. William was a solicitor for the daily paper.[458] The family's surname had been Americanized from Schmitz to Smith.

Numerous visits between the Hamilton County family and friends and the Illinois family occurred throughout the years, reflecting a healthy and loving relationship with the foster family. Mayme and her daughter, residing in Dixon, Illinois, visited relatives in Blairsburg, Iowa in 1908.[459] Blanche Smith of Dixon attended a party in Webster City in 1916.[460] Blanche visited her "aunt," Mrs. James H. O'Neill and her "uncles" Peter and Andrew Smith in July 1917.[461]

William and Mayme felt confident enough in their income that they purchased a lot in Dixon for $2500 in November 1919.[462]

---

[455] 1900 U.S. census, Hamilton County, Iowa, population schedule, Williams Township, ED 0114, dwelling 143, household 148, Peter C. Smith.
[456] "Real Estate Transfers," *Daily Freeman Tribune,* 9 June 1902, p. 5, col. 3.
[457] "Iowa, U.S., Marriage Records, 1880-1951," Hamilton County, vol 416, Schmitz-Smith marriage entry (9 November 1904).
[458] 1910 U.S. census, Lee County, Illinois, population schedule, ED 51, p. 7A, household 64, dwelling 64, William J. Smith.
[459] "Blairsburg," *Webster City Journal,* 20 August 1908, p. 8, col. 4.
[460] "Girls Give Picnic," *Webster City Journal,* 27 July 1916, p. 3, cols. 3 and 4.
[461] "Williams and Northeaster Hamilton County," *Webster City Journal,* 12 July 1917, p. 6, col. 3.
[462] Lee County, Illinois, mortgage, no. 138995, 1 November 1919, Wm. J. Smith & Mayme Smith to E.J. Countryman, Trustee for Lot 5, Block 19 in Dixon; County Clerk's Office, Dixon, Illinois.

One year later, William J. and Mayme Smith sold pianos, talking machines, musical merchandise and sewing machines at 109 W. 1st Street in Dixon. The store location was also their residence.[463]

William J. Smith divorced Mayme Smith in April 1924 in Lee County on the basis of desertion.[464] Just 40 days after the divorce was final, Mae Smith married Clifford V. Nation in Lake County, Indiana, a known "Gretna Green," a location for quick Illinois marriages. No age, residence ,or parents' names were recorded.[465]

In 1937 "Mayme Nation, formerly Mayme Smith" was identified with William J. Smith in Lee County, Illinois, making a claim against the estate of George C. Loveland.[466] In another court case, William A. Warner filed suit against "William J. Smith, Mayme Nation, formerly known as Mayme Smith," et al, over a lack of payment of $500 related to the 1919 mortgage.[467]

Mayme maintained her relationship with her foster family for the rest of her life. She traveled from Chicago with her "sister" to visit Mr. P. C. Smith. and visited her foster brother, Peter Smith, frequently in the 1940s.[468]

In 1940 Mayme, now going by Mae, and born in Iowa, resided in Evanston, Cook County, Illinois. The family rented their home for $40 a month. Clifford was a maintenance man for a public utility.[469]

---

[463] *Dixon (IL) City Directory*, 1920, Wm. J. Smith, p. 161.

[464] Lee County Circuit Court, Illinois, court proceedings, April 1924 term, divorce decree, William J. Smith-Mayme Smith; image of original supplied by Lee County Historical and Genealogical Society, Dixon, Illinois.

[465] "Indiana Marriages, 1811-2019," database with images, *FamilySearch* (https://familysearch.org : 22 January 2023), Lake > 1924 Volume 52 > image 247 of 312, Nation-Smith marriage license (74156) & certificate (27 May 1924); Indiana Commission on Public Records, Indianapolis. "Gretna Green" is a term used to denote a location that had lower or no residency standards or wait times and became a haven for couples that wished to marry quickly.

[466] "Legal Notices," *The Ashton Gazette* (Lee County, Illinois), 14 October 1937, p. 7, col. 6.

[467] Lee County, Illinois, Circuit Court Files,306-307, William H. Warner vs. William J. Smith, Mayme Nation, formerly Mayme Smith, et al, 1938; County Clerk's Office, Dixon.

[468] "Entertain in Honor of Guest," *Daily Freeman Journal*, 24 February 1938, p. 2, col. 3. Also, "Williams," *Daily Freeman Journal*, 5 June 1940, p. 5, col 1. Also, "Blairsburg," *Daily Freeman Journal*, 24 June 1944, p. 3, col 4. Also, "Smith Services Were Attended By Many Friends," *Daily Freeman Journal*, 2 April 1947, p. 6, col. 1.

[469] 1940 U.S. census, Cook County, Illinois, population schedule, Evanston, ED 16-192, p. 9A, dwelling 190, Clifford Nation. Mae was the informant.

Mary/Mayme/Mae (—?—/Smith) Smith Nation died 26 July 1958 in Evanston, Cook County, Illinois. Her husband stated she was born 10 April 1890 in Blairsburg, Hamilton County, Iowa.[470] Mae (Smith) Schmitz Nation was buried in Memorial Park cemetery, Skokie, Cook County, Illinois.[471]

Blanche, the only child of William and Mayme, is not found in records after 1917 when she would have been 12 years old.

Mayme Smith of Hamilton County, Iowa, fully assimilated into her foster family.[472] Her use of her foster parents' surname, given name changes, multiple marriages, use of Iowa as her birth location, and varying birth years made identifying Mayme challenging. The research is further complicated by Mayme marrying a man with the same common surname.

Two Blanche Smiths of approximately the same age resided in Illinois. One is a Smith by birth (parents' names William and Mayme (Smith) Smith. The other is a Smith by marriage named Blanche O'Dell who married Delbert Smith. Blanche married second Athol Durall in 9 January 1929 in Marian County, Illinois.[473] The former is the child of the orphan.

---

[470] "Illinois, Cook County Deaths, 1871-1998," Mae Nation death entry (26 Jul 1958). Also, "Mrs. Maye Nation," obituary, *Evanston (Illinois) Review*, 7 August 1958, p. 73, col. 1.

[471] Find a Grave, database and images (https://www.findagrave.com/memorial/234996551/mae-smith_schmitz_nation: accessed July 11, 2024), memorial page for Mae Smith Schmitz Nation (10 Apr 1886–26 Jul 1958), Find a Grave Memorial ID 234996551, citing Memorial Park Cemetery, Skokie, Cook County, Illinois, USA; Maintained by Mark Goebel (contributor 48218627).

[472] 1910 U.S. census, Lee County, Illinois, population schedule, Dixon, Ward 3, ED 51, p. 7A, household 64, dwelling 64, Walter J. Smith.

[473] Illinois, U.S. County Marriage Records, 1800-1940, Images > Marriage Register, Marian County, 1888-1934 > image no 151 of 173, certificate no. 19295613, Atholl Durall-Blanche Smith marriage entry (9 January 1929).

Figure 1-MS
Name, location and date of birth, foster and birth parents
of Mary/Mayme/Mae (—?—) Smith

Year	Name	Birth date	Birth location	Birth parents	Foster parents
1895	Mamie Smith[a]	1886	New York		Andrew Smith
1904	Mary (Mamie) Smith[b]	1885	Iowa		Andrew Smith
1910	Mamie (Smith) Smith[c]	1887	Iowa	b. New York	
1940	Mae Nation[d]	1894	Iowa		
1950	Maye Nation[e]	1895	New York		
1958	Mae Nation[f]	10 Apr 1890	Blairsburg, Hamilton Cty., Iowa		

a. 1895 State of Iowa census, Hamilton County, Iowa, population schedule, image 649 of 681, Marnie Smith in the household of Andrew Smith.
b. "Iowa, U.S., Marriage Records, 1880-1951," Hamilton County, vol 416, Schmitz-Smith marriage entry (9 November 1904).
c. 1910 U.S. census, Lee County, Illinois, population schedule, ED 51, p. 7A, household 64, dwelling 64, William J. Smith.
d. 1940 U.S. census, Cook County, Illinois, population schedule, Evanston, ED 16-192, p. 9A, dwelling 190, Clifford Nation.
e. 1950 U.S. census, Cook County, Illinois, population schedule, Evanston, ED 107-52, p. 10, dwelling 126, Clifford D. Nation.
f. "Illinois, Cook County Deaths, 1871-1998," database, *FamilySearch*, Mae Nation death registration (26 July 1958).

Based on the accumulated information Mayme (—?—) Smith was probably born 10 April 1885/1886, in New York City, New York. With the common name of Mary, no surname and no information about her New York parents, a search in the records results in too many candidates to assess.

CONCLUSION
Based on the accumulated information, Mary/Mayme/Mae (—?—) Smith was born possibly on 10 April 1886 or 1885 in New York City and came to Hamilton County, Iowa, in 1890. She fostered into the Andrew and Mary Smith family. Nothing is known about her birth parents. In August of 1904, Mayme Smith married W. J. Schmitz, from Dixon, Lee County, Illinois. The couple divorced and Mayme married Clifford V. Nation in May 1924. Mary/Mayme/Mae (—?—/Smith) Smith Nation died 26 July 1958 in Evanston, Cook County, Illinois.

Lulu (Knox) Strowbridge

B. 25 January 1884, New York City, New York
D. 28 September 1956, Cowlitz County, Washington
Birth family: Emma Strowbridge, unknown father
Foster family: Thomas and Sarah M. Knox

Photo courtesy of Barbara Homrighaus[474]

Signature from application for marriage

Lulu Strowbridge arrived in Hamilton County in the fall of 1890 and was placed in the home of Thomas and Sarah Knox.

> Mrs. Tom Knox has one of the little girls brought to Webster City from New York.[475]

The timing of this 1890 article confirms Lulu's status and implies that she arrived in the November delivery.

Thomas Knox, age 37 and born in Virginia, and Sarah M. Knox, age 27 and born Ohio, resided in Hamilton County in 1880. They had no

---

[474] Lulu (Knox) Strowbridge photograph, c1895; digital image, privately held by Barbara Knox Homrighaus, 414 W 7th St., Madrid, Iowa, 50156, from the June Knox Nemechek and Esther Knox Murray Collection, in the possession of Barbara Knox Homrighaus, first cousin twice removed of Lulu Strowbridge, 7 December 2022.

[475] "Jewell," *Webster City Freeman*, 3 December 1890, p. 4, col. 2.

children.[476] In 1895 Lulu Knox, age 10 and born in New York, resided with the family.[477]

Between 1895 and 1900, the family, composed of Thomas, Sarah, and Lulu, moved to Jay, Richland County, Indiana, where Thomas farmed. Lulu was born January 1884 in New York. Lulu was identified as their "adopted daughter."[478] No formal adoption has been discovered.

In 1901 Lulu brought charges against Charles Alexander for attempted assault. Alexander, 20 years old, was escorting her home from a party.[479] The outcome of the case is not known. On 17 August 1903, Lulu Strowbridge gave birth to a boy in Jay County, Indiana. The father was Earl Dangler. The baby was not named. The parents of the infant were not married.[480] This is the only known out-of-wedlock birth by any of the out-placed orphans.

In 1906 Lulu, now using Strowbridge as her surname, and Dwight Wise filed an application for a marriage license in Jay County on 25 August. Lulu, a music teacher, was born 25 January 1885, in New York City, New York. Her foster father was Thomas Knox. This was her first marriage. Lulu signed personally.[481] Strowbridge was probably her name at birth.

In 1910 Cecil T. Dangler, born in 1904 and described as a ward, resided with Thomas and Sarah M. Knox in Jay County, Indiana.[482] This child was the son of Lulu and Earl, not of Thomas and Sarah or Lulu and Dwight.

---

[476] 1880 U.S. census, Hamilton County, Iowa, population schedule, Lyon Township, ED 105, p. 231B, household 16, dwelling 19, Thomas Knox.

[477] 1895 Iowa state census, Hamilton County, Iowa, population schedule, Jewell, Lyon township, household 77, dwelling 80, Thomas Knox.

[478] 1900 U.S. census, Jay County, Indiana, population schedule, Richland, ED 70, p. 4, household 96, dwelling 98, Thomas Knox.

[479] "Youth is Held on Charge Preferred by a Redkey Girl," *The Star Press* (Muncie, Indiana), 8 June 1901, p. 3, col. 3.

[480] Indiana, U.S., WPA Birth Index, 1880-1920, unnamed baby boy Dangler, birth index (17 August 1903); Jay County, Indiana, Index to Birth Records, Vol. 1, book H-10, p. 52.

[481] "Indiana Marriages, 1811-2019, application for marriage license, Jay County, vol 1, p. 369, Dwight Wise-Lulu Strowbridge application for marriage entry.

[482] 1910 U.S. census, Jay County, Indiana, population schedule, Richland, ED 75, p. 1A, household 8, dwelling 8, Thomas Knox.

Lulu and Dwight Wise divorced between 1917 and 1920.[483] In 1920 Lulu Strowbridge declared herself a widow to avoid the stigma associated with divorce and resided in Mechanicsburg, Champaign County, Ohio. Living with her was her son, Cecil, with the newly assumed surname of Wise, age 16.[484] Lulu married second William Edward Stevens after 1920 and moved to the state of Washington before 1930.[485]

Cecil T. Wise, Lulu's son, married Burna Nelson in December 1924 in Kelso, Cowlitz County, Washington.[486] The couple had one stillborn child. No other known descendants have been identified.

From before 1930 to her death, Lulu and Will E. Stevens resided in Cowlitz County, Washington. Will was a roofer and earned $565 for 35 weeks of work in 1939.[487] In 1950, the family resided at 3335 Ocean Beach Rod, Longview.[488]

Lulu died of myocarditis on 28 September 1956, in her home in Longview,and was buried in Long View Cemetery Park.[489] The obituary mentioned no family members.[490] William died in 1959.[491]

---

[483] 1920 U.S. census Jay County, Indiana, population schedule, Richland, ED 81, p. 11A, Dwight Wise in the household of his sister, Lula Martten. Dwight declared himself divorced. For the earlier date: "U.S., World War I Draft Registration cards, 1917-1918, Indiana, Jay County, Dwight Wise. Dwight identified Lulu Wise as his nearest kin.

[484] 1920 U.S. census, Champaign County, Ohio, population schedule, Mechanicsburg, ED 4, p. 8B, no household or dwelling number noted, Lula Strowbridge. To avoid the stigma associated with being divorced, many woman stated they were widowed.

[485] 1940 U.S. census, Cowlitz County, Washington, population schedule, Longview, ED 8-27, p. 7B, household 154, William E. Stevens. Lulu's son, Cecil T. Wise and his wife are living in Cowlitz County, Washington in 1930.

[486] "Local News," *Laurel Outlook (Montana)*, 17 December 1924, p. 3, col. 2.

[487] 1940 U.S. census, Cowlitz County, Washington, population schedule, Longview, ED 8-27, p. 7B, household 154, William Stevens.

[488] 1950 U.S. census, Cowlitz County, Washington, population schedule, Longview, ED 8-40, p. 5, dwelling 48, Will E. Stevens.

[489] Washington State Department of Health, Public Health Statistics Section, Certificate of Death, Sate file no. 16437, Registrar's no 289, Lula M Stevens death entry (28 September 1956).

[490] "Funerals-Stevens," *Longview Daily News*, 13 October 1956, p. 15, col. 2.

[491] *Find a Grave*, database and images (https://www.findagrave.com), memorial page, William Edward Stevens Jr. (1889–1959), memorial 103588308, citing Cowlitz View Memorial Gardens, Kelso, Cowlitz County, Washington, USA; photo by Bee Charmer.

Multiple documents and an unusual surname help identify the New York City parents of Lulu (Strowbridge) Knox

Figure 1-LS
Name, location and date of birth, foster and birth parents
of Lulu (Knox) Strowbridge

Year	Name	Birth date	Birth location	Birth parents	Foster parents
1895	Lulu Knox[a]	1885	New York		Thomas Knox
1900	Lulu Knox[b]	Jan 1884	New York	b. New York	Thomas Knox
1906	Lulu Strowbridge[c]	25 Jan 1885	New York City	b. Unknown	Thomas Knox
1920	Lulu Strowbridge[d]	1887	New York	b. New York	
1940	Lulu Stevens[e]	1886	New York	b. New York	
1950	Lulu M. Stevens[f]	1889	New York		
1956	Lula M Stevens[g]	25 Jan 1888	Staten Island, NY	Unknown	

a. 1895 Iowa state census, Hamilton County, Iowa, population schedule, Jewell, Lyon township, household 77, dwelling 80, Thomas Knox.
b. 1900 U.S. census, Jay County, Indiana, population schedule, Richland, ED 70, p. 4, household 96, dwelling 98, Thomas Knox.
c. "Indiana Marriages, 1811-2019, application for marriage license, Jay County, vol 1, p. 369, Dwight Wise-Lulu Strowbridge application for marriage entry.
d. 1920 U.S. census, Champaign County, Ohio, population schedule, Mechanicsburg, ED 4, p. 8B, no household or dwelling number noted, Lula Strowbridge.
e. 1940 U.S. census, Cowlitz County, Washington, population schedule, Longview, ED 8-27, p. 7B, household 154, William E. Stevens.
f. 1950 U.S. census, Cowlitz County, Washington, population schedule, Longview, ED 8-40, p. 5, dwelling 48, Will E. Stevens.
g. Washington State Department of Health, Public Health Statistics Section, Certificate of Death, Sate file no. 16437, Registrar's no 289, Lula M Stevens death entry (28 September 1956).

Using the above information and assuming that Strowbridge was Lulu's birth name, Lulu's NYC mother was identified.

Figure 1-LS
Birth return, State of New York[492]
Lulu Strowbridge

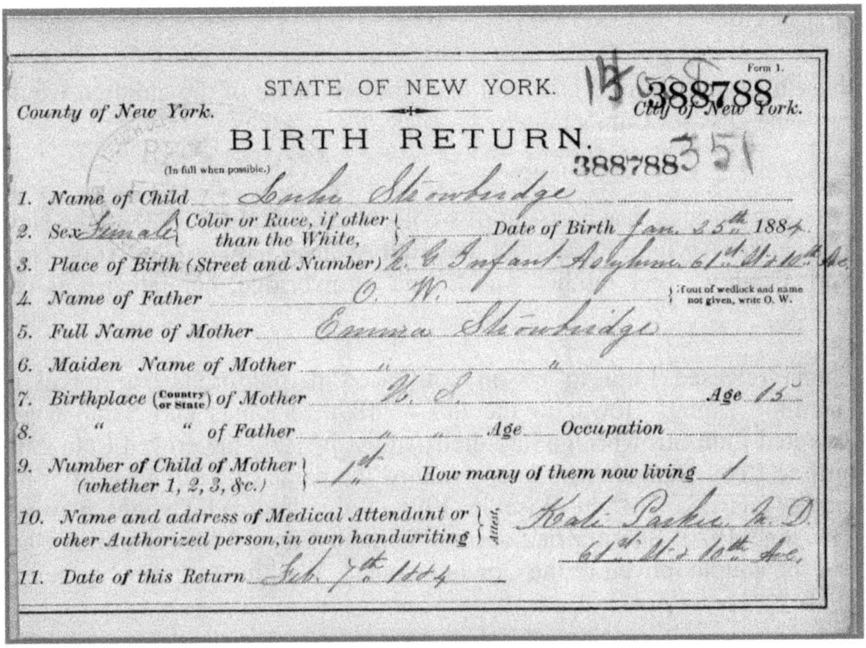

```
STATE OF NEW YORK.           Form 1.
County of New York.                                  388788
                                          City of New York.
              BIRTH RETURN.
                 (In full when possible.)        388788
 1. Name of Child          Lulu Strowbridge
 2. Sex Female  Color or Race, if other
                than the White,            Date of Birth Jan. 25th 1884
 3. Place of Birth (Street and Number) N. Y. Infant Asylum 61st St & 10th Ave
 4. Name of Father           O. W.                 { out of wedlock and name
                                                     not given, write O. W.
 5. Full Name of Mother     Emma Strowbridge
 6. Maiden Name of Mother        "          "
 7. Birthplace (Country or State) of Mother   U. S.              Age  15
 8.    "           "   of Father         "        Age    Occupation
 9. Number of Child of Mother }  1st
    (whether 1, 2, 3, &c.)         How many of them now living   1
10. Name and address of Medical Attendant or }  Kate Parker M. D.
    other Authorized person, in own handwriting   61st St & 10th Ave.
11. Date of this Return    Feb 7th 1884
```

Lulu Strowbridge was born to Emma Strowbridge, age 15 and unwed, on 25 January 1884 in Manhattan (not Staten Island). Lulu was the mother's first child. Emma gave birth to Lulu at the New York Infant Asylum at 61st Street and 10th Avenue[493] The Infant Asylum provided a haven for unwed mothers for their first child, and the children were often given to the orphanage. Emma, just 15, probably had few options.

In 1880 Emma Strowbridge, age 11, resided at the Free Home for Destitute Girls, located on 41 Seventh Ave. Established in 1870, it initially received thirty-five girls between 12 and 25 and trained them to serve as domestics.[494]

---

[493] State of New York, Birth Return, County of New York, certificate 388788, Lulu Strowbridge birth entry (25 January 1884.).

[494] To learn more about the Free Home for Destitute Girls: *Daytonian* (Tom Miller), "The 1844 Walsh House-No. 23 East 11th," blog, 1 August 2013. http://daytoninmanhattan.blogspot.com/2013/08/the-1844-walsh-house-no-23-east-11th.html

Emma was born in New York, and her parents were born in Ireland.[495] She also appeared in two non-population schedules in 1880. Emma's parents were not deceased. Emma was born to a married couple, but was separated from her mother.[496] Emma was temperate, able-bodied, and had never been convicted of a crime. Admitted on 12 April 1880, Emma had no brothers or sisters.[497]

Even if Emma married later and had children, none of the children would carry the DNA of Lulu's father.

CONCLUSION

Lulu Strowbridge was born out of wedlock on 25 January 1885 in the New York infant Asylum, 61st Street and 10th Avenue, City of New York, New York County. Her mother was Emma Strowbridge; her father was not named.

Emma released Lulu to be an out-placed partial orphan to travel to Hamilton County, Iowa, in the fall of 1890. Thomas and Sarah Knox accepted Lulu Strowbridge into their family. In 1903 the unwed Lulu gave birth to Cecil Dangler who later assumed the name of Cecil Wise after his mother married Dwight Wise in 1906. Lulu divorced Dwight between 1917 and 1920. She married second William Edward Stevens after 1920 and the couple moved to the Cowlitz County, Washington probably before 1930.

Lulu died 28 September 1956, in her home in Longview, Cowlitz County, Washington, and was buried in Long View Cemetery Park. William died in 1959.

No known descendants of Cecil exist.[498] DNA won't reveal the father's name.

---

[495] !880 U.S. census, New York County, New York, population schedule, New York, ED 180, p, 158A, line 25, Emma Strowbridge.

[496] U.S., 1880 Federal Census Schedules of Defective, Dependent, and Delinquent Classes, New York, New York, ED 180, "Homeless Children," Emma Strowbridge; The New York State Library, Albany.

[497] Ibid. "Pauper and Indigent Inhabitants," Free Home for Destitute Girls, Emma Strowbridge.

[498] "Cecil T. Wise," obituary, *Longview Daily News* (Washington), 29 October 1974, p. 23, col. 5.

Julia Mae Sumpter

B. 3 April 1884 in Manhattan, New York
D. 3 July 1977, Hamilton County, Iowa
Birth family: Annie Sumpter, father unknown
Foster family: Joseph and Elizabeth Adams

Julia Sumpter arrived in the fall delivery of children in 1890 to Hamilton County. In 1895 she resided with the Joseph and Elizabeth Adams family.

The Adams family was enumerated twice in 1895 with minor differences. The couple had no apparent children residing with the family, except for 11 year-old Julia who was born in New York.[499]

Between 1895 and 1900, the family moved to Crow Wing, Minnesota, where Julia Sumpter was described as a boarder in the Adams household. Julia attended school and was born April 1884 in New York. Elizabeth and Joseph had been married 30 years, also born in New York, and had no known children.[500]

Julia Sumpter married William Wright on 25 November 1902 in Crow Wing County, Minnesota.[501] She divorced William in early 1905.[502] Julia and her foster mother moved back to Hamilton County in time for the 1905 enumeration. Julia, now 21 and using the surname Sumpter, worked as a servant.[503]

Julia's foster mother, Elizabeth Adams died 7 July 1906 in Cherokee Hospital, Cherokee, Iowa, of a long debilitating illness.[504]

---

[499] 1895 State of Iowa census, Hamilton County, Iowa, population schedule, image 192 of 681, Julia Sumter in the household of Joseph Adams. Also Ibid., image 376 of 681, Julia Sumter in the household of J. H. Adams.

[500] 1900 U.S. census, Crow Wing County, Minnesota, population schedule, Township 43, ED 68, p. 4, household 55, dwelling 57, Julia Sumtor in the household of Joseph Adams.

[501] "Minnesota Marriage Index," Crow Wing County, certificate no. E-149, William Wright-Julia Sumpter marriage entry (25 November 1902).

[502] "Iowa, U.S., Marriage Records, 1880-1945," register of marriages, Louis Follett-Julia Wright (Julia M. Sumpter) marriage entry (29 August 1906).

[503] 1905 State of Iowa census, Hamilton County, Iowa, population census, Webster City, Julia Sumpter; for birth place of parents: card no. 537. For no parents: line no. 537.

[504] "Died in Cherokee," *Webster City Journal*, 12 July 1906, p. 2, col. 1.

On 29 August 1906, Julia M. Wright married second Louis Follett, a florist in Webster City.[505] In 1910 Louis Follet and his wife Julia of three years resided with Louis's parents. The couple had a child, Kathryn, about one and a half years old.[506] Ten years later Louis, Julia and their three children resided with Louis's father, a widower. The enumerator recorded Julia as "orphanage child," but the entry is crossed out and "U.S" inserted.[507]

In 1919 Louis Follett ran out of coal for his greenhouse. Remembering that there used to be coal mining in Hamilton County, he and another man went to the mill site and easily found the vein.[508]

In 1925 Julia M. and Louis Follett were enumerated with their four children in Webster City, Hamilton County, Iowa. Julia was 41 years old, and listed her foster parents as her parents. Louis's father James lived with the family.[509]

Julia had an active social live and served her community. The couple attended the state fair and visited friends and relatives.[510] In 1914 Royal Neighbors elected Julia as chancellor.[511] She served as secretary of the Westway Club in 1935; by 1939 Julia was president.[512]

Louis was the owner and horticulturist of his retail greenhouse. In 1939 he worked 52 weeks but had no income. The family did receive income from other sources and from their son, George, who earned $624 as an auto mechanic in a garage. Donald, the younger son, attended school.[513]

---

[505] "Iowa, U.S., Marriage Recods, 1880-1945," 1906-1907, 426 (Dallas-Iowa), register of marriages, Louis Follett-Julia Sumpter (Julia M. Wright) marriage entry (29 August 1906). Julia noted as divorced.

[506] 1910 U.S. census, Hamilton County, Iowa, population schedule, Webster City, Ward 2, ED 110, p. 10B, Julia Follett residing in the household of James Follett.

[507] 1920 U.S. census, Hamilton County, population schedule, Webster City Ward 2, ED 122, dwelling 63, household 72, Julia Follett in the household of James Follett.

[508] "Uncovers Good Vein of Coal," *Webster City Freeman*, 8 December 1919, p. 7, col. 4.

[509] 1925 State of Iowa census, Hamilton County, Webster City, image 719 of 884, Louis Follet.

[510] "Personal Gossip," *Daily Freeman Tribune*, 26 August 1907, p. 5, col. 4. Also, "Personal Briefs," *Daily Freeman Tribune*, 23 April 1913, p. 8, col. 4.

[511] "Royal Neighbors Install," *Webster City Freeman*, 13 January 1914, p. 5, col.4.

[512] "Westway Club, W.B.A. Have Annual Christmas Party at Goehring Home," *Daily Freeman Journal*, 19 December 1935, p. 2, col. 1. Also, "Installation of Officers," *Daily Freeman Journal*, 8 December 1939, p. 2, col. 2.

[513] 1940 U.S. census, Hamilton County, Iowa, population schedule, Webster City, ED 40-4, p. 14A, Louis Follett.

Louis Follett died on 2 March 1946 in Hamilton County, Iowa.[514] Julia (Sumpter) Wright Follett died 3 July 1977. Both are buried in Graceland Cemetery, Webster City, Iowa.[515]

Julia's birth date varied slightly across her lifetime. Even in 1895, her birth year was recorded as 1883 and 1884 in the two enumerations of the same household.

Figure 1-JS
Name, location and date of birth, foster and birth parents
of Julia Mae Sumpter

Date	Name	Birth date	Birth location	Birth parents	Foster parents
1895-1	Julia Sumter[a]	1883	New York		Joseph Adams
1895-2	Julia Sumter[b]	1884	New York		Joseph Adams
1900	Julia Sumtor[c]	April 1884	New York	b. New York	Joseph Adams
1906	Julia (Sumpter) Wright[d]	1882	New York, New York	Joseph and Elizabeth Adams, noted as foster parents	Joseph Adams
1910	Julia Follett[e]	1883	New York	b. Unknown	
1920	Julia Follett[f]	1885	New York	Orphanage child; b. U.S.	
1925	Jula M. Follett[g]	1884	New York	Joseph H. Addams & Elizabeth Walters (her foster parents)	Joseph Adams
1940	Julia Follett[h]	1884	New York		
1950	Julia Follett[i]	1884	New York		
1966	Jullia Follett[j]	3 April 1883			
1977	Julia Mae Sumpter Follett[k]	3 April 1884	Manhattan, New York		

---

[514] "Iowa, U.S., Death Records, 1889-1904, 1921-1952," Certificate of Death, no 40-?-29, Louis Follett death entry (2 March 1946).

[515] *FindAGrave,* database and images (http://findagrave.com), memorial page for Julia (Sumpter) Follett (1884-1977), memorial no. 185358672, Graceland cemetery, Webster City, Hamilton County, Iowa; the accompanying photographs by Michael are too small to read.

a. 1895 State of Iowa census, Hamilton County, Iowa, population schedule, image 192 of 681, Julia Sumter in the household of Joseph Adams.
b. "1895 State of Iowa census, Hamilton County, Iowa, population schedule, image 375 of 681, Julia Sumter in the household of J. H. Adams.
c. 1900 U.S. census, Crow Wing County, Minnesota, population schedule, Township 43, ED 68, p. 4, household 55, dwelling 57, Julia Sumtor in the household of Joseph Adams. Also, *Dixon (IL) City Directory*, 1920, Wm. J. Smith, p. 161.
d. "Iowa, U.S., Marriage Records, 1880-1945," 1906-1907, 426 (Dallas-Iowa), register of marriages, Louis Follett-Jullia Dumpter (Julia M. Wright) marriage entry (29 August 1906).
e. 1910 U.S. census, Hamilton County, Iowa, population schedule, Webster City, Ward 2, ED 110, p. 10B, Julia Follett residing in the household of James Follett.
f. 1920 U.S. census, Hamilton County, population schedule, Webster City Ward 2, ED 122, dwelling 63, household 72, Julia Follett in the household of James Follett.
g. 1925 State of Iowa census, Hamilton County, Webster City, image 719 of 884, Louis Follett.
h. 1940 U.S. census, Hamilton County, Iowa, population schedule, Webster City, ED 40-4, p. 14A, Louis Follett.
i. 1950 U.S. census, Hamilton County, Iowa, populations schedule, Webster City, ED 4, dwelling 87, household 99, Louis Follett.
j. "U.S. Social Security Death Index, 1935-2014," SS#: 485-66-1565, Julia Follet filed 1966, last payment to Webster City, Iowa. Birth recorded as 3 April 1883.
k. *FindAGrave*, database and images (http://findagrave.com : accessed 19 November 2022), memorial page for Julia (Sumpter) Follett (1884-1977), memorial no. 185358672, Graceland cemetery, Webster City, Hamilton County, Iowa.

Based on the documentary evidence, Julia was probably born on 10 April 1883, and possibly 1884. Sumpter, sometimes spelled Sumter, is probably the name of at least one New York City parent. Her birth parents may have been born in New York.

Only one white female Sumpter/Sumter was born between 1882 and 1884 in New York City.

Figure 2-JS
Birth Return for Baby Girl Sumpter, 3 April 1883
(O.W: out of wedlock)

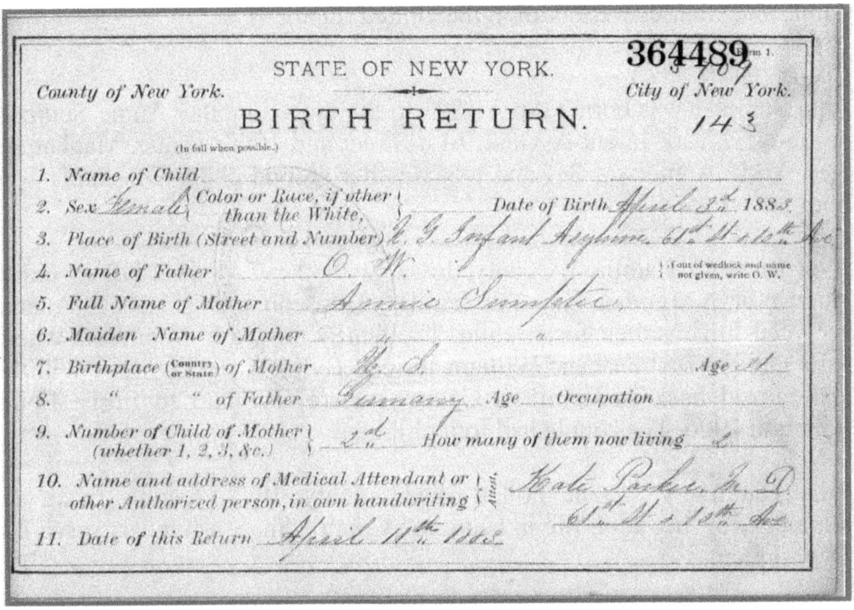
364489 Form 1.

STATE OF NEW YORK.

County of New York. City of New York.

BIRTH RETURN. 143

(In full when possible.)

1. Name of Child
2. Sex Female Color or Race, if other than the White, Date of Birth April 3rd 1883
3. Place of Birth (Street and Number) N. Y. Infant Asylum 61st St & 10th Ave
4. Name of Father O. W. (If out of wedlock and name not given, write O. W.)
5. Full Name of Mother Annie Sumpter
6. Maiden Name of Mother
7. Birthplace (Country or State) of Mother U. S. Age 31
8. " " of Father Germany Age Occupation
9. Number of Child of Mother (whether 1, 2, 3, &c.) 2nd How many of them now living 2
10. Name and address of Medical Attendant or other Authorized person, in own handwriting Attest. Kate Parker M. D. 61st St & 10th Ave
11. Date of this Return April 11th 1883

Annie Sumpter gave birth to an unnamed female on 3 April 1883. Annie Sumpter was 31 years old (b. 1852) and born in the United States. The only clue to the identity of the father was that he was born in Germany. Annie had given birth to two children, both living; one of them was the unnamed female. The birth was at the New York Infant Asylum at 61st Street and 10th Avenue.[516]

In 1870 Annie and Charles, her brother, lived with their parents, Michael and Margaret. Michael was a seaman.[517] Michael died in 1871 of kidney disease.[518]

---

516 New York City Municipal Archives, "Historical Vital Records," Birth Return, certificate no. 364489, Baby Girl Sumpter birth entry (3 April 1893).

517 1870 US census, New York County, New York, population schedule, New York City, Ward 16, District 16 (2nd enumeration), p. 4, Household 132, Michael Sumter.

518 "New York, New York City Municipal Deaths, 1795-1949", database, *FamilySearch* (https://www.familysearch.org/ark:/61903/1:1:2WJH-7TJ), Michael L. Sumter, death entry (8 November 1871).

In 1880 Annie Sumpter resided with her 48 year-old widowed mother Margaret, her brother and 1 year-old Mary. Mary was identified as a daughter to Margaret.[519] Based on her age, Margaret was not likely the mother of Mary. Mary was not the unnamed female born in 1883, but could be the first child born to Annie that she declared on the birth certificate as living. Both Michael and Margaret were born in Ireland, and Annie and Charles were born in the United States.[520]

CONCLUSION

Julia Sumpter was born 3 April 1883 to the unwed mother Annie Sumpter at the New York Infant Asylum, 61st Street and 10th Avenue, Manhattan, New York. Annie was 31, and this was her second child. The father was born in Germany.

Julia came to Hamilton County, Iowa, with the CAS in 1890 in either August or November, and the family of Joseph and Elizabeth Adams accepted Julia as their foster child. The family moved to Minnesota where Julia met her first husband William Wright. By 1905 she divorced William and moved back to Hamilton County, where she married florist Louis Follett in 1906. The couple had four children.

Julia (Sumpter) Wright Follett died 3 July 1977, having lived the remainder of her adult life in Hamilton County. She was the last surviving 1890 orphan.

Four children were born to the couple: Catherine E (b. 1908), James L. (b. 1919), George M. (b. 1921), and Donald H. (b. 1924) Follett.[521] DNA may help identify the father and confirm the mother.

(See https://iowaorphans.wordpress.com for any additional information about this family.)

---

[519] 1880 U.S. census, New York County, New York, population schedule, New York City, ED 425, household 17, dwelling 140, Annie Sumpter in the household of Margaret Sumpter.

[520] 1870 US census, New York County, New York, population schedule, New York City, Ward 16, District 16 (2nd enumeration), p. 4, Household 132, Michael Sumter.

[521] 1925 State of Iowa census, Hamilton County, Webster City, image 719 of 884, Louis Follett. Also *FindAGrave*.

CHARLES JOSEPH (NOLAN?) TARRANT

B. 16 JANUARY 1886; OR
8 DECEMBER 1884, NEW YORK CITY, NEW YORK
D. 30 JULY 1961, LAKE CRYSTAL, BLUE EARTH COUNTY, MINNESOTA
BIRTH FAMILY: —?— NOLAN
FOSTER FAMILY: W. C. WOOLSEY THEN RICHARD AND ELLEN TARRANT
BROTHER TO WILLIAM ANTHONY (NOLAN?) TARRANT

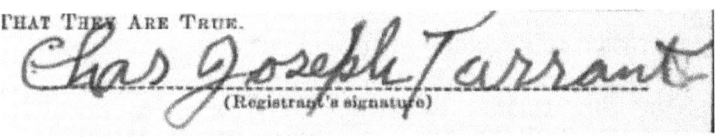

WWII Draft Registration Card

In the August delivery of children, it was noted that W. C. Woolsey took two boys.[522] No children born in New York or of the right age have been found with the W. C. (William Clark) Woolsey family in 1895 or in 1900.[523] The two boys were probably Charles and William, and they moved to the Tarrant family between 1890 and 1895 when the Woolsey family moved to Webster County.

Only two other orphan boys were known brothers- the Webers; however, they were documented in the October delivery as being accepted into the Briggs and the Gerber families. When two orphans of close age reside in the same household, like Charles and William, it is likely they were siblings.

No direct evidence exists that Charles and William came to the Woolsey family, but the location of their births in contrast to their foster parents, their ages, the advanced age of their foster father, the acceptance by Woolsey of two orphans, and living in Hamilton County identified the two boys as out-placed orphans accepted initially into the Woolsey family.

---

[522] E. Trott of the children's aid society…," *The Freeman (Webster City, Iowa)*, 3 September 1890, p. 5, col. 3.

[523] 1895 State of Iowa census, Webster County, Iowa, population schedule, image 830 of 1062, Wm. C. Woolsey. And, 1900 U.S. census, Webster County, Iowa, population schedule, Wahkonsa, ED 187, p. 10, household 190, dwelling 217, William Woolsey.

By 1895 both boys resided in the Richard and Ellen Tarrant household. Richard, age 65, and Ellen, age 52, were both born in Ireland. Both of the boys were born in New York and were of a similar age to be siblings.[524]

In 1900 Charles and William were the Tarrant's "adopted sons." Ellen had birthed five children, only a daughter survived.[525] With the advancing years of Richard, and no sons to help with the farm work, Richard accepted the orphans.

On 16 August 1907 Richard Tarrant died, survived by his wife, a daughter, a brother, and two "sons," Charles and William Tarrant.[526] From all appearances, the boys found a comfortable home in a loving family.

Shortly after Richard's death, the paths of the two boys diverged.

On 15 Sept 1909, Charles Tarrant married Pearl Rouse in the Catholic Church. Charles declared that he was born in New York; his father's surname was Nolan; but his mother's name was not known. After a short honeymoon in Omaha, Nebraska, the couple resided on the Tarrant farm. No mention was made of William.[527] By 1910 Charles and Pearl Tarrant with their one-month-old daughter, established their home on a rented farm in Hamilton County.[528] In 1911 Ellen Tarrant bought a farm in Kossuth County, Iowa, and Charles and the family moved and managed the farm for his foster mother.[529] Again, no mention was made of William.

Disaster struck the family a few years after moving to Kossuth County. In the morning of 2 February 1915, the Tarrant house caught fire and burned to the ground before any help arrived. Charles went into the building and rescued his wife and children who escaped in their nightclothes. Few possessions were saved. The day was bitterly cold and the family sat on a mattress in the yard before being taken to to a neighbor's home. Charles

---

[524] 1895 State of Iowa census, Hamilton County, Iowa, population schedule, image 334 of 681, Richard Torrent.

[525] 1900 U.S. census, Hamilton county, Iowa, population schedule, Fremont Township, ED 103, p. 3, household 45, dwelling 56, Richard Torenet.

[526] "R. Tarrant Passes Away," *Daily Freeman Tribune,* 15 August 1907, p. 4, col. 4.

[527] "Iowa, U.S. Marriage Records, 1880-1945," marriage register, 1909-1910, #436 (Emmet-Muscatine), Chas J. Tarrant-Pearl Terressa Rouse marriage entry (15 September 1909). Also, "Well known Young People are Wed," *The Daily Freeman Tribune,* 15 September 1909, Tarrant-Rouse marriage (15 September 1909).

[528] 1910 U.S. census, Hamilton County, Iowa, population schedule, Fremont Township, ED 113, household 156, dwelling 157, Charles Tarrant.

[529] "Irvington Localizer," *Kossuth County Advance (Algona Iowa),* 7 March 1912, p. 8, col 2,

vowed to rebuild that coming summer.[530] The cause of the fire was a stove pipe which became red hot and set the roof on fire. Pearl and the children went to Story City to stay with her parents while Charles took care of the stock on the farm.[531] In mid-April Charles started to rebuild the home after receiving a train car load of lumber.[532] By August 1915, the family moved into their new nine-room home. The neighbors gave Pearl a shower to assist in outfitting the home.[533] The house was listed in Ellen Tarrant's name. The insurance company noted that Ellen loss was $500.00.[534]

Charles registered for the World War I draft in Algona, Kossuth County, Iowa, declaring his birthday as 16 January 1886. He was a farmer and resided in Irvington.[535]

Perhaps recollecting his own beginnings, the Charles Tarrant family assumed the care of a 12 year-old boy, Harley Beck of Webster City in 1917. Harley was one of six children whose father, also named Harley Beck, could not care for them after the death of their mother. The Tarrants were "commended for their kind action."[536] It is not known how long Harley stayed with the family, but by 1929 young Harley was serving time for larceny in the Iowa Men's Reformatory in Anamosa.[537]

In 1919 Charles bought a quarter section in Blue Earth County, Minnesota, at $120 an acre.[538] They sold 80 head of livestock and farm machinery at a public sale in Kossuth County on 18 December 1919, and planned to move to Minnesota on 1 March.[539] The family reported that the crops were better in the north country due to more abundant rainfall. In 1930 the family, composed of Charles J., Pearl T., and six children, resided on a rented farm

---

[530] R.M. Watson, "Had to Flee Fire in Night-Clothes," *Kossuth County Advance*, 3 February 1915, p. 2, col 2.
[531] "Local News," A*lgona Courier (Iowa)*, 5 February 1915, p. 7, col 2.
[532] R.M. Watson, Editor, "Irvington," *Kossuth County Advance*, 21 April 1915, p. 7, col. 4.
[533] Ibid., 18 August 1915, p. 7, col. 3.
[534] Kossuth County Mutual Insurance Association, *Kossuth County Advance*, 5 January 1916, p. 12, col5 & 6.
[535] "U.S. World War I draft registration cards, 1917-1918," Local Board of Kossuth County, Algona, Iowa, serial no. 2759, Charles Joseph Tarrant.
[536] R. M. Watson, Editor, "Irvington," *Kossuth County Advance*, 22 August 1917, p. 6, col. 2.
[537] "Iowa, Consecutive Registers of Convicts, 1867-1970," Book 8, Men's Reformatory, Anamosa, 1921-1940; 10 April 1929, convict no. 12798, Harley Beck, age 24.
[538] A.E. Clayton, "Advance County Farm Department," *Kossuth County Advance*, 12 June 1919, p. 9, col 2.
[539] Ibid., 23 October 1919, p. 3, col. 1. Also, "Public Sale," *Kossuth County Advance*, 11 December 1919, p. 19, col 5 and 6.

in Minnesota.⁵⁴⁰ Since Charles rented the farm in Kossuth County from his foster mother, a similar arrangement was probably made for the Minnesota farm. One of the more unusual crops Charles planted and harvested was sixty acres of popcorn.⁵⁴¹

Charles stopped farming during the Depression. By 1940 the couple owned their home. Charles was a laborer and earned $468 the previous year, working 39 weeks. The three children at home attended school. Charles was born in New York and attended four years of high school, an unusual amount of schooling for the era and even more so for the orphans. Pearl had two years of college.⁵⁴² In 1942, Charles was a day laborer in Lake Crystal.⁵⁴³

By 1950 Charles set drainage tile to make more land viable for farming.⁵⁴⁴ Charles died on 30 July 1961 in Lake Crystal, Blue Earth County, Minnesota. His foster parents were identified as his parents.⁵⁴⁵ In his obituary, William "Bill" Tarrant was identified as a brother.⁵⁴⁶

Tarrant was an adopted name and not the name of the New York parents. Nolan, identified as a parent in the register of Charles's marriage, was the possible surname of the New York City parents of the brothers. To determine Charles's most likely date of birth and the birth location, a comparison of all entries was assembled.

---

⁵⁴⁰ 1930 U.S. census, Blue Earth County, Minnesota, population schedule, Lincoln Township, ED 16, household 8, dwelling 18, Charles J. Tarrant.

⁵⁴¹ "Irvington," The *Kossuth County Advance*, 6 November 1919, p. 12, col. 2.

⁵⁴² 1940 U.S. census, Blue Earth County, Minnesota, population schedule, Lake Crystal Township, ED 7-13, household 61, Charles Tarrant.

⁵⁴³ "U.S. World War II draft registration cards, 1942," fourth registration, Minnesota, Tanner, Elmer -Tenney, Albert, serial no. 1065, Charles Joseph Tarrant.

⁵⁴⁴ 1950 U.S. census, Blue Earth County, Minnesota, population schedule, Lake Crystal Township, ED 7-14, household 55, Charles J. Tarrant.

⁵⁴⁵ Minnesota Department of Health, Division of Vital Statistics, Certificate of Death, 1961-MN-001097, Blue Earth County, Charles Tarrant death certificate (30 July 1961).

⁵⁴⁶ "Charles Tarrant, 77, Dies in Minnesota," *Daily Freeman Journal,* 31 July 1961, p. 3, col. 5.

Figure 1-CJT
Name, location and date of birth, foster and birth parents of Charles Joseph (Nolan?) Tarrant

Year	Name	Birth date	Birth location	Birth parents	Foster parents
1890	Charles[a]				W. C. Woolsey
1895	Charles Tarrant[b]	1886	New York		Richard Tarrant
1900	Charles Torenet[c]	Dec 1885	New York	b. New York	Richard Torrent
1905	Charley Tarrant[d]	1886	New York	b.———	
1909	Charles Joseph Tarrant[e]	1885	New York	—?— Nolan & unknown b. New York	
1910	Charles Joseph Tarrant[f]	1885	New York	bUnknown	
1918	Charles Joseph Tarrant[g]	16 Jan 1886			
1930	Charles J. Tarrant[h]	1885	Iowa	b. New York	
1940	Charles Tarrant[i]	1884	Iowa	b. New York	
1942	Charles Joseph Tarrant[j]	6 Dec 1884	New York City, NY		
1950	Charles J. Tarrant[k]	1885	New York		
1961	Charles Joseph Tarrant[l]	6 Dec 1885	New York City, NY	Foster parents	

a. E. Trott of the children's aid society…," *The Freeman (Webster City, Iowa)*, 3 September 1890, p. 5, col. 3.
b. 1895 State of Iowa census, Hamilton County, Iowa, population schedule, image 334 of 681, Richard Torrent.
c. "1900 U.S. census, Hamilton county, Iowa, population schedule, Fremont Township, ED 103, p. 3, household 45, dwelling 56, Richard Torenet.
d. 1905 Iowa state census, Hamilton County, Iowa, population schedule, card no. 524, Charley Tarianl (Charley Tarrant).
e. "Iowa, U.S. Marriage Records, 1880-1945," marriage register, 1909-1910, #436 (Emmet-Muscatine), Chas J. Tarrant-Pearl Terressa Rouse marriage entry (15 September 1909).
f. 1910 U.S. census, Hamilton County, Iowa, population schedule, Fremont Township, ED 113, household 156, dwelling 157, Charles Tarent.
g. "U.S. World War I draft registration cards," 18 September 1918, Algona, Kossuth County, Iowa, serial no. 2759, Charles Joseph Tarrant.
h. 1930 U.S. census, Blue Earth County, Minnesota, population schedule, Lincoln Township, ED 16, household 8, dwelling 18, Charles J. Tarrant.
i. 1940 U.S. census, Blue Earth County, Minnesota, population schedule, Lake Crystal Township, ED 7-13, household 61, Charles Tarrant.
j. "U.S. World War II draft registration cards, 1942," fourth registration, Minnesota, Tanner, Elmer -Tenney, Albert, serial no. 1065, Charles Joseph Tarrant.
k. 1950 U.S. census, Blue Earth County, Minnesota, population schedule, Lake Crystal Township, ED 7-14, household 55, Charles J. Tarrant.
l. Minnesota Department of Health, Division of Vital Statistics, Certificate of Death, 1961-MN-001097, Blue Earth County, Charles Tarrant death certificate (30 July 1961).

Based on the documentary evidence, Charles Joseph (Nolan?) Tarrant was born between 1884 and 1886, possibly in December or January. Although Nolan may be the surname, the middle name sometimes reflects the birth surname or given name, i.e. Joseph. Only the birth location being New York (City) is consistent. Usually the date closest to the event is the most accurate, and the further away from the birth is the least. A candidate may remember the date and month of their birth, but forget the year.

The common name, the uncertainty of the birth year, and no known surname results in the inability to identify a New York family for either brother.

CONCLUSION

Based on the documentary evidence, Charles Joseph Tarrant was born 8 December 1884 in New York City, New York, but that date is not certain. His parents are unknown.

On 15 Sept 1909, Charles Tarrant married Pearl Rouse in the Catholic Church. Charles died on 30 July 1961 in Lake Crystal, Blue Earth County, Minnesota. In his obituary, William "Bill" was identified as a brother.

Charles and Pearl had a least six children: Mary E. (b. 1912), Margaret C. (b. 1917), Paul C. (b. 1921), Helen G. (b. 1923), Kenneth C. (b. 1926), and Duane R. (1929). DNA may provide clues to the NYC parents when the documents won't release their secrets.

(*See* https://iowaorphans.wordpress.com for additional information about the brothers.)

WILLIAM ANTHONY TARRANT

B. 16 JANUARY 1888 IN NEW YORK CITY, NEW YORK
D. 14 APRIL 1964, HAMILTON COUNTY, IOWA
BIRTH FAMILY: POSSIBLY —?— NOLAN
FOSTER FAMILY: W. C. WOOLSEY THEN RICHARD AND ELLEN TARRANT
BROTHER TO CHARLES JOSEPH TARRANT

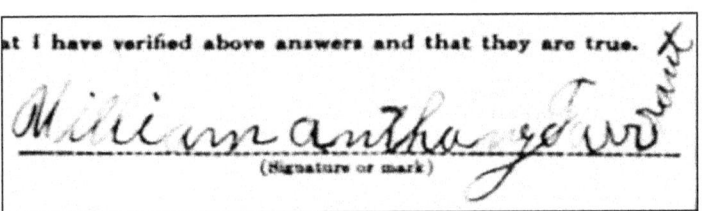

WWI Draft Registration Card

In the August delivery of children, it was noted that W. C. Woolsey took two boys.[547] No children born in New York or of the right age have been found with the W. C. (William Clark) Woolsey family in 1895 or in 1900.[548] The two boys were probably Charles and William, and they moved to the Tarrant family between 1890 and 1895 when the Woolsey family moved to Webster County.

Only two other orphan boys were known brothers- the Webers; however, they were documented in the October delivery as being accepted into the Briggs and the Gerber families. When two orphans of close age reside in the same household, like Charles and William, it is likely they were siblings.

No direct evidence exists that Charles and William came to the Woolsey family, but the location of their births in contrast to their foster parents, their ages, the advanced age of their foster father, the acceptance by Woolsey of two orphans, and living in Hamilton County identified the two boys as out-placed orphans accepted initially into the Woolsey family.

---

[547] E. Trott of the children's aid society...," *The Freeman (Webster City, Iowa),* 3 September 1890, p. 5, col. 3.

[548] 1895 State of Iowa census, Webster County, Iowa, population schedule, image 830 of 1062, Wm. C. Woolsey. And, 1900 U.S. census, Webster County, Iowa, population schedule, Wahkonsa, ED 187, p. 10, household 190, dwelling 217, William Woolsey.

By 1895 both boys resided in the Richard and Ellen Tarrant household. Richard, age 65, and Ellen, age 52, were both born in Ireland. Both of the boys were born in New York and were of a similar age to be siblings.[549]

In 1900 Charles and William were the Tarrant's "adopted sons." Ellen had birthed five children, only a daughter survived.[550] With the advancing years of Richard, and no sons to help with the farm work, Richard accepted the orphans.

On 16 August 1907 Richard Tarrant died, survived by his wife, a daughter, a brother, and two "sons," Charles and William Tarrant.[551] From all appearances, the boys found a comfortable home in a loving family.

Shortly after Richard's death, the paths of the two boys diverged.

In 1910 William worked on the Guy and Eunice Scott farm, a relationship that would re-establish itself after his service in The Great War.[552]

After working for the Scotts, William worked as a laborer for multiple farmers in the North Central Iowa area. In the spring and summer of 1914, William worked in Bancroft, Iowa.[553] In 1915 he went to Montana to stake a homestead claim. The newspaper commended William for striking out to obtain land. No claim was found for William in Montana.[554] By 5 June 1917 William was back in Kossuth County registering for the draft. He declared he was born on 16 January 1888 in New York City, New York.[555]

After trips to visit relatives in Webster City, Fort Dodge and his brother Charles in Kossuth County, William reported to the U.S. Army and was

---

[549] 1895 State of Iowa census, Hamilton County, Iowa, population schedule, image 334 of 681, Richard Torrent.

[550] 1900 U.S. census, Hamilton county, Iowa, population schedule, Fremont Township, ED 103, p. 3, household 45, dwelling 56, Richard Torenet.

[551] "R. Tarrant Passes Away," *Daily Freeman Tribune,* 15 August 1907, p. 4, col. 4.

[552] 1910 U.S. census, Hamilton county, Iowa, population schedule, Fremont Township, ED 113, p. 21A, household 209, dwelling 210, Wm. Tarrant is the household of Guy Scott.

[553] R. M. Watson, Editor, "Irvington Localizer," *Kossuth County Advance (Algona, Iowa)*, 27 May 1914, p. 6, col 1.

[554] Ibid., 31 March 1915, p. 7, col. 3. Also Bureau of Land Management, General Land office records, Search parameters: William Tarrant, Montana. https://glorecords.blm.gov/search; One mineral claim by a William Tarrant was found in Custer County, South Dakota, but probably not William Anthony Tarrant. If it was, shortly after filing, William Athony Tarrant was back in Iowa.

[555] "U.S. World War I draft registration cards, 1917-1918," Local Draft Board of Kossuth County, Iowa, serial no. 44, William Anthony Tarrant.

sent to Camp Gordon, Georgia, on 25 July 1918.[556] He was first assigned to serve in the 157th Depot Brigade.[557] The unit departed from Hoboken, New Jersey, on 31 August 1918. In case of an emergency, the Army was to notify his brother, Charles.[558] William informed his brother by letter that he landed safely in France on 11 September.[559]

William A. Tarrant and 83 others transferred into Company E of the 107th after the unit engaged in its last conflict.[560] William left Brest, France, on 28 February 1919 aboard the S/S *Neil Amsterdam*.[561] William was discharged on 30 March 1919.[562]

William is the only known orphan to participate in any military service.

William returned to Iowa and worked as a farm laborer for the James Devine family in Cresco, Howard County, Iowa.[563] The relationship with the Devines must have soured as William sued Devine in 1923, probably for past wages.[564] He continued his work as a farm laborer and moved to Fort Dodge for summer seasonal work in 1921.[565] Before 1930 William, single, moved back to Hamilton County and was again working as a hired

---

[556] "County's Quota for Camp Gordon, Ga., Cut from 337 Men to 299," *Kossuth County Advance*, 17 July 1918, p. 1, col. 6. Also, R.M. Watson, "Irvington Localizer," 24 July 1918, *Kossuth County Advance*, p. 6, col. 1.

[557] "U.S. Headstone Applications for Military Veterans, 1925-1970," 1965, Stout, Michael-Taylor, Elijah, for William A. Tarrant, death date 14 April 1964; NARA-St. Louis, RG 92, Records of the Quartermaster General.

[558] "U.S., Army Transport Service Arriving and Departing Passenger Lists, 1910-1939," Outgoing, USS *Leviathian*, 31 August 1918, Camp Gordon August Automatic Replacement, Draft Infantry Company #23, 218, William A. Tarrant, 4002992.

[559] R.M. Watson, "Irvington," *Kossuth County Advance*, 8 September 1918, p. 7, col 3.

[560] Gerald F. Jacobson, compiler, *History of the 107th Infantry, U.S.A.,* (New York City, Armory, 1920), 489, (https://www.google.com/books/edition/History_of_the_107th_Infantry_U_S_A/bGgyAQAAIAAJ?hl=en&gbpv=1&dq=Frank+Cornelius+awarded+DSC&pg=PT620&printsec=frontcover).

[561] "U.S., Army Transport Service Arriving and Departing Passenger Lists, 1910-1939," Incoming, USS *New Amsterdam*, 28 February 1919, Camp Dodge Detachment, 107th Infantry, 27th Division, William Tarrant, 4002992.

[562] Danni Altman-Newell, (danni@talkingboxgenealogy.com) email, "WWI records," 21 January 2024 to Jill Morelli (jkmorelli@gmail.com) Ms. Altman-Newell reported that the William A. Tarrant records were lost in the fire and no documents remained. Final payment, dated 30 March 1919 was attached.

[563] 1920 U.S. census, Kossuth County, Ioa, population schedule, Cresco, ED 168, p. 12B, household 221, dwelling 231, William Tarriut in the household of James L. Divina.

[564] "September Court to Open Monday," *Kossuth County Advance,* 18 September 1924, p. 6, col 4.

[565] "Irvington News," *Upper Des Moines Republican*, 9 March 1921, p. 11, col. 2.

hand for Guy M. and Eunice Scott's stock farm.⁵⁶⁶ William remained with the Scott family until his death.⁵⁶⁷

No newspaper article reported any activity of William while working for the Scotts.

When William registered for the World War II draft, he stated he was born in New York on 16 January 1887.⁵⁶⁸

After Guy Scott died, Eunice and William moved to Webster City and continued to reside together. William did yard work and cleaned private homes.⁵⁶⁹

William A. Tarrant died on 14 April 1964 at the home of Mrs. Eunice Scott, with whom he had farmed and lived for 54 years. He never married and had no descendants. He was buried in Graceland Cemetery in Webster City, Iowa.⁵⁷⁰ William died intestate. Mrs. Scott's son was named his executor. His assets did not cover his expenses in death.

Tarrant was an adopted name and not the name of the New York parents. His NY surname is unknown, but his brother Charles identified "Nolan" as his parents in his marriage register entry.

Based on documentary evidence William's birth date and place are consistent, but little is known of his New York City parents. He never mentioned the name Nolan in any records, as his brother did.

---

⁵⁶⁶ 1930 U.S. census, Hamilton County, Iowa, population schedule, Cass Township, ED 8, p. 6A, household 115, dwelling 115, William Tarrant in the household of Guy M. Scott.

⁵⁶⁷ 1950 U.S. census, Hamilton County, Iowa, population schedule, Webster City, ED 40-8, p. 7, household 74, William Tarrant in the household of Eunice M. Scott.

⁵⁶⁸ "U.S., World War II Draft Registration Cards, 1942, Hamilton County, Iowa, Sylvester, Reuel-Taylor, Robert, William Antony Tarant.

⁵⁶⁹ 1950 U.S. census, Hamilton County, population schedule, Webster City, ED 40-8, p. 7, household 73, William A. Tarrant in the household of Eunice M. Scott.

⁵⁷⁰ "W.A. Tarrant Dies Suddenly," *Daily Freeman Journal [Webster City, Iowa],* 14 April 1964, p. 1, col 8. Also, "U.S. Headstone Applications for Military Veterans, 1925-1970," 1965, Stout, Michael-Taylor, Elijah, for William A. Tarrant, death date 14 April 1964; NARA-St. Louis, RG 92, Records of the Quartermaster General.

Table 1-WAT
Name, location and date of birth, foster and birth parents of William Tarrant

Year	Name	Birth date	Birth location	Birth parents	Foster parents
1890	William[a]				W. C. Woolsey
1895	William Tarrant[b]	1888	New York		Richard & Ellen Tarrant
1900	William Tarrant[c]	Jan 1887	New York	b. NY	Richard & Ellen Torent
1905	William Tanaul[d]	1888	New York	b. Unknown	
1910	William Tarrent[e]	1886	New York	b. Unknown	
1917	William Anthony Tarrant[f]	16 Jan 1888	New York City, NY		
1918	William A Tarrant				
1919	William Tarrant[h]				
1920	William Tarruit[i]	1888	New York	b. U.S.	
1930	William Tarrant[j]	1887	New York	b. NY	
1942	William Anthony Taranto	16 Jan 1887	New York		
1950	William A Tarrant[l]	1888	New York		
1964	William A Tarrant[m]	16 Jan 1888	New York		Mr. & Mrs. John Tarrant

a. E. Trott of the children's aid society...," *The Freeman (Webster City, Iowa)*, 3 September 1890, p. 5, col. 3.
b. 1895 State of Iowa census, Hamilton County, Iowa, population schedule, image 334 of 681, Richard Tarrant.
c. 1900 U.S. census, Hamilton county, Iowa, population schedule, Fremont Township, ED 103, p. 3, household 45, dwelling 56, Richard Torenet.
d. 1905 Iowa state census, Hamilton County, Iowa, population schedule, Fremont Township, image 3911 of 6100, card no. 523, William Tanaul.
e. 1910 U.S. census, Hamilton county, Iowa, population schedule, Fremont Township, ED 113, p. 21A, household 209, dwelling 210, Wm. Tarrant is the household of Guy Scott.
f. "U.S. World War I draft registration cards, 1917-1918," Local Draft Board of Kossuth County, Iowa, serial no. 44, William Anthony Tarrant.
g. "U.S., Army Transport Service Arriving and Departing Passenger Lists, 1910-1939," Outgoing USS *Leviathian*, 31 August 1918, Camp Gordon August Automatic Replacement, Draft Infantry Company #23, 218, William A., Tarrant, 4002992.
h. "U.S., Army Transport Service Arriving and Departing Passenger Lists, 1910-1939," incoming, USS *New Amsterdam*, 28 February 1919, Camp Dodge Detachment, 107th Infantry 27th Division, William Tarrant, 4002992.
i. 1920 U.S. census, Kossuth County, Iowa, population schedule, Cresco, ED 168, p. 12B, household 221, dwelling 231, William Tarriut in the household of James L. Divina.
j. 1930 U.S. census, Hamilton County, Iowa, population schedule, Cass Township, ED 8, p. 6A, household 115, dwelling 115, William Tarrant in the household of Guy M. Scott.
k. "U.S., World War II Draft Registration Cards, 1942, Hamilton County, Iowa, Sylvester, Reuel-Taylor, Robert, William Antony Tarant.
l. 1950 U.S. census, Hamilton County, population schedule, Webster City, ED 40-8, p. 7, household 73, William A. Tarrant in the household of Eunice M. Scott.
m. "W.A. Tarrant Dies Suddenly," *Daily Freeman Journal*, 14 April 1964, p. 1, col 8.

William was one of the youngest orphans to arrive in Hamilton County.

William Anthony Tarrant, an assumed surname and perhaps given name, was born 16 January 1888 in New York City to unknown parents. Possibly 1887 was the year of his birth. William consistently used the day and month of 16 January, If Willian was a birth brother to Charles then he, too, should have same-named parents, perhaps named Nolan.

CONCLUSION
William Anthony Tarrant was probably born 16 January 1887 or 1888 in New York City. He was delivered to Hamilton County, Iowa, in 1890 from New York City with his brother Charles Joseph. His foster parents were Richard and Ellen Tarrant. After serving in World War I, he became a farm hand for the Guy M. and Eunice Scott family where he resided for the rest of his life.

William died 14 April 1964, at the home of Eunice Scott. William never married and had no descendants, limiting the ability of DNA to tie him to parents or to Charles.

(*See* https://iowaorphans.wordpress.com for additional information about the brothers.)

WALTER THOMPSON

B. 12 March 1883, New York City, New York
D. 29 October 1949, St.Louis County, Minnesota
Parents: Maggie Thompson; unknown father
Foster Family: James V. and Minerva Motheral

WWI Draft Registration Card

Walter Thompson was an out-placed orphan on the fall delivery of children in 1890 to Hamilton County, Iowa. In 1895 Walter Thompson, age 11 and born in New York, resided with the Motheral family in Hamilton County. James, age 44, Minerva Motheral, 39, and their 16 year-old daughter were born in Illinois. James was a farmer and needed help on the farm.[571]

No direct evidence exists that Walter was a New York City orphan. The location of Walter's birth in contrast to that of his foster family; Walter's age; the Motherals having only one daughter; and living in Hamilton County identified him as an out-placed orphan in 1890.

In 1900 Walter, as boarder and farm laborer, continued his residence with the Motheral family.[572] Walter participated in the life of a small town in Iowa and attended weddings and birthday parties. He competed in a shooting contest and won 4th place—a one pound bag of candy.[573]

---

[571] 1895 State of Iowa census, Hamilton County, Iowa, population schedule, image 210 of 681, Walter M. Thompson in the household of James Motherel.

[572] 1900 U.S. census, Hamilton County, Iowa, population schedule, Cass Township, Fremont, ED 103, p. 10, household 45, dwelling 45, Walter Thompson in the household of James Motheral.

[573] "Camp and Rifle Contest," *Daily Freeman Tribune*, 7 July 1908, p. 5, col. 3; "Wedding Bells," *Daily Freeman Tribune*, 3 January 1906, p. 4, col. 4; "Birthday Surprise," *Daily Freeman Tribune*, p. 5, col. 4.

By 1909 Walter had moved to Mason City, Cerro Gordo County, Iowa.[574] He continued close contact with his foster family in Webster City after he moved.[575]

In February 1917, Walter Thompson of Mason City, Iowa, age 34 and a painter, married Mrs. Ella (Hogen) Booth.[576] Ella died one month after the marriage due to complications of her pregnancy. Walter was the informant on the death certificate.[577]

Walter Thompson re-registered for the draft 9 November 1918 with the local draft board of Cerro Gordo County, Iowa, delayed due to a lost registration. He listed Mrs. J.V. Motheral as his closest relative. Walter described himself as single, self-employed painter.[578] He did not serve in the military.

During this time, Walter obtained information from the CAS about his New York City birth.

In 1925 Walter was a boarder in the household of Delos Fitzgerald. Walter was single, born in New York, and 41 years of age. Walter identified his foster parents as parents but took some license with the facts. He identified his father as Jim Thompson (b. Scotland, deceased); and his mother as Vanarrie [Minerva] Studely (b. England, still living).[579] The errors seem deliberate. He probably switched the surname of James to avoid questions.

By 1930 Walter, still working as a painting contractor, declared himself widowed. He lived in a boarding house in Mason City.[580]

---

[574] "Personal Mention," *Webster City Herald*, 4 March 1909, p. 5, col. 5.

[575] Ibid. and various articles, "Independence," *Webster City Journal*, 3 March 1910, p. 3, col. 6; 5 January 1911, p. 8, col. 1;

[576] Iowa, U.S., Selected Marriages, 1880-1951, Thompson-Booth marriage entry (17 February 1917).

[577] "Iowa, Death Records, 1904-1951," database with images, FamilySearch (https://familysearch.org/ark:/61903/3:1:3Q9M-CS6Q-3SSR-7?cc=2531337), > image 2921 of 4353.

[578] U.S. World War I draft registration cards, 1917-1918," Local Board of Cerro Gordo County, Iowa, serial no. 4402, Walter Thompson. The clerk has noted that this registration replaced a lost registration.

[579] 1925 State of Iowa census, Cerro Gordo County, Iowa, population schedule, Mason City, image 793 of 1079, Walter Thompson.

[580] 1930 U.S. census, Cerro Gordo County, Iowa, population schedule, ED 25, p. 2A, household 19, dwelling 48, Walter Thomson.

When Walter registered to receive his Social Security number, he provided his birth date and location as 12 March 1884 in New York City, New York, but identified the Motherals as his parents.[581]

Shortly after 1930, Walter moved to Minnesota.[582] In 1942 he resided in Austin, Minnesota, and worked for the Austin Mower Company.[583]

Walter drowned while duck hunting on 29 October 1949 (estimated), at Lake Kabetogama, St. Louis County, Minnesota, in the far north region of the state. He was found on 22 May 1950. His residence was the single-room-occupancy Frederic Hotel in International Falls, Mower County, Minnesota.[584] As a long-term residential hotel, Walter probably lived at the Frederic Hotel for a long time. Walter was buried in Mason City in an unmarked grave next to Ellen, "wife of Walter Thompson," at Elmwood-Saint Joseph Cemetery on 26 May 1950.[585]

As an adult, it appears that Walter received information about his NYC parents.

In his obituary, Walter was described as the adopted son of Mr. and Mrs. J. N. Motheral, but named his birth parents as O.W. and Maggie Thompson.[586] It is doubtful that there was a formal adoption, but rather that Walter was a part of the family in the real sense of the word. The contributor of the information for the obituary is not known.

In spite of Walter naming his foster parents as his birth parents much of his life, documentary evidence provides evidence of Walter's mother.

---

[581] U. S., Social Security Applications and Claims Index, 1936-2002, Walter Thompson, SSN 472-10-6263.
[582] R.L. Polk, *Mason City City Directory, 1932*, p. 268, Walter Thompson. He is not found in the 1933 directory.
[583] "World War II Draft Registration Cards, 1942," 12 September 1918, Austin, Mower County, Minnesota, Thompson, George-Thorpe, U767, for Walter Thompson.
[584] Minnesota Department of Health, Division of Vital Statistics, Certificate of Death, no. 15068, Walter Thompson (29 October 1949). "W. Thompson Rites Friday," *Mason City Globe Gazette*, 24 May 1950, p. 28, col. 3.
[585] Elmwood-St. Joseph's Cemetery (Mason City, Cerro Gordo County, Iowa), Ellen Thompson marker, 2nd Addition, personally read, 2023. Walter Thompson has no stone.
[586] "W. Thompson Rites Friday," *Mason City Globe Gazette*, 24 May 1950, p. 28, col. 3.

Maggie Thompson's unnamed boy born 12 March 1883 in Kings County, New York, is an obvious candidate.[587]

Figure 1-WT
Birth Certificate of unnamed boy Thompson, b. 12 March 1883

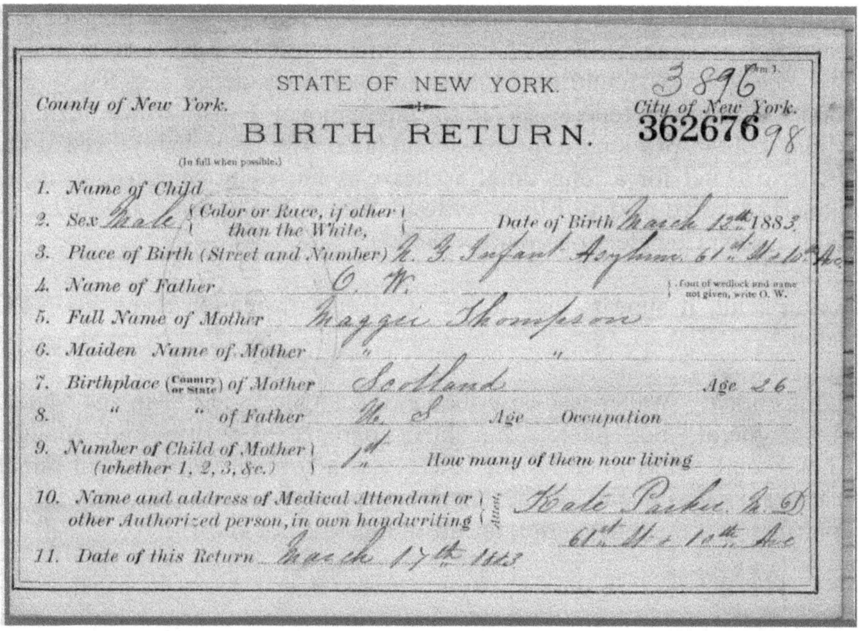

[Birth certificate image: STATE OF NEW YORK, County of New York, City of New York, BIRTH RETURN. No. 3896 / 362676 98. Showing fields for Name of Child (blank), Sex: male, Date of Birth: March 12th 1883, Place of Birth: N. Y. Infant Asylum, 61st St & 10th Ave, Name of Father: O. W., Full Name of Mother: Maggie Thompson, Birthplace of Mother: Scotland, Age 26, Birthplace of Father: U. S., Number of Child of Mother: 1st, Medical Attendant: Kate Parker M.D., 61st St & 10th Ave, Date of Return: March 17th 1883.]

The unnamed boy was born in the New York Infant Asylum, a laying-in hospital for poor women. The date is a reasonable match. The unnamed boy was the child of Maggie Thompson. The father's initials of O. W. refer to an "out of wedlock" relationship, and are not the initials of his father. A Scotland connection was mentioned in the 1925 Iowa State census, which was the mother's birthplace.

CONCLUSION
Walter Thompson was born 12 March 1883 at the New York Infant Asylum at 61st Street and 10th Avenue to the unmarried woman, Maggie Thompson. Nothing was recorded about the father other than him being born in the United States.

---

[587] New York City Municipal Archives, "Historical Vital Records," Birth Return, certificate no. 362676, male Thompson birth entry (12 March 1883).

Walter came to Hamilton County as an out-placed orphan in 1890 and married Mrs. Ellen (Hogen) Booth in 1917. Ellen died shortly after the marriage. Walter never married again, but lived and worked in Cerro Gordo County, Iowa, until 1931 or 1932 when he relocated to Minnesota, for the remainder of his life.

He drowned in Lake Kabetogama in St. Louis County, Minnesota in October 1949 while duck hunting and was found in May 1950. It is not known if he had established permanent residence in International Falls or if this was an extended hunting trip. He was buried in an unmarked grave next to Ellen Thompson in May 1950 in Mason City, Iowa.

(*See* https://iowaorphans.wordpress.com for more information.)

William (McKendry) Thompson

B. 1882, New York
D. Unknown
Birth family: —?— McKendry
Foster family: Barney and Betsy Thompson

William McKendry, age 8, arrived in Hamilton County in the October delivery of children. He was placed with the Barney Thompson family of Ellsworth.[588] In 1895 William Thompson, 13 years old and born in New York, resided in the household of Barney and Betsey Thompson and their 17 year-old daughter. The Thompsons were born in Norway and Illinois.[589]

In 1900 William, age 18, was not present in the Barney Thompson's household nor was he working out in Hamilton County.[590]

The New York City orphan, William (McKendry) Thompson, disappears from the records after 1895.

Thompson was an adopted name and McKendry the probable name of the New York parents. A spelling variation could be McHenry. This investigation revealed no identification of William (McKendry) Thompson or his parents.

(*See* https://iowaorphans.wordpress.com for more information.)

---

[588] Kialy Carson, Kansas, [(CURATOR@ORPHANTRAINDEPOT.COM),] to Jill Morelli, email, 7 March 2023, "Info from the CAS," OTR folder.

[589] 1895 State of Iowa census, Hamilton County, Iowa, population schedule, Lyon Township, image 468 of 681, William Thompson in the household of Barney Thompson.

[590] 1900 U.S. census, Hamilton County, Iowa, population schedule, Lyon Township, ED 111, p. 21, household 319, dwelling 323, Barney Thompson.

JACOB "FRED" WEBER

B. FEBRUARY 1883 IN NEW YORK
D. 23 MAY 1930 IN WARD, BOULDER COUNTY, COLORADO
BIRTH FAMILY: —?— WEBER
FOSTER FAMILY: FRANK BRIGGS
BROTHER TO: WILLIAM LOUELETTE WEBER

Jacob Weber, age 7, and his brother William arrived in Hamilton County in the October delivery of children, the second of two sets of brothers. Jacob was placed with the Frank Briggs family of Webster City.[591]

> Fred Weber was born in New York City in 1885. He came with his brother to Webster City when he was seven years of age. Being an orphan, for about 10 years he was a part of and grew to manhood in the Frank Briggs home in this community.[592]

Jacob and William are one of two identified sets of siblings who rode the train to Hamilton County.[593] While the other set of brothers (Tarrants) were placed with one family, Jacob and William were split between two households.

In 1895 Jacob Weber, age 12, resided with Frank Briggs, age 32 and single. Also living with Frank was his apparent mother, Ellen, age 76; a possible sister of his mother; and a possible sister, Thrisda.[594] Ellen's husband had died in August of 1890.[595]

---

[591] Kialy Carson, Kansas, [(CURATOR@ORPHANTRAINDEPOT.COM),] to Jill Morelli, email, 7 March 2023, "Info from the CAS," OTR folder.
[592] "Obituary-Fred Weber," *Daily Freeman Tribune*, 2 June 1930, p. 4, col. 2.This obituary is identified as "contributed," probably William, Fred's brother.
[593] "Taken from Hospital," *Daily Freeman Tribune,* 10 April 1914, p. 5, col. 4.
[594] 1895 State of Iowa census, Hamilton County, Iowa, population schedule, image 99 of 681, Jacob Weaver in the household of Frank Briggs.
[595] "Ullis Briggs Dead," *Webster City Freeman*, 27 August 1890, p. 5, col. 3.

The family experienced major changes in 1898. Thrisda Briggs married.[596] Ellen Briggs died that same year.[597] Ellen Briggs's will was specific and gave personal possessions and land to her daughter Thrisda, with a line of succession of goods if Thrisda died. Jacob was not named in the will of Ellen Briggs.[598]

The Briggs family were early settlers to the county, arriving in 1856, and were well known for the manufacturing of brick. They used raw materials from their farm to manufacture the brick for their farm home. This home was later occupied by their son, Frank and his family. A daughter Agnes was well known for her teaching skills.[599]

By 1900 Jacob worked for the John Brunkhorst family. Even when earning modest wages as a farm laborer, Jacob exhibited a generous nature, giving to the Indian Famine Fund $1, an amount larger than what most individuals donated.[600] By 1910 Jacob, now assuming the name of Fred, provided farm labor for the Frank Butto family. Again the family composition was a farming couple with girls and no boys to help with the heavier farm chores.[601] About this time, Fred spent time in the Dakotas before returning to Webster City.

Fred developed an aptitude for fixing machinery, and in 1912 worked for the New City Electric and Light Power Company as a stationary engineer.[602]

On 13 May 1912 a horrible work-place accident occurred that severely crippled Fred for the rest of his life. A large pressurized vessel filled with near-boiling water exploded, severely injuring Fred and two other employees. While fixing the the small steam pump under the boiler, Fred

---

[596] Iowa, U.S., Selected Marriages, 1880-1951, Aldrich-Briggs marriage entry (13 November 1898).

[597] *FindAGrave,* database and images, memorial page for Ellen Branch Briggs (1818-1898), Find A Grave Memorial no. 71022937, citing Glen Haven Memorial Park and Mausoleum, Winter Park, Orange County, Florida; the accompanying photographs by FlamilySleuth provide a legible image for year of death only. Other information is added by unknown.

[598] "Iowa, U.S., Wills and Probate Records, 1758-1997," Hamilton County, Will Record, vol 1-4, 1865-1901, dated 2 August 1894, Ellen Brigs.

[599] Bessie L. Lyon, *Early Days in Hamilton County: Then and Now* (Webster City, Iowa : Freeman-Journal Publishing Company, 1946) 43.

[600] 1900 U.S. census, Hamilton County, Iowa, population schedule, Freedom Township, ED 106, p. 4, household 87, dwelling 87, John J. Brunkhorst. Also, "India Relief Fund," *Hamilton County Journal*, 4 May 1900, p. 1, col 5.

[601] 1910 U.S. census, Hamilton County, Iowa, population schedule, Webster City, Ward 1, ED 109, p. 10B, dwelling 234, dwelling 240, Fred Weaver in the household of Frank Butto.

[602] "Obituary-Fred Weber," *Daily Freeman Tribune*, 2 June 1930, p. 4, col. 2.

received the brunt of the injuries. The pressure in the boiler was so extreme that parts were hurled across the room, and the top blew off piercing the roof. Fred was hit by shrapnel, but the escaping steam caused the worst damage, scalding him over most of his body.[603] At first it was thought that Fred's injuries were fatal, but it was determined he would live.[604] Skin replacement surgery began after Fred had spent three months in the hospital. Employees donated skin to aid in his recovery.[605]

In spite of the extent of his injuries, Fred maintained a positive outlook. Rev. Metcalf commented after a visit, "I went to cheer and encourage Fred, but he cheered and encouraged me instead." Council members and insurance company representatives assured Fred not to worry about his financial condition. The company always paid its obligations promptly and he would be "compensated in full for the damage inflicted."[606]

Fred was confined to the hospital for two years before being released into his brother's care in 1914. He was severely crippled, and suffered from large raw sores; the flesh of his calf had physically joined with the upper part of the left leg. It was reported that "he will be an almost helpless cripple for life."[607]

In spite of promises, and after the years in the hospital with no payment forthcoming from either the insurance company or the City, Fred filed a lawsuit. His medical bills had accumulated to $2,500. Fred wished to see a Chicago specialist who might be able to fix his left leg, at a cost of $1000. He had no money for such an expense.[608]

The newspaper was supportive of the Fred's suit, pointing out that the value of the company was $5,000,000; and the city was spending thousands of dollars on beautifying the city and continuing with building improvements. It also pointed out that the people of Hamilton County were generous towards "a poor young man who life is shattered." The newspaper editorialized that no one would go through what Fred had experienced for even $100,000, and Fred was asking for only $20,000.[609]

---

[603] 603 "Hot Water Heater at Power House Explodes," *Webster City Freeman*, 14 May 1912, p. 1, col. 3.
[604] "Explosion Injures Man at City Plant," *Webster City Journal*, 16 May 1912, p. 5, col. 3.
[605] "Skin-grafting Operation," *Webster City Freeman*, 16 July 1912, p. 1, col 63
[606] "Obituary-Fred Weber," *Daily Freeman Tribune*, 2 June 1930, p. 4, col. 2.
[607] "The Case of Fred Weber," *Daily Freeman Tribune*, 8 May 1914, p. 8, col. 2.
[608] Ibid.
[609] Ibid.

In 1914 Fred commenced a lawsuit against the city for medical care and damages for $20,000.[610] He won the case at the lower court and was awarded $25,000 in damages.[611]

Fred recuperated for the next four years in the care of his brother William, and his wife while his case weaved through the courts.[612]

It was rumored that the City tried to settle with Fred, but the newspaper reported that those rumors were untrue. Even the city's attorney asked the City to pay a small allowance between the filing, the court case and the hearing, but the city declined. Due to lack of money, the Chicago specialist was never engaged; by the time of the Supreme Court hearing, the opportunity for a successful surgery was lost.[613]

The case went to the Iowa Supreme Court in the January 1918 term. The court ruled that Webster City had not provided a safe workplace and found for the appellee J. F. Weber. The Supreme Court determined that the $25,000 granted by the lower courts was excessive and reduced it to $12,500 plus interest from the initial filing.[614] The City Council discussed the various available accounts for the payment; all accounts held more than the amount necessary to cover the remainder after the insurance was paid. Concern was expressed on account of the war.[615] The final amount due to Fred was $15,312.95. Because of offsets by insurance and utility companies, the City's share was $272.15.[616] The total settlement equated to $380,000 in today's dollars.[617]

Fred received the final installment of the court directed payment on 11 March 1918.[618] He moved almost immediately to Golden, Jefferson

---

[610] "The Case of Fred Weber," *Daily Freeman Tribune*, 8 May 1914, p. 8, col. 2.

[611] "Jury Gives Fred Weber Verdict for $25,000," *The Daily Freeman Tribune*, 27 October 1914, p. 8, col 1.

[612] "Obituary-Fred Weber," *Daily Freeman Tribune*, 2 June 1930, p. 4, col. 2.

[613] "Jury Gives Fred Weber Verdict for $25,000," *Daily Freeman-Tribune*, 27 October 1914, p. 8, cols. 1 and 2.

[614] U. G. Whitney, reporter, "Reports of Cases at Law and in Equity determined by the Supreme Court of the State Iowa," September term, 1917 and January Term, 1918, J.F. Weber, Appellee, v. City of Webster City, Appellant. P. 383. January 9, 1918. Most of the case centered around whether a regulation valve had been installed, and whose responsibility it was to make sure it was in proper position before work began. Weber v. Webster City, 182 Iowa 383, 165 N.W. 1009 (1918).

[615] "Arrange to Pay Weber Judgment," *Daily Freeman Journal*, 6 Mary 1918, p. 5, col. 1

[616] "The City Pays Weber Judgment," *Daily Freeman Journal*, 11 April 1918, p. 6, col. 1.

[617] U.S. Inflation Calculator, https://www.usinflationcalculator.com, using 1914 compared to 2023 and $12,500 as the base number.

[618] "City Council Proceedings," *Webster City Journal*, 14 March 1918, p. 5, col. 4.

County, Colorado.[619] In Denver, Fred underwent several operations on his legs which enabled him to trade the wheel chair for crutches.[620]

In February 1921, Fred purchased a number of mining claims from John O'Toole in Boulder County, Colorado:
- The Valley View Lode Mine, Lafayette Mill site, Hill Top Lode, Gold Cord Lode, and Valley View Mill site; purchased for $10.[621]
- The Gold Coin Mine, Canton Mine, Cardiff Mine and Lafayette Lode mine; purchased for $6000.[622]

In 1930 Fred resided in Ward, Boulder County, Colorado, and owned his own home valued at $400, a value considerably lower than that of his neighbors. Fred was a miner in a metal mining company.[623] Fred probably invested the remaining medical reimbursement funds by purchasing mines, although his physical limitations might have prevented him from doing the work.

Jacob "Fred" Weber died 23 May 1930 in Ward, Colorado.[624] Fred neither married nor had any children. His brother wrote a touching obituary.

> As a man he was industrious, dependable and always thoughtful of the interests and rights of others. In his general attitude he was quiet and reserved, unselfish and kindhearted.[625]

J. Fred Weber was buried in Graceland Cemetery in Webster City, Iowa.[626]

---

[619] "Fred Weber Here," *Webster City Freeman*, 22 December 1919, p. 1, col 4.

[620] SF "Obituary-Fred Weber," *Daily Freeman Tribune*, 2 June 1930, p. 4, col. 2.

[621] Indenture, no. 182729, John O'Toole to Fed Weber, both of Denver, Colorado; multiple mining claims 3 February 1921; Carnegie Library for Local History, Boulder, Colorado.

[622] Indenture, no. 182730, John O'Toole to Fed Weber, both of Denver, Colorado; multiple mining claims 3 February 1921; Carnegie Library for Local History, Boulder, Colorado.

[623] 1930 U.S. census, Boulder County, Colorado, population schedule, Ward, ED 10, p. 1A, household 5, dwelling 5, J. Fredrick Weber.

[624] "Fred Weber Dies in Ward Col., of Stroke Apolexy," *Daily Freedman Journal*, 23 May 1930, p. 1. col. 3.

[625] "Obituary-Fred Weber," *Daily Freeman Tribune*, 2 June 1930, p. 4, col. 2.

[626] Find a Grave, database and images (https://www.findagrave.com/memorial/119778737/j-fred-weber), memorial page for J. Fred Weber (1884–1930), Find a Grave Memorial ID 119778737, citing Graceland Cemetery, Webster City, Hamilton County, Iowa, USA; Maintained by Burt (contributor 46867609).

Several sources provided information concerning Fred's earliest life.

Figure 1-JFW
Name, location and date of birth, foster and birth parents
of Jacob "Fred" Weber

Year	Name	Birth date	Birth location	Birth parents	Foster parents
1890	Jacob Weber[a]	1883		—?— Weber	Frank Briggs
1895	Jacob Weber[b]	1883			Frank Briggs
1900	Jacob Weaver[c]	Feb 1885	New York	b. New York	
1910	Jacob Weber[d]	1885	New York	b. United States	
1930	J. Fredrick Weber[e]	1889	New York	b. New York	
1930	Fred Weber[f]	1885	New York City, New York		Frank Briggs

a. Kialy Carson, Kansas, [(CURATOR@ORPHANTRAINDEPOT.COM),] to Jill Morelli, email, 7 March 2023, "Info from the CAS," OTR folder.
b. 1895 State of Iowa census, Hamilton County, Iowa, population schedule, image 99 of 681, Jacob Weaver in the household of Ellen Briggs.
c. 1900 U.S. census, Hamilton County, Iowa, population schedule, Freedom Township, ED 106, p. 4, household 87, dwelling 87, Jacob Weber in the household John J. Brunkhorst.
d. 1910 U.S. census, Hamilton County, Iowa, population schedule, Webster City, Ward 1, ED 109, p. 10B, dwelling 234, dwelling 240, Fred Weaver in the household of Frank Butto.
e. 1930 U.S. census, Boulder County, Colorado, population schedule, Ward, ED 10, p. 1A, household 5, dwelling 5, J. Fredrick Weber.
f. "Obituary-Fred Weber," *Daily Freeman Tribune*, 2 June 1930, p. 4, col. 2.

Wide disparities are evident in the reporting of Fred's birth year. William L. Weber, identified as Fred's brother, was probably born 9 October 1885. (*See* William Louelette Weber) If William was a brother, Fred could not have been born in the same year, unless the boys were twins, of which no proof exists. The birth year of 1889 is an outlier. The year 1883 is the earliest declared birth year for Jacob/Fred, and is the most likely birth year.

Weber is consistent as a surname for both William and Fred. Weber is not the name of either of their foster parents. Jacob and/or Fred may be the given birth names of the younger brother. The location of birth in New York is consistent.

CONCLUSION
Jacob "Fred" Weber was born December 1883, in New York City and was brought to Hamilton County in 1890 on a train of orphans by the CAS with his brother William. The two brothers grew up in separate families.

While fixing a small boiler pump in 1912, Jacob was burned over most of his body when the large boiler exploded. He spent three years in a hospital and four years under the care of his brother.

The city and other parties refused to settle in spite of public sentiment to do so. Fred sued Webster City. Eventually the case went to the Iowa Supreme Court that upheld the claim but reduced the amount to be paid to $12,000 plus fees and interest.

After the city, insurance company and the utility company paid his claim, Fred left for Colorado where he received medical care enabling him to walk with crutches. Fred stayed in Colorado and invested in multiple mines near Ward, where he died in 1930. He was buried in Webster City, Iowa.

The brothers should have the same parents if they are brothers. No match has been found.

Fred did not marry and had no known descendants; DNA will not be helpful in determining his parentage.

(*See* https://iowaorphans.wordpress.com for efforts to identify Fred's and William's parents.)

WILLIAM LOUELETTE WEBER

B. 9 OCTOBER 1885, NEW YORK
D. 29 APRIL 1963 IN WEBSTER CITY, HAMILTON COUNTY, IOWA
BIRTH FAMILY: UNKNOWN WEBER
FOSTER FAMILY: CHARLES AND MARY GERBER
BROTHER TO JACOB "FRED" WEBER

WWI Draft Registration Card

William Weber, age 5, arrived in Hamilton County in the October delivery of children with his brother, Jacob. The brothers were separated. William was placed with the Charles Gerber family of Webster City. Jacob was placed with the Briggs family.[627] (*See* Jacob "Fred" Weber.)

William L. Weber, son of Mr. and Mrs. William Weber, was born Oct. 9, 1886, in New York. When he was five years old, he came to Webster City and was reared in the Charles Gerber home.[628]

The family was not found in the 1895 enumeration, as the Gerbers resided in Kamrar Township.[629]

---

[627] Kialy Carson, Kansas, [(CURATOR@ORPHANTRAINDEPOT.COM),] to Jill Morelli, email, 7 March 2023, "Info from the CAS," OTR folder.
[628] "Weber Rites Here Thursday," *Daily Freeman Journal,* 1 May 1963, p. 1, col. 8.
[629] Kamrar Township is not extant in the 1895 Iowa census.

In 1900 William resided with the Gerber family in Kamrar, composed of Charles, his wife Mary, and an adult daughter. William was born in October 1885 in New York. His parents were also born in New York. His foster parents were born in Germany and Illinois, respectively.[630]

In 1905 William, using the name William L. Gerber, lived on his own in Webster City, working as a janitor in the opera house. His parents' location of birth was unknown. William came to Iowa 15 years before (1890) and was described by the enumerator, F.A. Gerber, as an "adopted orphan."[631] The enumerator, related to the Gerber foster family, may have included the comment in order to make the non-familial relationship of William to the rest of the family clear.

William Weber and Harriet "Mae" Hutchinson married on 19 September 1910 in Webster City, Iowa.[632]

In 1912 William's brother, Fred Weber also an out-placed orphan, experienced a debilitating work-place accident while fixing a boiler pump. After release from the hospital, Fred recuperated in the household of William and his wife for four years. After receiving restitution from the City and other parties, Fred left Webster City and moved to Colorado.[633]

When William registered for the World War I draft, he worked in a restaurant.[634] Three years later, William was a cook in a restaurant in Webster City. The couple had one child, an infant daughter Evelyn.[635] Evelyn Dorthea Weber died of pneumonia in 1921.[636]

Just four years later, the prospects of the Weber family seemed to be improving. Mae's sister Mary lived with the couple, enumerated as a

---

[630] 1900 U.S. census, Hamilton County, Iowa, population schedule, Kamrar, ED 106, household 176, dwelling 176, Wm. Webber in the household of Charles Gerber.

[631] 1905 Iowa state census, Hamilton County, Iowa, population schedule, Independence Township, card no 522, image 4314 of 6894, William L. Gerber.

[632] "Weber Rites Here Thursday," *Daily Freeman Journal,* 1 May 1963, p. 1, col. 8. Also "Iowa, County Marriages, 1838-1934," index, Webster City, Hamilton county, Iowa, Weber-Hutchinson marriage entry (19 September 1910). William did not name his parents on the record.

[633] "Obituary-Fred Weber," *Daily Freeman Tribune,* 2 June 1930, p. 4, col. 2. Probably contributed by William Weber.

[634] U.S., World War I Draft Registration Cards, 1917-1918, Hamilton County, Iowa > all> draft card W, serial number 1778, William Louellette Weber.

[635] 1920 U.S. census, Hamilton County, Iowa, population schedule, Webster City, Ward 1, ED 121, p. 6B, household 125, dwelling 158, William Webber.

[636] "Iowa, Death Records, 1880-1972, death certificate, 1921-1929," no. 40-004, Evelyn Doretha Weber death certificate (13 July 1921).

Weber; no children resided with the couple. William owned his farm worth $1000 and had personal property, usually farm animals, worth $600. William was born in New York, but the informant did not know the names of his parents.[637] Going into the Depression decade, the family finances appeared more unsettled. William was doing odd jobs as a general laborer. The couple and their son, Wayne, resided in Webster City on Division Street.[638]

In 1940 William, Mae and Wayne were supported by the WPA Toy Project. The family had no other income.[639]

A federal government support program, the Toy Project, paid workers to make and fix toys for a children's lending library. The program began in Hamilton County in June 1938 and was modeled after many others in the area. The women sewed doll clothes for the toys made by the men. Over 500 children had enrolled in the program to borrow the toys. It was noted that the toy makers were exceptionally clever. Each doll and a chest of clothes accompanied the child home.[640] Besides employing numerous individuals who had no other livelihood, the program hired a supervisor and inspectors, paid rent, and bought supplies locally. The County Board of Supervisors managed the program.[641]

The Toy Project of Cedar Falls, Iowa, provides some context. Total costs for the Cedar Falls project, which employed 19 persons over 12 months, was anticipated to be $13,703. Of that amount, all but $690 was supplied by the government. In addition to repairing toys, toys would be manufactured from box crates. The project relieved the county's obligation for relief. Women received $48.64 per month working 128 hours and men received $48 for working 96 hours. Individuals received checks every two weeks. It was hoped that most of the money would be spent within the county.[642]

---

[637] 1925 Iowa state census, Hamilton County, Iowa, population schedule, Webster City, no page number, image 513 of 884, Wm L. Weber.

[638] 1930 U.S. census, Hamilton County, Iowa, population schedule, Webster City, ED 3, p. 1B, household 18, dwelling 21, William L. Weber.

[639] 1940 U.S. census, Hamilton County, Iowa, populations scheduled, Webster city, ED 40-3, p. 3B, household 68, Will. Weber. William was the informant.

[640] "Toy Library is Popular," *Daily Freeman Journal*, 22 November 1938, p. 1, col. 3

[641] "Proceedings of the Board of Supervisors," *Daily Freeman Journal*, 26 June 1939, p. 5, col 1 and 3.

[642] "Two New WPA Projects considered for Cedar Falls," *The Courier* (Waterloo, Iowa), 17 November 1938, p. 8, cols. 1-3.

In 1939 William was placed in charge of the handiwork section (making and fixing the toys) of the WPA Toy Project.[643] The program lasted from June 1938 until at least September 1941 in Hamilton County.

By 1940 William, Mae and Wayne resided in Kamrar. The family owned their home valued at $1200, a lower value than other homes in the area. William still worked on the Toy Project, earning $561 for 44 weeks of work.[644] In 1942 William was unemployed, but living at the same address on Division Street.[645] In 1950 William was a doorman at the local theater.[646] Did he see the irony of being a janitor in the opera house as a young man and now being the door man in the theater?

William Weber died 29 April 1963 in Webster City. Wayne Weber of Crescent City, California, was named guardian and executor.[647] A parcel of farm land in Minnesota, a town lot in Webster City, and two mining claims were passed to Wayne, the only heir:
> Two mining claims of undetermined value in the state of Colorado, the Free Gold Mining Claim Survey o.15699 and Janet Lode Mining Claim Survey o.15810 in the Ward Mining District.

Total value of the estate was $10,159.64.[648]

The mining claims were probably inherited by William from his brother Fred, but do not carry the same claim names as those which were initially purchased.[649]

At the time of William's death, Wayne had not married, nor had any identified children.[650] Wayne died in 16 August 2005 in Crescent City, Del Norte County, California, without known issue.[651]

---

[643] "New Project for Children," *Daily Freeman Journal*, 2 February 1939, p. 4, col. 6.

[644] 1940 U.S. census, Hamilton County, Iowa, population schedule, Kamrar, ED 40-3, p. 3b, household 68, Will. Weber, indexed as Weger. William Weber was the informant.

[645] U.S., World War II Draft Registration Cards, 1942, Iowa > all > Watson, Frank-Wedeking, Herman, Serial number 1182, William L. Weber.

[646] 1950 U.S. census, Hamilton County, Iowa, population schedule, Webster City, ED 40-3, p. 2, dwelling 29, W.L. Weber.

[647] "Weber Rites Here Thursday," *Daily Freeman Journal*, 1 May 1963, p. 1, col 8.

[648] Hamilton County, Iowa, probate file number #7732, William L. Weber; Office of the Court Clerk, Hamilton County Courthouse, Webster City, Iowa.

[649] Hamilton County, Iowa, probate file number #7725 & #7732, guardianship & probate, William Weber; Office of the Court Clerk.

[650] Weber Rites Here Thursday," *Daily Freeman Journal*, 1 May 1963, p. 1, col. 8.

[651] Social Security Death Index, 481-24-3587, Wayne F. Weber death date (16 August 2005), last residence, Crescent City, Del Norte, California.

Many sources provide evidence to the various identifiers of William Louelette Weber.

Figure 1-WLW
Name, location and date of birth, foster and birth parents of William L. Weber

Year	Name	Birth date	Birth location	Birth parents	Foster parents
1890	William Weber[a]	1885			Charles Gerber
1900	Wm Weber[b]	Oct 1885	New York	b. New York	Charles Gerber
1905	William L. Gerber[c]	1885	New York		
1910	William L. Weber[d]	1886		Weber	
1917	William Louellette Weber[e]	9 Oct 1885			
1920	William Webber[f]	1886	New York	b. United States	
1925	Wm. L. Weber[g]	1886	New York	Don't know	
1930	William L. Weber[h]	1888	New York	b. United States	
1940	Will Weber[i]	1888	New York		
1942	William L. Weber[j]	9 Oct 1888	New York City		
1950	W.L. Weber[k]	1887	New York		
1963	William L Weber[l]	9 Oct 1886	New York	Mr. & Mrs. William Weber	Charles Gerber

a. Kialy Carson, Kansas, [(CURATOR@ORPHANTRAINDEPOT.COM),] to Jill Morelli, email, 7 March 2023, "Info from the CAS," OTR folder
b. 1900 U.S. census, Hamilton County, Iowa, population schedule, Kamrar, ED 106, household 176, dwelling 176, Wm. Webber in the household of Charles Gerber.
c. 1905 Iowa state census, Hamilton County, Iowa, population schedule, Independence Township, card no 522, image 4314 of 6894, William L. Gerber.
d. "Weber Rites Here Thursday," *Daily Freeman Journal*, 1 May 1963, p. 1, col. 8. Also "Iowa, County Marriages, 1838-1934," index, Webster City, Hamilton county, Iowa, Weber-Hutchinson marriage entry (19 September 1910).
e. U.S., World War I Draft Registration Cards, 1917-1918, Hamilton County, Iowa > all> draft card W, serial number 1778, William Louellette Weber.
f. 1920 U.S. census, Hamilton County, Iowa, population schedule, Webster City, Ward 1, ED 121, p. 6B, household 125, dwelling 158, William Webber.
g. 1925 Iowa state census, Hamilton County, Iowa, population schedule, Webster City, no page number, image 513 of884, Wm L. Weber.
h. 1930 U.S. census, Hamilton County, Iowa, population schedule, Webster City, ED 3, p. 1B, household 18, dwelling 21, William L. Weber.
i. 1940 U.S. census, Hamilton County, Iowa, population schedule, Kamrar, ED 40-3, p. 3b, household 68, Will. Weber, indexed as Weger.
j. U.S., World War II Draft Registration Cards, 1942, Iowa > all > Watson, Frank-Wedeking, Herman, Serial number 1182, William L. Weber.
k. 1950 U.S. census, Hamilton County, Iowa, population schedule, Webster City, ED 40-3, p. 2, dwelling 29, W. L. Weber.
l. "Weber Rites Here Thursday," *Daily Freeman Journal*, 1 May 1963, p. 1, col. 8.

William Weber was the birth name of the New York City orphan. The 9 October 1885 birth date seems the date most logical. "Mr. & Mrs. William Weber" may be the name of the NYC parents—or it could be a fabrication. The middle name of Louelette is unusual and could be a surname or a given name in the birth family. Numerous Louelettes resided in the New York City area.

If brothers, Jacob and William would have the same parents and both would have been released to the orphanage. In correlating the likely parents of Jacob and William, no parents were in common. No conclusion can be drawn concerning the parents of Jacob and William.

There is a likely set of parents for William; however, there is no comparable birth registration for Fred.

CONCLUSION

William Louelette Weber was born 9 October 1885 in New York City. He and his older brother Jacob "Fred" were included in the 1890 deliveries of children to Hamilton County. William Weber and Harriet "Mae" Hutchinson married on 19 September 1910, in Webster City, Iowa.[652] William and Harriet resided in Hamilton County until their deaths; William died 29 April 1963 in Webster City, Iowa. His apparent birth parents have not been identified.

Fred had no descendants; William had one descendant, Wayne, who never married and had no descendants. DNA will not be helpful in resolving the parentage of the brothers.

(*See* https://iowaorphans.wordpress.com for efforts to identify Fred and William's NYC parents.)

---

[652] "Weber Rites Here Thursday," *Daily Freeman Journal,* 1 May 1963, p. 1, col. 8. Also "Iowa, County Marriages, 1838-1934," index, Webster City, Hamilton county, Iowa, Weber-Hutchinson marriage entry (19 September 1910). William did not name his parents on the record.

Belle (Welch) Wientjes

B. 4 OR 14 APRIL 1882, NEW YORK
D. 4 FEBRUARY 1947, WAVERLY, IOWA
BIRTH FAMILY: FATHER: UNKNOWN; MOTHER: MAGGIE WELCH
FOSTER FAMILY: FRED AND MINNIE WIENTJES

Belle (Welch) Wientjes
Photo used with permission of the family

Bella Welch, age 7, arrived in Hamilton County in the October delivery of children. She was placed with the Fred Wientjes family of Kamrar.[653]
    Bella Welch came to the Children's Aid in April 1890 at age 7…On October 30, 1890, the Rev. Mr. Dickmausser [sic, (Dickman)] reported that the Wissitzer's [sic, (Wientjes)] were well pleased…[654]

Fred and Minnie were not found in the 1895 Iowa census as the enumeration of Kamrar Township is not extant. In 1900 Fred and Minnie Wientjes were an older couple at 54 and 65. Minnie stated that she had given birth to one surviving child; she counted Belle. Minnie had given birth to no children. In 1900 Belle was 18 years old and born in New York.

---

[653] Kialy Carson, Kansas, [(CURATOR@ORPHANTRAINDEPOT.COM),] to Jill Morelli, email, 7 March 2023, "Info from the CAS," OTR folder.he agent's name (Trott), 13 children by name, and their foster parents. Ten boys, three girls.

[654] Paul Clarke, Archivist, Children's Aid (117 W. 124th Street, New York, New York 10027] to Kathleen Beebe via email {address for private use], 29 April 2022, re: Bella Welch, scan of document in the Wientjes File, possession of the author.

Fred and Minnie were both born in Germany.[655] Conversation with the family revealed that Belle had a close relationship with her foster mother.

Communication with the CAS occurred intermittently throughout Belle's life. In 1895 the CAS file described her as "a nice, bright young girl who spoke, read and wrote German."[656] In 1900 Katie Hines, another New York City orphan wrote a note to the CAS stating Bella was "well and doing nicely."[657] Mr. Fry of the CAS visited in March 1901. A note was included in her record that Belle had just returned from Webster City. "She had a good home with people who were attached to her."[658]

On 22 February 1905, Belle married Dick Eckhoff of Kamrar. Belle named her foster parents as her parents.[659] The couple first moved to Grundy County where Dick rented a farm and did general farm work. By 1910 Belle had given birth to three children, two of whom survived.[660] Within five years, the Eckhoff family had moved to Washington Township, Butler County, Iowa.[661] Dick was a laborer in a lumber yard supporting Belle and their four daughters. They rented their home.[662]

In 1924 Dick and Belle Eckhoff confessed their faith and became members of the Christian Reformed Church of Austinville, Iowa. It was recorded that Belle Wientjes was born on 14 April 1883.[663]

Prior to 1925, Belle received information concerning her birth mother from the CAS.

---

[655] 1900 U.S. census, Hamilton County, Iowa, population schedule, Liberty Township, ED 98, p. 7B, household 131, dwelling 131, Belle Wientjes in the household of Fred Wientjes.

[656] Ibid.

[657] Paul Clarke, Archivist, Children's Aid (117 W. 124th Street, New York, New York 10027] to Kathleen Beebe via email {address for private use], 29 April 2022.

[658] Ibid.

[659] "Iowa Marriages 1880-1945," 1905-1906 > 421 (Emmet-Jones), Dick Eckhoff & Belle Wientjes marriage record (22 February 1905). Also, "Liberty," *Daily Freeman Tribune*, 3 March 1905, p. 8, col. 4.

[660] 1910 U.S. census, Grundy County, Iowa, population schedule, German Township, ED 48, p. 5B, household 74, dwelling 74, Dirk H. Eckhoff.

[661] 1915 Iowa state census, Butler County, Iowa, populations schedule, Washington Township, image 4082 of 5261, card no. 49, Bell Eckhoff.

[662] 1920 U.S. census, Butler County, Iowa, population schedule, Washington Township, ED 93, p. 7A, household 118, dwelling 118, Dick H. Eckhoff.

[663] Christian Reformed Church, membership book, 1918-1914, Austinville, Iowa, p. 7, Dick & Belle (Wientjes) Eckhoff membership entry.

Within five years, the family had moved to another rented home within Butler County. Dick worked as a laborer. Belle noted that her mother was Maggie Welch, but named her father as her foster father, Fred Wientjes.[664]

In October of 1926 and in response to some family legal matters, Dick Voogd, an attorney in Aplington, Iowa, inquired to the CAS concerning any indication of an adoption. The CAS did not note their response.[665] No court adoption occurred.

Dick died on 28 December 1928 in the Illinois Central Hospital in Chicago.[666] Now a widow and entering the Depression decade, Belle, four of her daughters, and her mother-in-law lived in a house which they rented for $5 per month. The family did not own a radio. The oldest daughter was a school teacher in a rural school and was the only employed individual in the family.[667] The family resided in the same home through the difficult 1930s. By 1940 Belle's two daughters and a son-in-law lived with her. The family now owned their home valued at $1000. Belle was a nurse, worked 20 weeks in the past year, and had earned $150. Her son-in-law farmed; one of the daughters was a teacher and contributed $560 to the welfare of the family. [668]

Belle died 4 February 1947 at Mercy Hospital in Waverly, Iowa, of a cerebral hemorrhage.[669] Belle and Dick were buried in Memorial Park in Austinville, Iowa.[670]

---

[664] 1925 Iowa state census, Butler County, Iowa, population schedule, Washington Township, image 47 of 82, lines 18-24, Dick Eckhoff.

[665] Paul Clarke, Archivist, Children's Aid (117 W. 124th Street, New York, New York 10027] to [private] via email [address for private use], 29 April 2022. No formal adoption has been identified.

[666] "Deaths—Austinville," *Waterloo Evening Courier*, 1 January 1929, p. 12, col 1. Also, Christian Reformed Church, membership book, 1918-1914, Austinville, Iowa, p. 7, Dick & Belle (Wientjes) Eckhoff membership entry.

[667] 1930 U.S. census, Butler County, Iowa, populations schedule, Washington Township, ED 27, p. 8A, dwelling 149, Belle Eckhoff.

[668] 1940 U.S. census, Butler County, Iowa, population schedule, Washington Township, ED 12-27, p. 1B, dwelling 14, Belle Eckhoff.

[669] Iowa, U.S., Death Records, 1880-1904, 1921-1952, certificate, Belle Wientjes Eckhoff death certificate (4 February 1947). Also, "Waverly," obituary, Mrs. Belle Eckhoff (4 February 1947), *Waterloo Daily Courier*, 5 February 1947, p. 7, col. 2.

[670] Find a Grave, database and images (https://www.findagrave.com/memorial/108018312/belle-eckhoff: accessed July 12, 2024), memorial page for Belle Wientjes Eckhoff (14 Apr 1884–4 Feb 1947), Find a Grave Memorial ID 108018312, citing Memorial Park Cemetery, Austinville, Butler County, Iowa, USA; Maintained by Hooked On Family (contributor 47448897).

Documentary evidence provides information about Belle:

Figure 1-BWW
Name, location and date of birth, foster and birth parents of Belle (Welch) Wientjes

Year	Name	Birth date	Birth location	Birth parents	Foster parents
1890	Bella Welch[a]	4 April 1882	Nursery & Childs Hospital, Staten Island	Maggie Welch	Mr. & Mrs. Wizzitser
1900	Belle Wientjes[b]	Apr 1882	New York		Fred Wientjes
1905	Bell Weintjes[c]	1883	New York	b. Germany	
1905	Belle Wientjes[d]	1882	New York, New York	Freidrk Wientjes & Mina Hobbas	
1910	Bell Eckhoff[e]	1882	New York		
1915	Bell Eckhoff[f]	1882	New York		
1920	Bell Eckhoff[g]	1883	New York		
	Belle (Wientjes) Eckhoff[h]	14 April 1883			
1925	Belle Eckhoff[i]	1884	New York	m. Maggie Welch, b. New York	Fred Wientjes
1930	Belle Eckhoff[j]	1885	New York	b. New York	
1940	Belle Eckhoff[k]	1884	New York		
1947	Belle Wientjes Eckhoff[l]	14 April 1883	New York City	Fred Wientjes	

a. Paul Clarke, Archivist, Children's Aid (117 W. 124th Street, New York, New York 10027] to [a grandchild] via email [address for private use], 29 April 2022.
b. 1900 U.S. census, Hamilton County, Iowa, population schedule, Liberty Township, ED 98, p. 7B, household 131, dwelling 131, Belle Wientjes in the household of Fred Wientjes.
c. 1905 Iowa state census, Hamilton County, Iowa, population schedule, Liberty Township, Image 5095 of 6100, card no. A65, Bell Wientjes.
d. "Iowa Marriages 1880-1945," 1905-1906 > 421 (Emmet-Jones), Dick Eckhoff & Belle Wientjes marriage record (22 February 1905).
e. 1910 U.S. census, Grundy County, Iowa, population schedule, German Township, ED 48, p. 5B, household 74, dwelling 74, Dirk H. Eckhoff.
f. 1915 Iowa state census, Butler County, Iowa, populations schedule, Washington Township, image 4082 of 5261, card no. 49, Bell Eckhoff.
g. 1920 U.S. census, Butler County, Iowa, population schedule, Washington Township, ED 93, p. 7A, household 118, dwelling 118, Dick H. Eckhoff.
h. Christian Reformed Church, membership book, 1914-1918, Austinville, Iowa, p. 7, Dick & Belle (Wientjes) Eckhoff membership entry.
i. 1925 Iowa state census, Butler County, Iowa, population schedule, Washington Township, image 47 of 82, lines 18-24, Dick Eckhoff.
j. 1930 U.S. census, Butler County, Iowa, population schedule, Washington Township, ED 27, p. 8A, dwelling 149, Belle Eckhoff.
k. 1940 U.S. census, Butler County, Iowa, population schedule, Washington Township, ED 12-27, p. 1B, dwelling 14, Belle Eckhoff.
l. Iowa, U.S., Death Records, 1880-1904, 1921-1952, certificate, Belle Wientjes Eckhoff death certificate (4 February 1947).

The CAS provided clues to help identify the New York family:
- Bella Welch came to the CAS in April 1890, from Nursery & Childs Hospital on Staten Island. She had been abandoned.
- The CAS stated that Bella was born at the Hospital on 4 April 1882.
- Bella's mother was Maggie Welch, an Irish Catholic, 28 years old (b. 1854) who was admitted to the hospital for the birth on 26 March 1882. By revealing only the mother, it implies that Belle was born out of wedlock.
- Maggie had a sister, Mrs. Kate McCarthy, 59 Cedar St., or 160 Fulton St. or 35 Washington St. No explanation was given for the miscellaneous addresses, but it implies regular contact.
- Bella's mother worked for Mrs. M. M. Delaney of Sea View cottage, Rockaway Beach [Queens, New York].
- Maggie's whereabouts in 1892 was unknown.
- Bella was sent "west" by request of her mother.[671]

Some information seems to conflict. Staten Island birth records are only digitized from 1898 to 1909, preventing identification of Bella's parents and other information.[672]

In spite of numerous clues to her birth family, common names and origins of the family create difficulty in identifying the mother and her family. Women giving birth outside of wedlock often concealed the truth of critical facts.

CONCLUSION

Bella Welch was born in April of 1882, probably on the 4th. She was brought to Hamilton County in the October delivery of children and was fostered into the Fred and Minnie (Hobbs) Wientjes family, a farm family in Kamrar. On 22 February 1905, Belle married Dick Eckhoff, a laborer. They resided in Butler County, adjacent to Hamilton County. Dick died 28 December 1928, leaving Belle a widow with five young girls. By 1940 Belle owned her own home in Webster City. Belle died 4 February 1947 in Waverly, Iowa.

With five children, the family might be identified with DNA.

(See https://iowaorphans.wordpress.com for additional information.)

---

[671] Paul Clarke, Archivist, Children's Aid (117 W. 124th Street, New York, New York 10027] to [private] via email [address for private use], 29 April 2022. No formal adoption has been identified.

[672] NYC Historic Vital Records, "Digital Vital Records," graphs illustrate the various records and their chronology of digitization (https://a860-historicalvitalrecords.nyc.gov/digital-vital-records).

198

George R. (Warden) Witte

B. February 1887/1885 in New York
D. May 1923, Montreal, Quebec Province, Canada
Birth Family: —?— Warden
Foster Family: August & Minnie Witte.

George Warden, age 5, arrived in Hamilton County, in the October delivery of children. He was placed with the A. Witte family of Webster City.[673]
...Mr. and Mrs. Witte adopted George Witte into their home when he was three or four years old. He was an orphan and was brought to this city with a group of other orphan children from New York City....[674]

In 1895 George, age 8 and born in New York, appeared in the household of August Witte with his apparent wife Minnie and daughter Anna.[675] In 1900 George Witte, identified as a "son," still resided with August, a grocer, and Minnie Witte in Webster City. Annie Witte, a daughter; Lillian Bohning, a granddaughter; and Albert Arends, a servant also resided in the household. George was a student in the 9th grade. George's parents were born in Germany and Wisconsin, reflecting the birth locations of his foster parents.[676]

In October 1902, George Witte, described as August Wit's adopted son, ran away from home. The reporter wrote that the Witte family created a loving home. George needed "unrestrained freedom of which he would find unappealing after a short sojourn."[677] George returned to the Witte family by February 1903.[678]

---

[673] Kialy Carson, Kansas, [(CURATOR@ORPHANTRAINDEPOT.COM),] to Jill Morelli, email, 7 March 2023, "Info from the CAS," OTR folder.

[674] "Former Local Boy Dies in Montreal," *Webster City Daily News*, 31 May 1923, p. 2, col. 2.

[675] 1895 State of Iowa census, Hamilton County, Iowa, population schedule, image 156 of 681, Geo. Witte in the household of Aug Witte.

[676] 1900 U.S. census, Hamilton County, Iowa, population schedule, Webster City, ED 99, p. 4, household 97, dwelling 101, August Witte household.

[677] "George Witte has Disappeared," *Daily Freeman Tribune*, 29 October 1902, p. 8, col. 1.

[678] "A Good Time Party," *Daily Freeman Tribune*, 21 February 1903, p. 4, col. 4. George Witte was listed as an attendee.

In June 1903, August Witte posted a notice that "I have given George Witte his time and will not hereafter collect his wages or pay his debts contracted by him."[679] George was 16 years old. The informal agreement with the CAS stated the foster parent could collect the wages of the child until age 18.[680] What compelled the family to release George from these obligations early is not known.

In spite of his youthful transgressions, George participated in the social life of the county with his peers. He was one of thirty-eight young men and women invited to a party at the home of Orle Bateman and Garfield Ferrell. Picnics and card parties were other occasions for interaction with young people of the county.[681]

George left Hamilton County in 1909 to work for the railroad. In the fall of 1922, George returned to Hamilton County from Laramie, Wyoming, to care for his foster father who suffered a protracted illness. It had been 13 years since he left his home in Hamilton County.[682] George was a member of the Railroad Brotherhood.[683]

One year later, George Witte unexpectedly died in Montreal, Quebec Province, Canada, at age 35. He had recently undergone an operation for a perforated ulcer. George never married.[684] August Witte died 18 May 1926. August's will referred to George Warden as "deceased—no known heirs."[685]

George was buried in Graceland Cemetery in Webster City, Iowa, in the same plot as August Witte, Minnie Witte, and their daughter Anna (Witte) Schroder.

---

[679] "I hereby give notice…," *Daily Freeman Tribune,* 5 June 1903, p. 4, col. 5.
[680] "E. Trott of the children's aid society…," *The Freeman,* 3 September 1890, p. 5, col. 3.
[681] "A Picnic Supper," *Daily Freeman Tribune,* 27 July 1904, p. 4, col 5. Also, "Card Party," *Daily Freeman Tribune,* 16 September 1903, p. 4, col 4.
[682] "George Witte arrived here Friday Morning…," *Webster City Daily News,* p. 2, col. 2.
[683] "Former Local Boy Dies in Montreal," *Webster City Daily News,* 31 May 1923, p. 2, col. 2.
[684] Ibid.
[685] Hamilton County, Iowa, probate file number #2873, will, August Witte; Office of the Court Clerk.

Witte was an adopted name; his New York surname was Warden. This investigation revealed no additional evidence of the identification of George Warden Witte's NYC parents.

Figure 1-GWW
Name, location and date of birth, foster and birth parents
of George (Warden) Witte

Year	Name	Birth date	Birth location	Birth parents	Foster parents
1890	George Warden[a]	1885	New York		A. Witte
1895	Geo. R. Witte[b]	1887	New York	b. Denmark	August Witte
1900	George Witte[c]	Feb 1887	New York	b. Germany & Wisconsin	August Witte
1923	George Witte[d]	1886/1887	New York		August Witte

a. Kialy Carson, Kansas, [(CURATOR@ORPHANTRAINDEPOT.COM),] to Jill Morelli, email, 7 March 2023, "Info from the CAS," OTR folder.
b. 1895 State of Iowa census, Hamilton County, Iowa, population schedule, image 156 of 681, George Witte in the household of August Witte.
c. 1900 U.S. census, Hamilton County, Iowa, population schedule, Fremont, ED 99, p. 4, household 97, dwelling 101, George Witte in the household of August Witte.
d. "Former Local Boy Dies in Montreal," *Webster City Daily News*, 31 May 1923, p. 2, col. 2.

Based on documentary evidence, George Warden was born probably in February 1885 or 1887. There is not enough data to identify his NYC parents.

CONCLUSION

George Warden, age 5, arrived in Hamilton County in 1890 in the October delivery of children and was fostered into the August Witte family. He assumed their surname for the rest of his life and resided with them until after 1900. In 1902, George ran away from the Witte home but returned shortly after. He went to work for the railroad, but returned to the family to care for August. George died in 1923 in Montreal, Canada, of a perforated ulcer.

George never married and had no known children. DNA will not be able to identify George's New York City parents.

(*See* https://iowaorphans.wordpress.com for efforts to identify George's NYC parents.)

AUGUST HILBERT ZAHN

B. 11 APRIL 1880, NEW YORK CITY, NEW YORK
D. 24 AUGUST 1951, IN WEBSTER CITY, HAMILTON COUNTY, IOWA
BIRTH FAMILY: WILLIAM AND FREDRICKE (VETTER) ZAHN/ZAUN
FOSTER FAMILY: JOHN AND ELIZABETH ESSIG

Cropped photo: Dskoglund_1, "Lyon Public Tree,"
used with permission.

WWI Draft Registration Card

Superintendent Trott recorded J. Essig as a recipient of an unnamed boy in the 29 August 1890 delivery of children to Hamilton County.[686] In 1895 August Zahn, age 17, born 1878 in New York, appeared in the Hamilton County home of John Essig, his apparent wife Elizabeth and their four children ages 2-10.[687] August was the oldest out-placed orphan to arrive in Hamilton County.

John Essig was born in Germany and emigrated with his family when he was seven, first settling in New Haven County, Connecticut. He went into the the brass finishing business for 14 years on the East coast, but left for the Midwest in 1887 because of his health. John Essig began working on

---

[686] "E. Trott of the children's aid society...," *The Freeman*, 3 September 1890, p. 5, col. 3.

[687] 1895 Iowa State census, Hamilton County, Iowa; population schedule, p. 34 [handwritten], 109 [stamped], image 99 of 681, household 366, dwelling 393, Aug. Johnn (August Zahn) in the household of John and Elizabeth Essig.

the 283 acre Bernnake farm, in Hamilton County, which he purchased a few years later.[688]

By 1900 August Zahn worked on the farm of William Rupple as a farm laborer.[689]

On 4 September 1907, August married Lizzie Lyon in Eagle Grove, Wright County, Iowa. Shortly after the marriage, the couple moved to Blue Earth, Minnesota.[690] By 1910 August and Elizabeth rented a farm in Pilot Grove Township in Faribault County, Minnesota.[691] The couple lived in Minnesota for four years before returning to Hamilton County.[692] August stopped farming at that time, and began working at the Closz & Howard Sieve factory.[693]

By 1915 August had attended one year of college and lived in Iowa 20 years. August earned $1000 the preceding year.[694]

The next year, August rented the W. T. Fisher farm, located two miles southwest of Webster City.[695] Two years later, He auctioned 37 head of livestock, including 7 horses, 11 cattle, and 29 Poland China hogs. He also sold all his farm machinery, 7 dozen chickens, seed corn, and silage.[696] August quit farming and returned to the Closz Company as a solderer.[697]

By 1930 August H. Zahn and Elizabeth moved to Webster City and resided at 1206 Second Street with August's sister Elsie R. Zahn. They owned their own home valued at $4000 and had a radio. Elsie was born in New York

---

[688] *The Biographical Record of Hamilton County, Iowa* (Chicago: S.J. Clarke Publishing Company, 1902) 565.

[689] 1900 U. S. census, Hamilton County, Iowa, population schedule, Independence Township, ED 106, p. 8B, household 166, dwelling 167, August Zahn in the household of William Rupple.

[690] "Miss Lizzie Lyon, daughter of....," *Webster City Journal*, 12 September 1907, p. 6, col. 3.

[691] 1910 U.S. census, Faribault County, Minnesota, population schedule, Pilot Grove Township, ED 80, p. 9A, household 133, dwelling 136, August H. Zahn.

[692] "A.H. Zahn, 71, dies in City," *Daily Freeman Journal*, 25 August 1951, p. 1, col. 4.

[693] 1920 U.S. census, Hamilton, Iowa, population schedule, Webster City, Ward 4, ED 124, p. 7B, household 165, dwelling 180, August Zoln.

[694] 1915 Iowa State census, Hamilton County, Iowa; population schedule, Fremont Township, card number 396, August Zahn. Lizzie, his wife, is card no. 395.

[695] "W.T. Fisher Buys Farm," *Webster City Freeman*, 28 November 1916, p. 3, col 2.

[696] "Closing Out Sale," advertisement, *Webster City Freeman*, 18 February 1918, p. 2, col. 5 & 6.

[697] U.S., World War I Draft Registration Cards, 1917-1918, Hamilton County, Iowa, > ALL > Draft Card Z, August Hilbert Zahn.

like her parents; she was 31 years old (b. 1889) and widowed.[698] Correspondence between August and his New York City parents and siblings certainly occurred during this period of time. This is the only known example of a birth family member visiting their relative, an out-placed orphan.

The couple continued their residence at 1206 Second Street in 1940 and owned their home valued at $3000, a value similar to that of their neighbors, but 25% less than it was valued in 1930. August was now a watchman at the sieve factory. The family seemed financially stable. In 1940 August had worked 50 hours the previous week and 52 weeks the previous year. He had earned $416 but also had access to other income.[699] The other income may have been from the farm sale.

By 1950 August was unable to work, but Elizabeth was taking in laundry, ironing and house cleaning.[700] August suffered an extended illness for nine years, requiring bedrest for the nine months prior to his death. August died 24 August 1951 in Webster City. His parents, Mr. and Mrs. William Zahn and a brother predeceased him.[701]

The documentary evidence created by August in Iowa identifies his parents.

August is one of only two Hamilton County arrivals born in 1880 or before, and the only one enumerated in the 1880 census. The parents of August have been identified as William and Fredricke Zahn, spelled also as Zaun.[702]

---

[698] 1930 U.S. census, Hamilton County, Iowa, population schedule, Webster City, ED 6, p. 13A, household 293, dwelling 318, August H. Zalm.

[699] 1940 U.S. census, Hamilton County, Iowa, population schedule, Webster City, ED 40-6, household 255, p. 12A, August H. Zahn. August was the informant.

[700] 1950 U.S. census, Hamilton County, Iowa, population schedule, Webster City, ED 40-9, household 208, p. 19, August H. Zahn.

[701] "A.H. Zahn, 71, dies in City," *Daily Freeman Journal*, 25 August 1951, p. 1, col. 4.

[702] New York City Municipal Archives, "Historical Vital Records," Birth Return, certificate no. 282744, August Laun birth entry (11 April 1880). Also, State of Iowa, Certificate of Death, certificate 17895, Hamilton County, August Zahn death certificate (24 August 1951).

Figure 1-AHZ
Name, location and date of birth, foster and birth parents
of August Hilbert Zahn

Year	Name	Birth date	Birth location	Birth parents	Foster parents
1895	Aug. Zahn[a]	1884	New York		John Essig
1900	August Zahn[b]	Dec 1876	New York	b. New York	
1910	August H. Zahn[c]	1880	New York	b. New York	
1915	August Zahn[d]	1881	New York	b. Germany	
1917	August Hilbert Zahn[e]	11 April 1881			
1920	August Zalm[f]	1881	New York	b. US	
1925	August Zalm	1881	Illinois	b. US	
1930	August H. Zalm[g]	1881	New York	b. New York	
1940	August H. Zahn[h]	1880	New York		
1950	August H. Zahn[i]	1881	New York		
1951	August H. Zahn[j]	11 April 1880	New York City, New York		Mr. & Mrs William Zahn
1951	August H. Zohn[k]	11 April 1880	New York		William & Fredricka Zahn

a. 1895 Iowa State census, Hamilton County, Iowa; population schedule, p. 34 [handwritten], 109 [stamped], image 99 of 681, household 366, dwelling 393, Aug. Johnn in the household of John and Elizabeth Essig.
b. 1900 U. S. census, Hamilton County, Iowa, population schedule, Independence Township, ED 106, p. 8B, household 166, dwelling 167, August Zahn in the household of William Rupple.
c. 1910 U.S. census, Faribault County, Minnesota, population schedule, Pilot Grove Township, ED 80, p. 9A, household 133, dwelling 136, August H. Zahn.
d. 1915 Iowa State census, Hamilton County, Iowa; population schedule, Fremont Township, card number 396, August Zahn. Lizzie, his wife, is card no. 395.
e. U.S., World War I Draft Registration Cards, 1917-1918, Hamilton County, Iowa, > ALL > Draft Card Z, August Hilbert Zahn.
f. 1920 U.S. census, Hamilton, Iowa, population schedule, Webster City, Ward 4, ED 124, p. 7B, household 165, dwelling 180, August Zoln.
g. 1930 U.S. census, Hamilton County, Iowa, population schedule, Webster City, ED 6, p. 13A, household 293, dwelling 318, August H. Zalm.
h. 1940 U.S. census, Hamilton County, Iowa, population schedule, Webster City, ED 40-6, household 255, p. 12A, August H. Zahn.
i. 1950 U.S. census, Hamilton County, Iowa, population schedule, Webster City, ED 40-9, household 208, p. 19, August H. Zahn.
j. "A.H. Zahn, 71, dies in City," *Daily Freeman Journal*, 25 August 1951, p. 1, col. 4.
k. State of Iowa, Certificate of Death, certificate 17895, Hamilton County, August Zahn death certificate (24 August 1951).

Figure 2-AHZ
Return of a Birth, August Zahn[703]

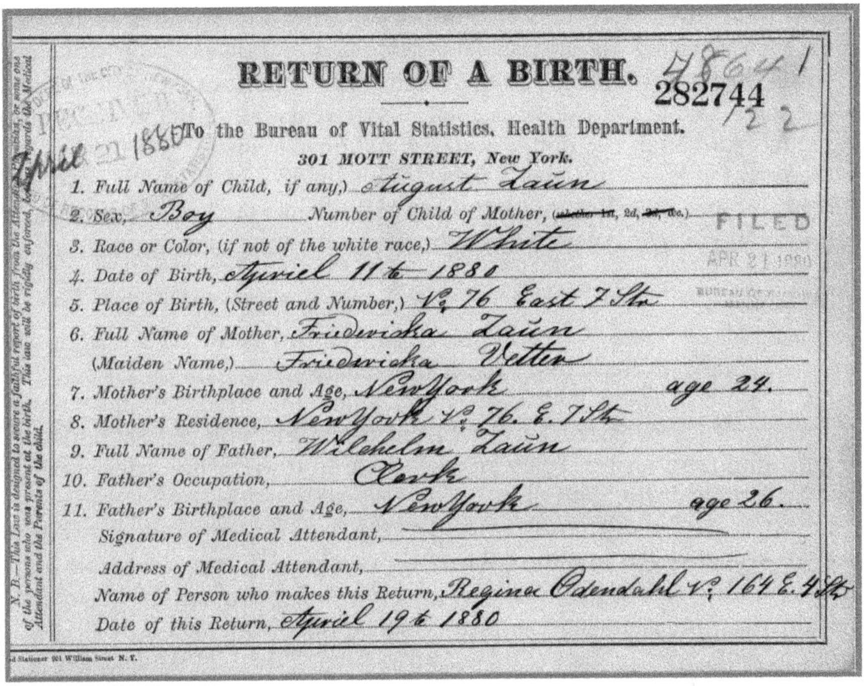

RETURN OF A BIRTH. 282744

48641 / 22

To the Bureau of Vital Statistics, Health Department.
301 MOTT STREET, New York.

1. Full Name of Child, if any,) August Laun
2. Sex, Boy Number of Child of Mother, (whether 1st, 2d, 3d, &c.)
3. Race or Color, (if not of the white race,) White
4. Date of Birth, April 11th 1880
5. Place of Birth, (Street and Number,) No. 76 East 7 Str
6. Full Name of Mother, Friedericka Laun
(Maiden Name,) Friedericka Vetter
7. Mother's Birthplace and Age, New York age 24.
8. Mother's Residence, New York No. 76. E. 7 Str
9. Full Name of Father, Wilhelm Laun
10. Father's Occupation, Clerk
11. Father's Birthplace and Age, New York age 26.

Signature of Medical Attendant,
Address of Medical Attendant,
Name of Person who makes this Return, Regina Odendahl No. 164 E. 4 Str
Date of this Return, April 19th 1880

FILED APR 21 1880

April 21 1880

Multiple records confirm this relationship:

- Fredericka (Vetter) Zaun gave birth to August Zaun on 11 April 1880 at 76 East 7th Street. The father Wilhelm, age 26, was a clerk, born in New York. August was the second child of Fredericka, age 24.[704]
- In 1880 August Zahn, 1 month old, and his brother, William, lived in the household of Reinhardt Vetter, his wife Charlotte, and their three daughters, Fredricke (25), Mary (17) and Louisa (7). William and August were identified as grandsons. While the mother of William and August was not identified, Fredricke was the only married daughter. Her husband was not living with the family.[705] Brother William was noted in

[703] New York City Municipal Archives, "Historical Vital Records," Birth Return, certificate no. 282744, August Laun birth entry (11 April 1880).

[704] New York City Municipal Archives, "Historical Vital Records," Birth Return, certificate no. 282744, August Laun birth entry (11 April 1880).

[705] 1880 U.S. census, New York, New York, population scheduled, City of new York, ED 274, dwelling 43, household 256, August Zahn in the household of Rienhardt Vetter, 76 Seventh Street.

the 1880 census was one year old, born 1878/1879; he went by the name George the remainder of his life.
- In 1930 August H. Zahn, Elizabeth E. his wife, and Elsie R. Zahn, identified as a sister, resided in Webster City. Elsie was born in New York as were her parents; she was widowed.[706] Louisa C. "Elsie" Zahn was born 16 November 1889 to William and Fredericka Zahn.[707]
- August's death certificate named his parents as William Zahn and Fredericka Vetter. His obituary stated that his parents and his brother had predeceased him.[708] August's father, William, died in 1914;[709] Fredericka died in 1932.[710] His brother George/William died in 1927.[711] The information is consistent with his obituary and death certificate.

CONCLUSION

August Hilbert Zahn was born 11 April 1880 in New York City to the married couple William and Fredricka (Vetter) Zahn. The family had two other children, a son and a daughter, who remained with the couple. Correspondence occurred between August and his siblings, as evidenced by the long-term visit by his widowed sister, Louisa "Elsie" Zahn, in 1920 and his knowledge of a brother.

August was fostered into the John Essig family, and, married Lizzie Lyon in Eagle Grove, Wright County, Iowa, on 4 September 1907. He tried farming in Minnesota and Hamilton County, but abandoned it in 1918 and went to work for the Closz & Company. August died 24 August 1951, in Webster City, Iowa.

August had no children; DNA won't confirm August's biological parents' names.

(*See* https://iowaorphans.wordpress.com for more information.)

---

[706] 1930 U.S. census, Hamilton County, Iowa, population schedule, Webster City, ED 6, p. 13A, household 293, dwelling 318, August H. Zalm.

[707] New York City Municipal Archives, "Historical Vital Records," Birth Return, certificate 10606, Louisa Catharine Zaun birth entry (16 November 1889). Louisa, born in 1873, must have died before 1889.

[708] "A.H. Zahn, 71, dies in City," *Daily Freeman Journal*, 25 August 1951, p. 1, col. 4. Also, State of Iowa, Certificate of Death, certificate 17895, Hamilton County, August Zahn death certificate (24 August 1951).

[709] New York City Municipal Archives, "Historical Vital Records," Death Return, certificate 20507, William Zaun death entry (2 November 1914).

[710] New York City Municipal Archives, "Historical Vital Records," Death Return, certificate 1921, Fredricka Zaun death entry (14 March 1932).

[711] New York, New York, U.S. Index to Death Certificates, 1862-1948, certificate 7237, George Zaun death entry (6 April 1927); index, not available on the NYC Historic Vital Records site.

By the Numbers

In a review of existing literature about out-placed orphans, the authors usually tell the story of a single successful life. These stories are undoubtedly true, but are they indicative of the whole?

Forty-six unnamed orphans arrived in Hamilton County, Iowa, from New York City in the fall of 1890, bringing with them the hopes and dreams of any child. Some grew up, received an education, married, settled down and contributed to their communities. Others faced significant struggles.

The goal of this book is to identify and share the stories of these unnamed orphans and to compare the cohort with any availablestudies. We developed two hypotheses:
1. The trauma of out-placement made it more difficult for the orphan to develop meaningful and long-lasting relationship and
2. Male orphans were more negatively affected than females.

Georgia G. Ralph, (Department of Child Welfare, New York School of Philanthropy) conducted a study for the Children's Aid Society in 1922 (Ralph Study). She analyzed every available CAS orphan, including the Hamilton County orphans. Although the complete study is unavailable, summary sections appeared in an article written by Henry W. Thurston in 1927.[712] Other data was compared with state or national norms.

This chapter is separated as follows:
1. Characteristics of Hamilton County orphans
2. Characteristics of foster families of the orphans
3. Characteristics of NYC parents of the orphans
4. Comparison of the Hamilton County orphans to the Ralph Study
5. Summary of findings

---

[712] Henry W. Thurston, *The Dependent Child* (New York: Columbia University Press, 1930) 133. The location of the study is now not known, but Thurston included the entire table that summarized the data as described (1922). Ms. Ralph's compilations were recorded every 10 years between 1865 to 1905 and would have included the Hamilton County cohort. Her credential from J.E. Hansan, "The Early History of the Child Welfare League of America," (2013. https://socialwelfare.library.vcu.edu/programs/child-welfarechild-labor/child-welfare-league-history-1915-1920/

The forty-six unnamed orphans that arrived in Hamilton County are divided into four groups:

Table 1-A
The Orphans of Hamilton County, Iowa who arrived the Fall of 1890 "By the Numbers"

		Total	Boys	Girls
1	Arrived in Hamilton County	46	35	11
2	Identified orphans	35	25	10
3	Unidentified orphans	11	10	1
4	Lost orphans	6	6	0
5	Arrival to Death orphans (AtoD)	29	19	10
6	NYC parent(s) identified	12	6	6

Clarification of the categories follow:
- Arrived in Hamilton County: These orphans came to Hamilton County in 1890 and form the studied cohort.
- Identified orphans: They were identified by name and foster family
- Unidentified orphans: The orphans' identity remains obscured.
- Lost orphans: These orphans were initially identified at arrival, but disappeared from the records as young adults. Row 4 is a subset of row 2.
- Arrival to death (AtoD): Identified orphans were tracked from their arrival in Iowa to their death. Subtracting row 4 from row 2 results in row 5.
- NYC parent(s) identified: These orphans' New York City parents were identified through direct and indirect evidence. This is a subset of row 2.[713]

The lost orphans disappear from the records between 1900 and 1912 for a variety of reasons:
1. They had a common name and left the area upon reaching majority age.
2. They reverted to their unknown New York name.

---

[713] The term "NYC parents" will refer to those individual(s) who appear on the birth certificate or are known through other means. Since names can be falsified and information incorrect, the term "birth parents" will not be used until DNA can confirm parentage.

3. They changed their name arbitrarily.
4. They did not participate in activities that resulted in the creation of records, e.g. they moved frequently, died early or lived a life of crime.

Some of the seventeen unidentified and lost orphans possibly returned to New York City; however, no orphan has been identified as having done so.

Twenty-nine orphans, nineteen boys and ten girls, were possiblyn traced from arrival to death (AtoD).

New York City parent(s) were identified for twelve of the identified orphans, six boys and six girls. The identified birth parents of two individuals (Krohn, Schlosshauer) are based on one likely candidate. In four cases (Wientjes, Doyle, Krohn and Zahn), birth certificates were not found, but other evidence identifies the parent(s).

No DNA studies were conducted.

The New York Historic Vital Records site indicates that between 1880 tand 1890, birth records are not available for Richmond County (Staten Island), the Bronx and Queens. Kings County (Brooklyn) and Manhattan records are complete for this period, but may be missing records. The site notes that many Irish did not register births with the municipality opting for registration with the church.[714]

CHARACTERISTICS OF HAMILTON COUNTY ORPHANS

Two hypotheses about the orphans developed during the writing of the biographies:
1. Childhood trauma made it difficult for the orphans to develop meaningful and long-lasting relationships.
2. Males were more negatively affected than females.

The CAS expected foster parents to utilize the boys as laborers on the farms. In 1890 Hamilton County was promised deliveries of only boys.[715]

Of the 46 orphans delivered to Hamilton County, Iowa, in the fall of 1890 ,thirty-five (76%) were boys, and eleven (24%) were girls. All

---

[714] NYC Historic Vital Records, https://a860-historicalvitalrecords.nyc.gov/digital-vital-records.
[715] "Persons wishing to adopt a boy...," *Webster City Freeman*, 25 July 1890.

children were selected by Hamilton County families. Only the children of the October delivery were identified by the CAS.[716]

None of the Hamilton County orphans were identified as having a physically handicap or being of color.

Only one child (Doyle) was born outside New York City or its boroughs.

Although many of the children were identified as "adopted," only one was adopted through court action—Lillian Lingreen Roop. Lottie Krohn stated that her foster child Clara was formally adopted, but all documents were lost. No indication of a formal adoption has been found for Clara other than Lottie Krohn's document testified before a Notary Public.[717]

Table 2 - A
Average age at arrival & birth data of cohort

	Boys	Girls	Both
Average age in years	6.16	6.0	6.11
Oldest	Richard Doyle, 11	Minnie Busing, Katie Hines, Belle Wientjes, 8	Richard Doyle, 11
Youngest	Wm. Tarrant, 2	Anna McIntyre, 3	Wm. Tarrant, 2

The average age of the identified boys and girls at arrival was similar, but the age range was broader for the boys than the girls, particularly in older boys. This supports the hypothesis that older boys were desired to work on the farm, and the CAS tried to accommodate this preference.

---

[716] Kialy Carson, Kansas, [(CURATOR@ORPHANTRAINDEPOT.COM),] to Jill Morelli, email, 7 March 2023, "Info from the CAS," OTR folder.

[717] Sworn statement by Lottie Krohn sworn to Notary Public, Clara Temsland, Lynden, Whatcom County, Washington, copy of original, dated 26 October 1935, identifying Clara L. (Mason) Kuchenreuther, born 16 January 1884 as her adopted daughter. Document in the family papers of Randall Kuchenreuther, Bellingham, Washington, and the Whatcom County Historical Society, and collected by Linda Lawson, 16 November 2023.

Four boys transferred to a second family. (the Tarrants, Bittner, and Bringolf). Bittner (age 6), Smith (13) and Minnie Busing (11) experienced the sudden death of their foster mothers at a young age. When they were older, Richard Doyle and George Jensen Myers chose to remain in Hamilton County rather than move with their foster families. Several others moved with their foster families: Lucy Fay, Lulu Strowbridge, Clara Krohn, Julia Sumpter, John Bringolf, John Burnett, and James Baldwin.

Education
The CAS recognized the importance of education for the children and outlined the responsibility of the foster parents' to support it.
- Boys between 12 and 15 were expected to attend school at least part of the year.
- Boys under 12 were expected to attend school alongside the family's other children through the 8th grade. it was difficult for farm children to continue high school while helping with the farm chores.
- No specifics were outlined for girls.

Claudia Goldin and Lawrence Katz (G&K Study) investigated educational attainment in ten Iowa counties (excluding Hamilton) and three metropolitan areas, based on the 1915 Iowa state census.[718]

The G&K Study found that children in metropolitan areas could attend school more easily and were not burdened with farm chores, increasing the days of education.[719] The inclusion of metropolitan areas may inflate some data points in the study compared to data from the orphans in rural Hamilton County.

To maintain consistency with the G&K Study, each orphan's education level was first assessed based the 1915 Iowa census. If they were not enumerated in the 1915 census, e.g. if they lived outside the state, the 1940 census was used. Anomalies were found between censuses. For instance, in 1915 August Zahn's education level was reported as eight years of schooling.[720] In 1940 the informant reported August had three years of high school. No indication exists of Zahn's of additional schooling.[721]

---

[718] Claudia Golden and Lawrence F. Kat, "Education and income in the early 20th century: Evidence from the prairies," *The Journal of Economic History* 60(3): 782-818; JSTOR, permalink: https://www.jstor.org/stable/2566438, available through your academic library.

[719] Ibid., 801.

[720] 1915 Iowa State census, Hamilton County, Iowa; population schedule, Fremont Township, card number 396, August Zahn. Lizzie, his wife, is card no. 395.

[721] 1940 U.S. census, Hamilton County, Iowa, population schedule, Webster City, ED 40-6, household 255, p. 12A, August H. Zahn.

Table 3-A
Formal Schooling Indicators in 1915 Iowa Census +, Compared to the Hamilton County, Iowa AtoD orphans (Living in 1915/1940)

	Boys	Girls
Iowa, average years of schooling, 1915[a]	8.40	8.99
AtoD orphan cohort, average years of schooling, 1915/1940 (boys, n=14; girls, n=8)	7.57	8.00
Iowa, percentage graduating from high school[a]	15.2%	17.9%
AtoD orphan cohort, percentage graduating from high school (12 years+)	14.2%	25.0%

a. Claudia Goldin, & Lawrence F. Katz, "Education and Income in the Early 20th Century: Evidence from the Prairies," *The Journal of Economic History* 60(3): for average years in school: 792, Table 2; for percentage graduating from high school: 790, Table 1.

Iowa's ethnic and immigrant groups understood the importance of education and established "country school" districts, one for every four sections.[722]

Typical Iowa Country School, Grant No. 5
Photo by author in Winnebago County, Iowa

"*The School-house stood about a mile away on the prairie with not even a fence to shield the blast.... It was merely a square, box-like structure with three windows on the side and two on the front. It was painted a glaring white on the outside and a drab within...*"

Hamlin Garland, *A Boy's Life on the Prairie*, p. 35.

Since female orphans tended to go to families who resided in town, they received about a half a year more schooling than the boys and attained a higher graduation rate. The average number of years of schooling the AtoD orphans experienced is lower than the Iowa average by almost one full year for both sexes.

---

[722] Bessie L. Lyon, *Early Days in Hamilton County, Then and Now* (Webster City, Iowa: Freeman Journal Publishing Co., 1946) 72. Also, *Iowa's Country Schools: Landmarks of Learning*, (Parkersburg, Iowa: Iowa State Education Association, and Mid-Prairie Books 1998) 5; Internet Archive. A section is one mile x one mile.

The agreement with the CAS required schooling of the orphans through high school graduation (c. 12 years), yet only two girls and two boys attained that level of education. While high school graduation was stipulated by the CAS, eighth-grade completion predominated and could be achieved in the country schools. Charles Bjustrum and George Breckfeldt completed just three years of schooling.

Findings relating to the two hypotheses concerning education:
Childhood trauma made it more difficult for the orphans to develop meaningful and long-lasting relationships.
- While level of education might affect future earning opportunities, it does not appear to negatively impact relationship-building.

Male orphans were more negatively affected than females.
- Males completed fewer grades than females, perhaps due to working on the farm.
- Neither gender's average achieved the CAS-desired education level.

Marriage & Children

If these orphans experienced difficulty in establishing long-erm relationships, evidence should be found in the longevity of their marriages, and numbers of children when compared to norms.

The US average considers all people, age fifteen to sixty-five, both urban and rural. Our comparison cohort, however, are thirty to forty years old and entirely rural or small town.

When compared with the US averages, it is predictive that the Iowa orphan cohort should see the following:
- A higher percentage of orphans who are married, as the orphans are of the age when families have been formed, but not yet affected by death.
- A similar age at first marriage.
- The US average of "never/not marrieds" should be lower than that of the orphans, and male orphans should have a higher percentage of "never married" than the female orphans.
- A lower percentage of divorces because the longer the span of time of measurement the greater the possibility of multiple divorces.
- A higher average number of children, as the orphans are in their child-bearing years; children are still young and living at home; and death would not yet have affected the count.

- A lower percentage of childlessness, as the orphans are in their child-bearing years.

All AtoD orphans who were going to marry had done so by 1920.

Table 4-A
Comparison of Marriage & Children of AtoD orphans in 1920

	US average	AtoD orphans n= 28	AtoD males n= 18	AtoD females n=10
Married[a]	60%	78%	72%	90%
Average age of first marriage[b]	Males: 24.6 yrs Females: 21.2 yrs		28.5 yrs	20.6 yrs
Never married[c] (1920)	M: 15% F: 8%	21.4%	27.7%	10%
Divorces[d]	1.8 per 1000 population	5 divorces	1 divorce	4 divorces
Percentage with a divorce[e]	0.18%	17.8%	5.5%	40%
no. of children per family	3.17	2.05	1.57	3.33
No children compared to norm		64% below	49.5% below	105% above

a. Julissa Cruz, "Marriage: More than a Century of Change," *National Center for Family & Marriage Research*, Bowling Green State university, not dated, but last data point is 2010.
b. *Infoplease*, "Median Age at First Marriage, 1890-2010," updated 28 July 2023.
c. National Center for Health Statistics (U.S.) "100 years of marriage and divorce statistics, United States 1867-1967", no. 24, 1973. Some orphans had multiple divorces.
d. Julissa Cruz, "Marriage: More than a Century of Change."
e. *Population Connection*, "Average number of children per U.S. Family (Historic)," https://populationeducation.org/wp-content/uploads/2020/04/average-number-children-per-us-family-historic-infographic.pdf.
f. "Childless Couples," *New York Times,* 7 August 1935, p. 18, col 3.

Married: No orphan married another. True to predictions, both male and female orphans, were married more than the general US population. However, since the number of marriages would be predicted to be higher due to the differences in measurement, only the percentile of marriageable females (91%) appears significant when compared to the U. S. average.

Age at marriage: Male orphans married 15.8% later than the national norm, which might account for their fewer divorces. Female orphans married 2.8% earlier than the national norm.

Never married: Six AtoD orphans never married.[723] None of the orphans married for the first time after 1920. Only one female did not marry (McIntyre) and given the small cohort, the percentage seems reasonable. Male orphan marriages exceeded the norm by 42%.

Divorce: Male orphans were twenty times more likely to divorce than national norms; female orphans were 138 times more likely to divorce than national norms. Despite the severe stigma surrounding divorce at the time, divorces among the orphans were much higher than norm. The high orphan divorce rate suggests poor initial marriage choices. However, in every case, the females married again and formed long-lasting relationships. Regardless of perspective, the high number of divorced couples with one orphan partner indicates difficulty in choosing initial life partners for both males and females.

Two first marriages appeared to just dissolve (Fay, Lyons). Efforts were made to see if the other partner was still living, with no success.

Children: Male orphans had 50.4% fewer children compared to the norm, the female orphans had 5.0% more children than the norm. There was one illegitimate birth (Strowbridge). In an era of larger families and with the need for children to provide labor, this is a significant data point for both genders.

Five married couples had no descendants of twenty-one orphans who married.[724] This lack of descendants negatively impacted the average children per couple.

---

[723] Six AtoD orphans never married: McIntyre, Moore, Wm. Tarrant, J.F. Weber, Witte, and Bittner (died at age 14).

[724] Five AteD orphans married, but no children: Baldwin, Bjustrom, Breckfeldt, Lyons, and Wa. Thompson. Four AtoD orphans had one child who had no descendants: Busing, Smith, Wm. Weber, and Strowbridge. By 1920, the female orphans would be nearing the end of their birthing years.

Findings related to the two hypotheses concerning marriage and the children of the orphans:
Childhood trauma made it more difficult for the orphan to develop meaningful and long-lasting relationships.
- The average age at first marriage of male orphans is older than US norms, but slightly younger for female orphans.
- The percentage of male orphans who never married is much higher than US norms.
- The divorce rate among the orphans is significantly higher than the US population for both males and females;
- The number of children among married male orphans is lower than the norm, possibly reflecting their delay in getting married or a desire to not expose children to trauma.

Male orphans were more negatively affected than females.
- A higher percentage of male orphans never married compared to US norms. Females married at a rate similar to national norms.
- Male orphans married much later and had significantly fewer children than average couple.
- The number of childless couples is higher than average for males, but not for females.

Life & Death
Some observations of the Hamilton County orphans:
- Unidentified and lost orphans comprise 37% of the total number of orphans who arrived in Hamilton County in the fall of 1890.
- Twenty-nine (83%) of the identified orphans went to foster families who lived on farms.
- Only 26% of the adult orphans farmed or attempted to farm for a living compared to 30.2% of the US population in 1920. Farming usually requires generational wealth to be passed on to the next generation. A foster child was rarely is the line of succession to receive a farm. The Depression disrupted many of the orphans' plans to continue farming.[725] The remainder worked in factories, ran small businesses, or were laborers, some in the agricultural sector.
- 23% of the AtoD orphans resided in and died in Hamilton County; 31% died in other Iowa counties or Midwest states (IA, IL, MN, WI, SD); and 20% died elsewhere (CA, WA, CO and Canada). No AtoD orphan resided east of Indiana at the time of death.

---

[725] J. Z. Kalbacher & D. Deare, "Farm Population of the United States, 1985," *Current population reports. Series P-20, Population characteristics*, 59 (1986): i-1-20.

A review of the probates of Hamilton County foster family members revealed that orphans or their descendants were mentioned in only three instances.[726] Viola Meyer, daughter of Minnie (Busing) Meyer received an allocation from her mother's foster mother; Annie McIntyre received $200 from the Crane estate; and George Witte was noted as deceased.

Three orphans received assistance from their foster family during their lifetimes.
- Clara (Krohn) Kuchenreuther received land from her foster mother.
- John Bringolf received support from his foster father to invest in a farm in Kansas.
- Charles Tarrant rented the farm from his foster mother after his foster father died. His brother, William, did not.

In an exception, Harry Guseka Moore willed his property to his foster sister, Clara.

Training on the farm with no likelihood of inheritance created stress about future job opportunities for orphans. Job seekers may take riskier positions to earn enough money to sustain a family. With lower levels of education, fewer job opportunities were available.

If these scenarios created stress and stress shortens lifespan, then male orphans should die earlier than female orphans when compared to US norms.[727] We should expect to see longer life spans of women as medical advances in child birth reduced the causes of death for females, especially when combined with the reduced number of children born to female orphan families.

Two comparisons were made- the average age at death for a child born in 1890 and the average age of death if the person lived to 1950. Only those orphans who survived to 1950 were averaged in the second comparison.

---

[726] Probate records were reviewed at the Hamilton County Courthouse in August 2024 for Geerd Hassebroek (2986); Jennie Hassebroek (5528); Fred Ashpole (1473); Charles Young (1737); Joseph Bjustrom (2853); Olaf Angstrom (3746); Aalderk Busing (577); John Grensberg (1712); Grietje Grensberg (2382); Robert Crane (1178); David McFarland's probate unavailable due to insanity; Eliza McFarland (2324); W. R. Wilson (589); Etta Pruismann (12317); Jackson Mickle (1626); Benjamin Segar (no number, P.R. 1, p. 189, file #1); Andrew Smith (974 and Joseph Adams (1734); William A. Tarrant (7905); Barney Thompson (2319); Frank Briggs (6763); Charles Gerber (3505); Fried Wientjes (2931); August Witte (2873); and John Essig (3518).

[727] Chelsea Hetherington, PhD, "Stress Can Shorten Your Lifespan," Health News, 11 September 2023, https://healthnews.com/family-health/healthy-living/can-stress-shorten-your-lifespan.

Table 5 - A
Comparison of average age at time of death by gender of AtoD orphans
(Orphan average is average age at death if living at in the year noted.)

	US Average		Diference	Orphan Average		Difference
	Men	Women	Difference between male and female	Men	Women	Difference between male and female
Est. age at death if alive in 1890[a]	45.8 (white)	42.9 (white)	2.9 (adv. males)	58.6	73.0	14.4 yrs. (adv. female)
Est. age at death if died in 1950	65.6	71.1	5.5 yrs. (adv. females)	72.5	82.6	10.1 yrs. (Adv. female)

a. J. David Hacker, "Decennial Life Tables of the White Population of the United States, 1790-1900," Table 1, 'Life Tables Estimates of Infant Mortality and Life Expectancy at Selected Ages, United States 1798–1901,' *National Library of Medicine* (https://www.ncbi.nlm.nih.gov/pmc/articles/PMC2885717/)
b. *"Life Expectancy in the USA, 1900 to 1998, men and women," University of California Berkeley*, https://u.demog.berkeley.edu/~andrew/1918/figure2.html. This gives the reader an idea of the change over time and the expectation if one lived to 1950.

In both comparisons the average age at death for the AtoD females was significantly higher than that of the AtoD males, whether assessed from arrival date or if the orphan survived to 1950. Additionally, both male and female orphans lived longer than the averages would indicate. Ten male orphans and three female orphans died before 1950.

Three female orphans lived into their 90s (Fay, Krohn, Sumpter). No male lived into this 90s and only one lived into his 80s (Myers). The men's lives were cut short by childhood diseases, heart issues, and illness. Using the 1890 data, the male orphans outlived the US average by 27.9%, but the female orphans outlived the US average by 70.1%.

> Findings relating to our two hypotheses and life and death of the orphans:
> Childhood trauma made it more difficult for the orphan to develop meaningful and long-lasting relationships.
> - The large number of unidentified and lost male orphans indicates unsatisfactory relationships with their assigned foster families or other external issues.
>
> Male orphans were more negatively affected by out-placement than females.
> - Males comprised 94% of all unidentified or lost orphans.
> - Male orphans were raised and trained on farms, but could not receive any long-term benefit through inheritance.
> - Any situation that increases stress will affect the projected lifespan. Stress related diseases predominated amongst the males.
> - Age at the time of death for male orphans was significantly younger then that of the female orphans, but ages were still above the U.S. average.

CHARACTERISTICS OF FOSTER FAMILIES

Two documents identified foster parents. The newspaper article for the August delivery of orphans identified seventeen foster families but did not name the foster children.[728] The October manifest from the CAS identified thirteen foster families and their assigned children.[729] A total of thirty heads of household were identified as taking orphans, with one family taking two.

Eight of seventeen (47%) families that accepted a child in the first delivery did not have an orphan child in their family in the next census (1895). These children either died, moved to another unidentified family, or returned to New York City. Of the October delivery, thirteen foster family heads of household were identified, and twelve retained their orphan (92%).

Four scenarios describe the situations of foster parents:
- The family gave birth to no children and/or had no children survive (Wientjes, Krohn, Adams).

---

[728] "E. Trott of the children's aid society…," *The Freeman (Webster City, Iowa)*, 3 September 1890, p. 5, col. 3.

[729] Kialy Carson, Kansas, [(CURATOR@ORPHANTRAINDEPOT.COM),] to Jill Morelli, email, 7 March 2023, "Info from the CAS," OTR folder.

- The couple had only daughter(s) (Tarrant, B. Thompson, Motheral).
- The couple was much older, and/or the older children had moved on. (Crane, Ashpole, T. Johnson).
- The couple was younger and had only young children to assist (Hassebroek).

It wasn't just older individuals who desired and received an orphan.

Table 5 - A
Foster Families characteristics

	US average	Foster Father	Foster Mother
Ave. birth year		1845.5 (Range 1827-1863)	1847.4 (Range 1826-1867)
Natural children	3.56[a]		2.8 born/ 2.1 surviving
Foreign-born	14.6%[b]	54.5%	43.8%

Data not available for every family, e.g. if the wife died before 1900, then the children in the 1895 census were counted and it was assumed that no children died.

a. Population Connection, "Average number of children per U.S. Family (Historic)," https://populationeducation.org/wp-content/uploads/2020/04/average-number-children-per-us-family-historic-infographic.pdf.
b. US Census Bureau, "Historical Census Statistics on Foreign-born Population of the United States, 1850-1950: Introduction," https://www.census.gov/library/working-papers/1999/demo/POP-twps0029.html.

Birth year: In 1890, the average age of foster fathers and mothers was forty-five, beyond the mother's birthing years. All foster parents were married, with two exceptions. Frank Briggs, single, supported his mother, her sister, and an uncle, and received a male orphan. (J. F. Weber). Thea Johnson, widow, received a female orphan. (Fay)

Natural Children: At arrival of the thirty-five identified children, eleven foster families had no children, and twelve had no surviving children. The average number of children per family is affected by four families who had ten or more children, but no children lived at home.

The number of children born to the families of foster parents is in stark contrast to the US average for that time. Foster families had 41% fewer surviving children than the U.S. average at the time when one would assume children were valued for their work on the farm.

Foreign-born foster families:
- While the foreign-born population comprised 14.6% of the total U.S. population, foreign-born foster parents comprised 50% of foster families. Most heads of households of foster families immigrated from England, Ireland, and Germany. Illinois was the predominate birthplace for those born in the United States. Only three of 64 foster parents were born in Iowa.
- The ethnicity of foster families who received male orphans is split evenly between U.S.-born and foreign-born. The U.S.-born foster parents hailed from Illinois (6), Iowa (4), Wisconsin (3), Ohio (2), Pennsylvania (2), and Kentucky. Foreign-born foster parents came from Germany (9), England (5), Scandinavia (4) and Ireland (4).
- The ethnicity of the foster parents who received a female orphan is split evenly between U. S.-born and foreign-born. The U.S.-born foster parents hailed from New York (2), Ohio (2), Wisconsin (2), Virginia, Illinois (1) and Indiana (1). The immigrant foster parents came from Germany (4), England, Canada, Denmark and Ireland.
- New York City parents for male orphans are predominantly unidentified United States (4) and New York (2). Foreign-born parents came from Germany (2), England, Ireland and Scotland.
- The ethnicity of New York City parents for U.S.-born female orphans are unidentified as United States (7), and New York (2). The foreign-born parents came from Germany and Ireland.

Iowa had a higher percentage of immigrant residents available to be foster parents because of the availability of land for farming through the Homestead Acts.

Crises in Foster Families
Foster families seemed to have experienced significant and numerous crises. The national 1895 Depression may have contributed to familial stress, but personal factors were also present.

Circumstances often challenged foster families and their decisions to accept orphans. Harry Bittner was seven years-old when his initial placement family, the Olmsteads, moved and did not take Harry with them. Mayme Smith was 14 when her foster father died two years after experiencing a devastating and uninsured fire on the family farm.

Other examples of crises in the foster families include:
- Geerd Hassebroek feuded with his neighbor, George Strever, over water drainage. The case was taken to court, and the judge ruled in favor of Strever. In 1900 William Allison, the foster child assigned to Hassebroek, worked for George Strever. This might have be enviewed by the Hassebroeks as disloyalty by William.
- Around 1900 David McFarland spent a few years in the Cherokee Hospital for the Insane and was later officially declared insane.[730] This was not a good environment for raising orphan, Iris Doutrich, who spent his teen years at the Eldora Training School for Boys.
- Aeilt Hinderks, a deacon in the First Presbyterian Church in Kamrar, was excommunicated in 1893 for adultery. The family seemed to overcome the crisis. Aeilts, wife Hilke, and Henry remained in the Hamilton County area as a nuclear family.
- About 1900 Nels and Nellie Jensen moved to Michigan and was promptly divorced by his wife. George Jensen, now using his New York City surname Myers, stayed in Hamilton County.
- A more common disruption was the removal of the foster family from the county, even if the orphan stayed with their foster family. While most children were still in Hamilton County in 1900, early removals occurred with five children—Burnett (Missouri); Johnson/Baldwin (California); Strowbridge (Indiana); Sumpter (Minnesota); and Krohn (Kossuth County, Iowa and Washington).
- William Tarrant remains an enigma. He is the only foster child who served in World War I. He was sent to France, but his unit never saw action. How this affected him is unknown, yet his life was a solitary one, residing with one family for his post-war life. This may now be called PTSD, but it is unclear what precipitated his almost hermit-like behavior.

If a child, already traumatized by a move from New York and separation from their NYC family, experienced trauma within their foster family, their lives would be probably unsettled as adults.

Midway through their lives, some orphans desired answers about their New York parentage. These orphans communicated with the CAS requesting information. The NYC parental information would suddenly appear in documents. That was the case for Belle (Welch) Wientjes who used her foster parents' names and birth locations consistently until the

---

[730] The Cherokee Hospital for the Insane was opened in 1902 and initially housed about 700 patients. It was the fourth hospital for the insane in the state and was modeled after the Utica hospital under the classic Kirkbride plan. See "A Tourist in the Land of Reason, "The Cherokee State Hospital for the Insane, 1902 to Present," https://www.youtube.com/watch?v=WQLYCW4Awuc

1925 Iowa census. Walter Thompson shared information about his NYC parents with the hospital intake person. Clara (Mason) Krohn must have remembered the name of her NYC mother evidenced by her use of Lavinia as a middle name; but in 1998 her daughter requested information from the CAS.

Findings relating to the two hypotheses and crises in the foster families:
   Childhood trauma made it more difficult for the orphan to develop meaningful and long-lasting relationships.
- The preponderance of families with few or no children or only daughters might create an atmosphere that is either welcoming or one of servant-employer.
- Any instability in the foster family to a child who has only known instability will be damaging to the child and to their orphan's future ability to handle similar situations.

Males were more negatively affected than females.
- Expectations of the foster parents, especially those on the farm, were that the male orphan would be a farm laborer. Female orphans did not have that burden.
- There is no observable tie between crises in foster families and increased stress in male orphans.

Although the percentage of foreign-born individuals was higher in Hamilton County in 1890 compared to the U. S., ,no identified correlation between additional stress because of the immigration status of the foster parents has been identified. Belle (Welch) Wientjes integrated so completely with her German community, that she learned the language and married a German.

Contrary to the above stories, most of the AtoD girls and 50% of the AtoD boys led satisfactory lives, perhaps experiencing the average amount of pain and happiness of any typical family. However, crises within a foster family had to be unsettling to young orphans dealing with their own challenges.

COMPARISON OF NEW YORK CITY PARENTS OF ORPHANS

Only 12 orphans have their New York City parents identified. One might hypothesize that there would be more single mothers in the identified subgroup than parental couples.

Table 2 - A
NYC Parents

	All	Boys	Girls
Identified NYC parent(s)	12 7 (both parents) 5 (single mothers)	6 5 (both parents); 1 (single mother)	6 2 (both parents); 4 (single mothers)

This hypothesis is incorrect. Single mothers comprise less than half of the Hamilton County orphans identified through a New York City birth certificate (42%). Couples predominate, particularly for the boys.

Eight orphans have their New York City birth certificates, determined using records supplied by orphans in their lifetime in Iowa. The CAS supplied two orphans with their information (Wientjes, Krohn). Traditional genealogical research identified parents of another orphan (Zahn), and clues provided in a family story defined another (Doyle).[731]

Two facilities predominate in birth locations—the New York Infant Asylum (61st Street & 10th Avenue) and the Nursery & Childs Hospital (61st Street & Amsterdam Avenue).[732] Starting in the mid-1800s both provided laying-in services, and maternity care for single mothers or the poor starting in the mid 1800s, but the primary focus of the Infant Asylum was post birth care of orphans until they could be placed with foster parents. Nursery and Childs provided medical care.[733] Six of the orphans with a birth certificate were born in one of these two facilities; one was born at Bellevue Emergency; and two were born at home.

One might also hypothesize that the child would be the parent's first born. While that is mostly true, George Breckfeldt was the seventh child; John Burnett was the third child; and Lucy Fay was the fourth.

---

[731] Ken Norstrud, [(ADDRESS FOR PRIVATE USE)] to Jill Morelli, email, 12 March 2023, 12:10 pm, "Richard Doyle," OTR email collection, privately held by Morelli [(ADDRESS FOR PRIVATE USE)], Seattle Washington. Mr. Norstrud is a Richard Doyle's grandson. See the individual biographies for the others.

[732] 10th Ave. and Amsterdam are the same street. These facilities were probably on opposite corners.

[733] Wikipedia, "New York Infant Asylum," "New York Nursery & Childs Hospital."

COMPARISON OF ORPHANS TO THE RALPH STUDY

In 1922, Georgia G. Ralph (with the Children's Aid Society) conducted a longitudinal study of the out-placement of children.[734] The author's definitions of the following categories is not known. One would expect the conclusions of the larger study to be similar to those of the Hamilton County orphans.

Table 6 - A
Comparison of the Ralph Study and the identified orphans (n = 46) of Hamilton County, Iowa

Col 1	Col 2	Col 3	Col 4	Col 5	Col 6	Col 7	Col 8	Col 9	Col 10
Yr. Placed	N =	Group 1 no info	Group 2 left foster homes	Group 3 returned to NY	Group 4 unfavor-able	Total unfavor-able	Group 5 in foster homes	Total favor-able	Total favorable %age
BOYS									
1885	182	5	36	25	8	74	108	40	60%
1890	**35**	**10**	**2**	**0**	**3**	**15**	**13**	**13**	**48%**
1895	127	0	12	23	11	46	81	38	62%
GIRLS									
1885	29	3	0	1	3	7	22	31	69%
1890	**11**	**1**	**0**	**0**	**2**	**3**	**8**	**8**	**73%**
1895	42	0	0	5	1	6	36	14	86%

Group 1: No information.
This is a sizable group for the Hamilton County cohort, with no information for 28.6% of the boys. Only one girl (9%) has no information.

---

[734] Henry W. Thurston, *The Dependent Child* (New York: Columbia University Press, 1930) 133. The location of the study is now not publicly available, but Thurston included the entire table that summarized the data as described and allocated children based on that point in time (1922). Ms. Ralph's compilations were recorded every 10 years between 1865 to 1905 and included all children in the CAS files for those years. Only years 1885 and 1895 are shown. The data associated with 1890 is the data of the Hamilton County orphans.

Group 2: Left foster homes
This category includes children who left their foster homes before they reached age 18. Because of the lack of records for the Hamilton County orphans, it is difficult to accurately identify the age any individual left their foster family. It is unknown if Ralph considered the common practice of working on an adjacent farm as "leaving the foster home." (Allison, Doyle).

Group 3: Returned to New York
Although this category comprised a large number of Ralph's study group (24%), no orphans in the cohort were identified as returning to New York City. One instance of a family member from New York City visiting an adult orphan in Iowa exists (Zahn). Some of the lost orphans in Group 1 possibly returned to New York City. Contrary to Ralph's assessment, returning to New York City might be favorable if the New York City family had stabilized and the child desired to return.

Group 4: Unfavorable
This category defined orphans residing in an institution as unfavorable. Two boys were sent to Eldora Training School for Boys (McFarland/ Doutrich, Bringolf). MacFarland/Doutrich continued his incorrigible ways, spending time in state and federal prison before he was 25 years old. Somewhat arbitrarily, Harry Bittner is also counted in this group because he died at age 14 of an unidentified illness. One girl (McIntyre) spent thirty years of her adult life in a hospital for the insane and one (Busing) was committed later in life. These individuals were placed in Group 4.

Group 5: In foster homes
Members of the Hamilton County cohort were included if they stayed in their foster homes, kept close contact with their foster families or left when marrying.

Some general observations regarding the Ralph Sstudy:
- Ralph had access to all CAS records from 1854 to 1922. Her study would have included the Hamilton County cohort.
- In the Ralph Study, the discrepancy between the number "In Foster Homes" (Group 5) and the number "Total Favorable" (Column 9) cannot be reconciled.
- "Total Favorable Percentage" (Column 10) is calculated by dividing Column 8 (108) by n=182.
- The Hamilton County assessment assumed that staying with the assigned foster family was "Favorable." Unfortunately, this is not always true—foster families could be abusive, view the orphan as slave labor, or not comply with their CAS agreement.

A comparison to the Ralph Study can be made but several conditions need to be taken into account.
- The thirty-five identified orphans were characterized over time rather than at a single point.
- N = 35 is a small cohort.

Comparing the unfavorable outcomes recorded by the Ralph Study to the Hamilton County orphan boys cohort yields the following:
- In 1885 40.6% of the Ralph Study male orphans had unfavorable outcomes.
- In 1895 36.2% of the Ralph Study male orphans had unfavorable outcomes.
- Hypothesis: In 1890 38.4% of male orphan should have unfavorable outcomes.
- Results: In 1890 48% of Hamilton County male orphan had unfavorable outcomes, 25% worse than hypothesized.

Given the high demand for orphans in Hamilton County, did the CAS send the more vulnerable boys to Hamilton County in 1890? Without the manifest for November, the question cannot be answered.

Comparing the unfavorable outcomes recorded by the Ralph Study to the Hamilton County orphan girls cohort yields the following:
- In 1885 24.1% of the Ralph Study female orphans had unfavorable outcomes.
- In 1895, 14.2% of the Ralph Study female orphans had unfavorable outcomes.
- Hypothesis: In 1890 19.15% of female orphan should have unfavorable outcomes.
- Results: Only 9.1% of Hamilton County female orphan had unfavorable outcomes, a 52.4% better than hypothesized.

The Hamilton County orphans girls defied the Report's trend. Orphan girls had significantly more favorable outcomes that would be predicted based on the Ralph Report.

Focus on the unfavorable outcomes is easy, but examples exist of warm relationships between orphans and their foster parents. William Bringolf lived next door to his foster son in Hamilton County and when the foster son moved to Kansas. William was eventually cared for within the John's home until his death. George Witte left Hamilton County for thirteen years, but returned to care for his terminally ill foster father. Julia Sumpter moved with her family to Minnesota, married, and divorced there. When her widowed foster mother moved back to Hamilton County, Julia returned with her. Mayme Smith moved to Illinois after she married, but maintained a close relationship with her foster family despite her subsequent adultery, divorce, and second marriage.

Sometimes, it's the extraordinary lives quietly lived that speak loudest to the program's success. Belle (Welch/Wientjes) Eckhoff. Clara (Mason/Krohn) Kuchenreauther, John Henry Burnett, George (Jensen) Myers, August Zahn, and others married, had on-going relationships with their foster parents, and became the citizens that Charles Loring Brace envisioned when he initially conceived his plan.

SUMMARY OF FINDINGS

Almost half of the males and one-tenth of the females suffered unfavorable outcomes, including mental illness and/or a propensity for crime. The stories of these dispossessed orphans are rarely told or even highlighted except when examining a cohort. We cannot overlook that half the males and nine-tenths of the females had successful outcomes, which probably would not have been true if they stayed in New York City. Their adult lives reveal an experience they would never have known without the out-placement program. The bucolic environment of an Iowa farming community created a good environment for some.

Eleven orphans cannot be identified and another eight became lost after adulthood. One might hope that the eleven integrated into their families so completely that they, too, found loving homes. However, it is equally possible that they reverted to their New York City names and became lost or returned to New York City. These children may be identified in the future.

The two hypotheses are valid for the orphans of Hamilton County and are consistent with the 1922 Ralph study.
- Childhood trauma made it more difficult for the orphans to develop meaningful and long-lasting relationships.
- Male orphans were more negatively affected than females.

Crises are not uncommon in children's lives, but the out-placed children started with a personal crisis—rejection by their living parents or a lack of knowledge of either parent. As adults the children experienced their own crises—the early death of a foster parent, transference to another family, divorce, mental illness, or criminal activity resulting in imprisonment.

This pattern of damage to an orphan's psyche affected their ability to create and sustain lasting relationships. The number of divorces; delayed marriages; and fewer children all point to difficulty in establishing and maintaining relationships.

Female orphans sustained relationships better than the males, probably due to the lower expectations by society and their foster parents. They also had a significantly longer life than the males. This was possibly due to different expectations while growing up that reduced their stress; they possibly had fewer instances of childbirth deaths, due to having fewer children or a lack of participation in hazardous occupations.

One cannot generalize about the outcome of the orphans as a whole based on the anecdotal evidence of one life lived.

Please go to my website to see any new documentation which arrived after publication; the research invested in the failed searches; and for any new information about the identity of the children.

(*See* https://iowaorphans.wordpress.com)

Conclusion

Our journey began with five questions:
1. What were the characteristics of the Hamilton County orphans?
2. What were the characteristics of the foster parents of the orphans?
3. What were the characteristics of the New York City birth parents?
4. How do attributes of the cohort compare with the results of the Georgia G. Ralph Study in 1922?
5. What qualitative observations can be made concerning the success of placement of theorphans in Hamilton County?

The result is complicated. For every child that had a rough time, another rose above similar adversity.

Iris Doutrick/Harry Dawson and John Bringolf both spent time in the Eldora Training School for Boys for petty crimes. Both boys committed crimes after they were released from the school. But their outcomes differ radically. Iris committed a federal crime and was imprisoned in Leavenworth. John continued to live with the Bringolf family throughout his escapades, moved with them to Minnesota, married, and eventually moved to Kansas where he farmed and raised a family. His foster father either lived adjacent to or with John until his death.

Two boys; two different paths taken. Is the difference the level of trust exhibited by the foster fathers? Iris's foster father spent time in Cherokee Hospital for the Insane, eventually being declared insane. Iris could not expect support from his foster father while he dealt with his own issues.

Alternatively, William was an advocate for John. He appealed and received a governor's release for his foster son from Eldora. William forced the issue when John gambled the harvest money away by threatening to sue. This type of advocacy of a foster parent towards their foster child is the kind of emotional support one does not routinely see in the stories of the orphans.

The female orphans had a seemingly better time. Only two, Anna (Crane) McIntyre and Minnie Bussing were institutionalized. Anna spent three decades until hr death in an institution for the insane. Minnie suffered from mid-life dementia. Belle Wientjes, attended the church of her foster parents, learned German, and married a man of the same ethnicity as her foster parents. Belle loved her foster mother who died when she was 18. Belle married and had five daughters. It's remarkable in its un-remarkability. This type of story is told over and over for the girls. Yes, they suffered through the Depression and lost farms, but their families hung together.

Some statistics stand out.

The orphan cohort had a significantly higher divorce rate than the average American, at a time when a stigma was attached to the dissolution of marriage. Some of these divorces were almost immediate. Julia Sumpter married, divorced within two years and married again a few years later. She and her husband raised three children and lived in Webster City for the rest of their lives. George Breckfeldt married and, within three years, was divorced from his wife for "cruelty and inhuman treatment." George died at age 36 of dementia.

Two second marriages were identified but the resolutions of the first marriage are not known. The first spouse could have died or divorced.

Boys seemed to have a more difficult time than girls, as explained by the disappearance of six of the boys and none of the girls. Their reasons for leaving were unfavorable—a time in federal prison, an accidental fatal shooting, and death at a young age of an unidentified sickness. One may be in a California prison (Allison); another likely changed his name (Ashpole); and one's name is too common to be found (Wm. Thompson). We have to ask ourselves why would they leave so abruptly?

TBut for each crisis in a foster family, there is an opposite outcome. Geerd Hassebroek was a well regarded, deeply religious man, yet he engaged in an acrimonious relationship with his neighbor. Geerd's foster son, William Allison, disappeared. Contrast that to Henry Aielts Hinderks, foster son to Aeilts Hinderks. Aeilts was also a deeply religious man and served as a deacon of the First Presbyterian Church of Kamrar. In 1893 Aeilts was removed from his duties as deacon and excommunicated from the church for committing adultery. This crisis in the family possibly had negative effects on Henry, yet Henry stayed with the family, kept his foster father's name, married, and lived in Hamilton County the rest of his life.

William and Charles Tarrant were placed in the Richard and Ellen Tarrant home. Charles attended school to at least the 8th grade and aspired to farming, an occupation supported by his foster mother. He stopped farming early in the Depression years, but continued working in agriculturally related occupations.

In contrast to Charles, William Tarrant, Charles's brother did not seem to reap the benefits from the foster parents that Charles did. William worked as a farm laborer, served in World War I, and worked as a farm hand for the same family in Hamilton County for the rest of his life. William continued his solitary life and never married. At death William's debts were greater than his assets.

Split between two families, the Weber brothers took different paths. William was raised by the Gerber family, but by age 20 he was working on his own in Webster City. Ten years later he was employed in a WPA program, making and fixing toys. The Depression seem to have hit this family harder than some. In 1940 William was still working through a governmental support program.

William's brother, "Fred," was raised in the Frank Briggs home. By age 15, Fred was working as a farm laborer. When he was 27, he suffered a terrible workplace accident and spent years in the hospital. After Fred was released from the hospital, William and his wife cared for him for four years. Fred moved to Colorado and invested in multiple mines. In the obituary of Fred, which was contributed by William, Fred was described as and industrious, thoughtful and kindhearted person.

What is clear is that the orphan boys of Hamilton County suffered more unfavorable outcomes than did the orphan girls. The boys had more unfavorable outcomes than boys in the Ralph Study. The Hamilton County orphan girls had more favorable outcomes than orphan boys and the girls in the Ralph study.

John Burnett, Richard Doyle, George (Jensen) Myers, and August Zahn grew up in stable homes, married and had children, and led relatively unremarkable lives.

The many stories of the orphans that came to Hamilton County, Iowa are more complicated than a single story might reveal.

Attachment 1
Methodology

In 1890 46 unnamed orphans arrived in Hamilton County, Iowa. The newspapers announcing their arrival mentioned no names.

A total of 98 candidate orphans were identified by conducting the following:
- A line-by-line search of the 1895 Iowa state census of Hamilton County, the most contemporaneous census available (The 1890 federal census is not extant.);
- A search of the 1900 and 1910 U.S. census databases;
- A line-by-line search of the 1905 Iowa state census;
- A review of orphan candidates proposed in the Iowa GenWeb Orphan Train Project assembled by Madonna Harms;[735]
- A review of adoptions in Hamilton County between 1890 and 1892;
- A search of the Hamilton County newspapers for the terms "adopted son," "adopted daughter," "foster son," and "foster daughter;"
- A search for foster parents identified in the August delivery; and
- A search for the October orphans identified by the CAS through the Orphan Train Depot in Kansas.

Of those 98 candidates, the thirty-five can be positively identified as Hamilton County orphans arriving in 1890.

The investigation and analysis contained four parts:
1. Identification of the orphans;
2. Creation of the biographical narrative of each orphan based on documentation;
3. Research of the New York City parents of each orphan; and
4. Assessment of the results of the cohort as a whole.

IDENTIFICATION OF THE ORPHANS
The identity of an out-placed orphan was based on them living in Hamilton County, birth in New York between 1880 and 1890, and not living in New

---

[735] IAGenWeb, ""Orphan Train Riders to Iowa," a special project, incomplete, http://iagenweb.org/history/orphans/index.htm.

York after that date. Name variations and changes were factored into the searches.
1. Three articles in the newspaper announced the visits by the Children's Aid Society. The articles recorded the numbers of boys and girls. The August article listed the foster parents. All were accepted by Hamilton County families.
   Issue: The CAS releases orphan file information to descendants only. The author is not a descendant of any of these children. The CAS released the list of children of the October delivery, but not the August or November deliveries at the time of publication.
   Issue: If the accepting foster parents released their child to another, family between arrival and the 1895 census, no record exists.
   Issue: If the family moved out of the county between 1890 and 1895 and was not one of the seventeen foster parents identified, no record exists.
   Issue: If the child died before 1895, the child cannot be identified unless the death and his/her orphan status were noted in the newspaper.
   Issue: If the child requested to be returned to New York, there would be no record in Hamilton County.
   Issue: If a young child subsumed their identity with that of their foster parents, they cannot be identified.
2. The 1890 US census was destroyed in the 1920s due to water damage during a fire. This census, taken in the summer of 1890 would have included the names of many of these orphans.
3. The 1890 New York Police Census and the 1892 state census for Kings County, New York are available.
   Issue: No orphans will be found in these censuses as the enumeration occurred after the children left for Iowa; but candidates can be eliminated if found in these schedules.
4. A line-by-line search was conducted in the 1895 Iowa census for New York-born children.
   Issue: If one or more of the parents were born in New York, additional documents were reviewed. If those parents arrived before 1890, they were still candidates for being a foster family.
   Issue: the enumeration of Kamrar Township in 1895 is missing. If a foster family lived in Kamrar Township, the family would not be enumerated until 1900. An older orphan could have married, have died or have moved out of the county in that time span.
5. The 1900 U. S. census for Hamilton County was sorted by location of birth (New York) and for births between 1880 and 1890. Each family was reviewed to determine if the child and the family fit the profile.
   Issue: Individuals could be missed by the enumerator, miss-

identified, not identified, or moved from the county in the intervening years.

Issue: By 1900 older children could be married or working away from the foster family.

6. It was possible that a child might not be identified by name, but by the term "adopted" or "foster." A search was conducted in the Hamilton County newspapers between 1890 and 1910. Thirteen candidates not already identified were investigated. No additional orphans were found.
7. Newspaper articles made special note that the children went "to good Hamilton County families." It was assumed that no one from another county received a child in the Hamilton County deliveries.
8. No other deliveries of children to Hamilton County have been documented until a statewide request was noted in the newspaper in 1913.[736]

Issue: A special request for a child made directly to the CAS after 1885 but before 1900, would make the child difficult to differentiate from the 1890 orphans.

A case that illustrates the difficulty of identification is Harry Caroon, who was born in New York City in 1886 and resided in Hamilton County in 1895. His identifiers all point to him as being part of the 1890 cohort. However, Harry arrived in Iowa in 1888 and stayed with Reverend Father Brennan of Mason City. When Rev. Brennan came to Hamilton County with his change of pastorate, he brought Harry with him. Harry was fostered into the family of Patrick and Ellen Caroon before 1895. Letters sent in 1888 and 1889 confirm the timing.[737] Harry did not arrive with the cohort in 1890, but his identifiers are deceiving.

The placement of the orphan into a foster home under this program did not involve compensation for the family. Generally families were to provide room, board, access to schooling, and to treat the child as their own.

In spite of children frequently identified as adopted or as a son/daughter, most children were not adopted.

---

[736] "Some Good Homes Wanted for Children," *Daily Freeman Tribune*, 9 September 1913, p. 8, col. 2.

[737] 1895 State of Iowa census, Hamilton County, Iowa, population schedule, image 652 of 681, Harry Caroom in the household of Patrick Caroom. Also, Betty Jo Stockton, Central Florida Genealogical Society, "Papers Found in an Abandoned Office: The Search for Harry Caroon, 1886-1973," *Buried Treasures,* 38 (September-December 2006):4, 84-86. Harry was placed by the New York City Foundling Hospital managed by the Sisters of Charity.

BIOGRAPHICAL NARRATIVES

As the children aged, they had opportunities to record the names of their parents—at the time of their marriage; in the 1925 Iowa state census; and at death. When they reached adulthood, their curiosity about their origins compelled some of them to seek answers from the CAS. This is evidenced by the greater specificity in the responses about names of parents and birth locations later in life.

While many resources were used, five online record sets provided the most significant evidence of the orphans and their foster parents—the 1895 and 1925 Iowa state censuses, the 1900 United States census, Hamilton and other county newspapers, and vital records for marriage and death.

THE ORPHANS' PARENTS IN NEW YORK CITY

By using New York City information found in the orphans' records, twelve of thirty-five children's birth parents were identified.

Five online record sets provided the most significant evidence for the New York City parents—the 1880 and 1900 United States censuses, the 1892 state census for Kings County and the 1890 New York Police census taken after the children left New York. The New York City Municipal Archives posted digitized vital records which provided significant additional information about the parents. Unfortunately, birth records for the Bronx, Queens, and Richmond County (Staten Island) start about 1888 and are sporadic. Manhattan and Kings County (including Brooklyn) are available for the desired years with some exceptions.

Using these methods and resources, eight birth certificates were tied to an orphan; two descendants shared information they obtained from the CAS and two descendants identified the birth parents of their ancestor.

While identification of birth parents met with some success, many obstacles prevented additional identifications. Names and birth dates used by the orphans appear fungible. Even if the name of the birth mother was known, a single mother could give an alias when she went into the hospital to give birth. Not all births were registered in New York City or its boroughs. Foundlings may have had no name, no birthdate, or no records associated with them.

Efforts were made to achieve "reasonably exhaustive search," a standard for genealogical research set by the Board for Certification of

Genealogists.[738] While the orphans left a wide variety of records, the foster parents and NYC parents were not as thoroughly explored.

Other documentation may exist that supports, conflicts or even eliminates one or more of the orphans. It is more likely that descendants of the orphan or their foster families have stories about the child and may come forward. While efforts were made to identify and interview descendants, most knew little about the experiences of their grandparent or great grandparent. Some genealogists had also placed the orphan in their public tree as if they were a natural child of the foster parents.

As orphans are identified, and additional information is obtained about the orphans after the publication of this book, the information will be placed on the following website: https://iowaorphans.wordpress.com

---

[738] Board for Certification of Genealogists, *Genealogy Standards,* (Nashville: Ancestry.com, 2019) p. 1. "Reasonably exhaustive research" is the first principle of the Genealogical Proof Standard and requires one to investigate "all evidence that might answer a genealogist's question."

Attachment 2
Summary List of Identified Orphans

	Name	Hamilton County, Iowa, Foster parents	Birth Date	Arrival Date (if known)	Name of Birth Parents
	Boys				
B1	William Allison	Geerd & Etta Hassebroek	Feb 1882	August	
B2	Fred Ashpole	Fred & Elizabeth Ashpole	Nov 1881	August	
*B3	Harry Bittner	H.S. Olmstead > Charles & Harriet Young	13 Nov 1885	August	
B4	Arthur "Charles" Bjustrom	Joseph & Matilda Bjustrom	18 Aug 1884	October	? Muller
B5	George Breckfeldt	Olaf F & Eva Angstrom	29 June 1885	November	George & Mary (Cusick) Breckfeldt
B6	John Bodger Bringolf	Philip Morris > William & Clara Bringolf	4 May 1887	October	? Bodger
B7	John Henry Burnett	John & Mary Burnett	8 June 1883	October	Patrick & Emily (Lee) Murtha
B8	Iris Doutrich/Harry Dawson	David & Eliza McFarland	March 1885	November	? Doutrich
B9	Richard Doyle	Wiliam R. & Matilda Willson	12 Oct 1878	October	John & Annie (Newell) Doyle
B10	Edward Graham Pruismann	Frank & Henrietta Pruismann	15 July 1884	August	
B11	Henry Aeilts Hindirks	Aielts & Hilke Hinderks	May 1885	August	
B12	George Jensen Myers	Nels & Nellie Jensen	18 June 1882	August or November	? Myers
B13	James G. Baldwin	Perry O. & Amelia Baldwin	22 Oct 1883	October	? Johnston
B14	James Wilfred Lyons	Kearance & Mary Lyons	July 1885	August or November	
B15	Harry Guseka Moore	Alfred & Sarah Moore	7 Oct 1884	August or November	? Guseka

B16	Nelson Morris	Luther & Eva Bozell	May 1883	August or November	? Morris
B17	William Schlosshauer	Benjamin & Maria Segar	23 June 1883	October	Jacob Dubert & Carrie Schlosshauer
B18	Charles Joseph Tarrant	W.C. Woolsey > Richard & Ellen Tarrant	6 Dec 1885	August or November	? Nolan; brother to William
B19	William Anthony Tarrant	W.C. Woolsey > Richard & Ellen Tarrant	16 Jan 1888	August or November	? Nolan; brother to Charles
B20	Walter M. Thompson	James & Minerva Motherel	12 Mar 1883	August or November	Maggie Thompson
B21	William Thompson	Barney & Betsy Thompson	1882	October	? Mcendry
B22	Jacob "Fred" Weber	Frank Briggs	Feb 1883	October	? Weber: brother to William
B23	William Louillette Weber	Charles & Mary Gerber	9 Oct 1885	October	?? Weber; brother to Fred
B24	George R. Witte	August & Minnie Witte	Feb 1887	October	? Warden
B25	August Zahn	John & Elizabeth Essig	11 April 1880	August	William & Fredricke (Vetter) Zahn
B26					
B27					
B28					
B29					
B30					
B31					
B32					
B33					
B34					
B35					

	Name	Hamilton County, Iowa, Foster parents	Birth Date	Arrival Date, if known	Name of birth parents
	Girls				
G1	Minnie Busing	Aalderk & Grietje Busing	21 June 1882	August	
G2	Lucy (Johnson) Fay	Thea Johnson	17 April 1882	October	William Henry & Hester (Parisen) Fay
G3	Katie (Mickle) Hines	N. Jackson & Elsie Mickle	13 June 1882	August	Frank & Ellen (Leahy) Hines
G4	Clara (Mason) Krohn	Christ & Lottie Krohn	16 Jan 1884	August	Sarah Lavinia Mason
G5	Anna (Crane) McIntyre	Robert & Mary Crane	March 1887	August or November	? McIntyre
G6	Lillian L. Roop	Henry C. & Sophronia Roop	Feb 1886	October	? Lengren
G7	Mary "Mae/ Mayme" Smith	Andrew & Mary Smith	10 April 1886	August or November	
G8	Lulu (Knox) Strowbridge	Thomas & Sarah Knox	25 Jan 1884	August or November	Emma Strowbridge
G9	Julia Sumpter	Joseph & Elizabeth Adams	3 April 1884	August or November	Annie Sumpter
G10	Belle (Welch) Wientjes	Fred & Minnie Wientjes	14 Apr 1882	October	Maggie Welch
G11					

ATTACHMENT 3
Other Foster Families

One newspaper identified seventeen foster parents of the August delivery for eighteen children.[739] Nine of those foster families had no children in the 1900 federal or 1895 state census. Thirteen heads of households were named in the October delivery of children.[740] Only two families had no children five years later.

Named foster families without children from August delivery:

Horace Segar:
Horace Segar died in 1892 in Hamilton County.[741] This orphan child could have died or been moved to an unidentified family. Since Benjamin Segar, Horace's son, is an identified recipient in the October delivery of orphan William "Willie" Schlosshauer. William was not moved from Horace and then moved to Benjamin's household.

Alexander Ashpole:
Elich Alexander Ashpole was born in 1868 in Iowa and was the youngest recipient of an orphan at age 23.[742] Alex married Minnie King on 4 July 1888. The couple had one child, Glenna Fern. Minnie, without Alex, moved to Dickinson County in 1895.[743] Alex cannot be found in the 1895 or the 1900 censuses. In 1900 Fern G. King, born March 1894, resided with her divorced mother, Minnie King, in Lake

---

[739] "E. Trott of the children's aid society…," *The Freeman,* 3 September 1890, p. 5, col. 3.

[740] Kialy Carson, Kansas, [(CURATOR@ORPHANTRAINDEPOT.COM),] to Jill Morelli, email, 7 March 2023, "Info from the CAS," OTR folder, privately held by Morelli, [(E-ADDRESS), & STREET ADDRESS FOR PRIVATE USE], Seattle, Washington, 2023. The email referred to an email from the archivist, Paul Clarke [(ARCHIVIST@CHILDRENSAIDNYC.ORG)] of the CAS to the Depot. listed the agent's name (Trott), 13 children by name, and their foster parents. Ten boys, three girls.

[741] "Administrator's Notice," *Webster City Freeman,* 24 February 1892, p. 4, col. 7.

[742] 1885 Iowa state census, Hamilton County, Iowa, population schedule, Blairsburg, household 25, dwelling 26. Elich Ashpole.

[743] "Obituary of Mrs. M. Palmer," *The Lake Park News (Dickinson County, Iowa),* 10 November 1955, p. 1, col 7.

Park, Dickinson County, Iowa.[744] The selected boy could have stayed with Alex after the divorce and not moved with Minnie in 1895. Alex possibly selected an older boy who left the family by the 1900 census or was transferred to another family before 1900.

John E. Young:
John E. Young received a boy in the August delivery of children. In 1895 the Young family had no children residing with them.[745] The orphan could have died or been moved to another family.

William Peitsch:
William Peitsch immigrated to Iowa in 1882. He first married Bena Tapper in 1888 in Hamilton County.[746] William cannot be found in the 1895 Iowa census. In 1900 William, now married to his second wife, Fredericka, was enumerated with six children. Only one was born before 1890.[747] Nothing identifies the child as being born in New York. The 1890 orphan probably moved to another family, perhaps at the time of the second marriage.

John L. Ford:
John L. Ford received a boy in the August delivery of children, but did not have children in the 1895 census.[748] The child could have died or moved to another family.

W.C. Woolsey
See the biographies of the Tarrant brothers.

Charles M. France:
Charles Marston France was allocated a girl in the August delivery of children. In 1895 the France family was composed of Charles, his apparent wife Rachel, and daughter Myrtle, age seven and born in Hamilton County.[749] In 1900 the France family included Charles, his

---

[744] 1900 U.S. census, Dickinson County, Iowa, population schedule, Lake Park, ED 36, p. 15, household 280, swelling 280, Fern King in the household of Minnie King.

[745] 1895 State of Iowa census, Hamilton County, Iowa, population schedule, image 38 of 681, John E. Young.

[746] "Iowa, Marriage Records, 1880-1945, 1915-1916" > 352 (Emmet-Jones), Return of Marriages in the County of Hamilton, fiscal year ending, 1 October 1888, p. 492, Pritsch-Tapper marriage entry (5 November 1888).

[747] 1900 U.S. census, Moody County, South Dakota, population schedule, Lynn, ED 271, household 197, dwelling 199, William Getch.

[748] 1895 State of Iowa census, Hamilton County, Iowa, population schedule, image 411 of 681, John ford.

[749] 1895 State of Iowa census, Hamilton County, Iowa, population schedule, image 13 of 681, Charles M. France.

wife and Myrtle, born in April 1888. Myrtle was Charles and Rachel's biological child, or she was an out-placed orphan who so totally assimilated into that of her foster family that the identification cannot be made.

Peter H. Dickman:
Reverend Peter "Henry" Dickman served on the selection committee for the August and October deliveries of children.[750] Two families of sisters were assigned girls from the August delivery—Christ & Lottie (Rosenau) Krohn and Rev. Peter Henry and Paulina (Rosenau) Dickman. Both couples lived in Hamilton County for only a short time before leaving. Peter Henry Dickman died in 1893 in Stephenson County, Illinois.[751] Before 1895 his widow had moved to Kossuth County with her two children, both born in the 1890s.[752] Neither of the children are the right age to be one of the New York City orphans.

In 1900 Pauline still resided in Kossuth County with her two children.[753] The female child fostered into the Dickman family in 1890 could have died, or moved to another family.

The families of France and Dickman both had girls, but only one female orphan is yet to be identified; therefore, one of the known girls moved to another family.

---

[750] "E. Trott of the children's aid society…," *The Freeman,* 3 September 1890, p. 5, col. 3.

[751] "From Forreston," *Deutscher Anzeiger, (Illinois)*, 4 October 1893, p. 1, col. 5. Text is in German but my rudimentary German is enough to translate this short article about Pastor Dickman's death due to "nerve fever." Thanks to Kathy Pasch for finding this article.

[752] 1895 State of Iowa census, Kossuth County, Iowa, population schedule, image 391 of 733, Polina Dickman.

[753] 1900 U.S. census, Kossuth County, Iowa, population schedule, Germania Township, ED 149, p. 2, household 38, dwelling 39, Pauline Dickman.

Absent foster families from the October delivery:[754]

> Philip Morris
> In 1895 no children resided with Philip Morris and his apparent wife Fannie in Hamilton County, Iowa.[755] John Bodger was initially placed with the Philip Morris family; but John appeared in the household of William Bringolf in 1895.[756]
>
> William R. Wilson
> William Robert Wilson of Stanhope, accepted Richard Doyle as his foster son in 1890. As an older orphan (b. 1879), Richard probably struck out on his own after Wilson died in November of 1894.[757] In 1895 Richard Doyle, 16 years old and a farm laborer, resided with Leonard Hill and family.[758]

The October delivery of children generated a higher rate of successful placement. Individuals who desired an orphan in October probably discussed the process with those who received a child in September. The risks and rewards of a foster child in the family could be assessed more realistically, perhaps increasing successful placement.

---

[754] Kialy Carson, Kansas, [(CURATOR@ORPHANTRAINDEPOT.COM),] to Jill Morelli, email, 7 March 2023, "Info from the CAS," OTR folder.

[755] 1895 State of Iowa census, Hamilton County, Iowa, population schedule, image 84 and 11 of 681, Phillip Morris.

[756] 1895 State of Iowa census, Hamilton County, Iowa, population schedule, image 42 of 681, Wm. H. Bringolf.

[757] "Died," *Webster City Freeman*, 7 November 1894, p. 5, col. 4.

[758] 1895 State of Iowa census, Hamilton County, Iowa, population schedule, image 514 of 681, Richard Doyle in the household of Leonard Hill.

ATTACHMENT 4
Diagrammatic Map of Hamilton County, Iowa
Noting locations of residence of known foster families.

This map identifies the location of the farms or residences of the identified orphans and their foster families. Rose Grove, Lincoln, Scott, and Ellsworth townships had no foster families. Clear Lake and Marion Townships, located in the most northern tier of sections, had only one each.

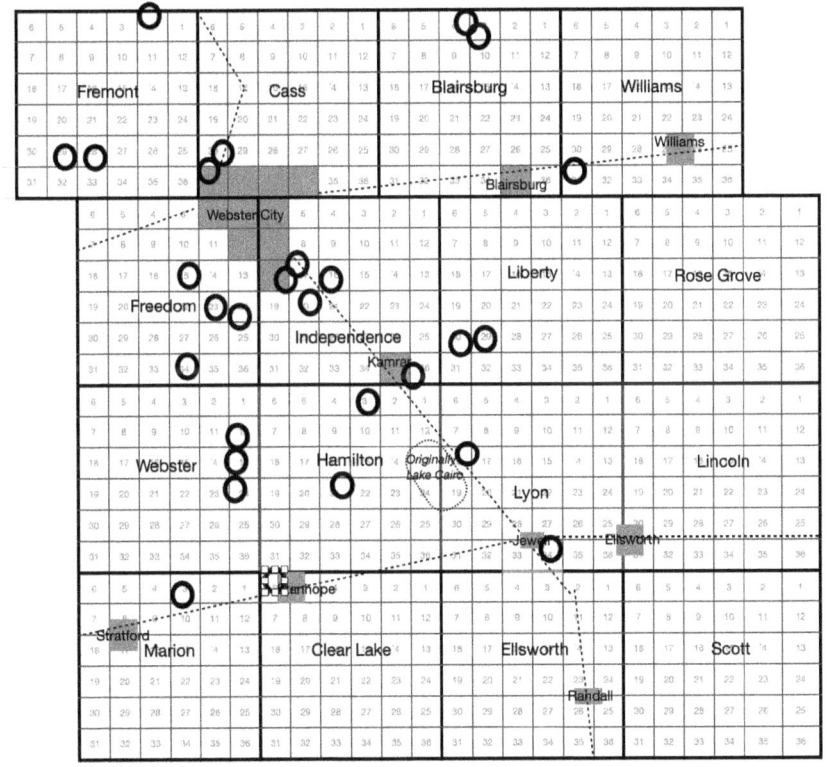

Map drawn by Jill Morelli, showing town locations, foster parents locations, Lake Cairo and railroads
Source: Hamilton County Plat Book, 1896; Kendall Young Public Library, Webster City, Iowa
Foster parent locations from plat map and/or deeds; County Recorder's Office, Hamilton County, Webster City, Iowa

Hamilton County is composed of 16 townships; each township is composed o 36 sections; each section is 640 acres and is 1 mile by 1 mile in dimension. Railroads criss-crossing the county are shown; but the roads are not shown, as most occurred on section lines.

There will be some inconsistencies in the location of foster families. Some families owned multiple parcels of land, and Christ Krohn's rented farm location cannot be identified.

Webster City, located in the northwestern quadrant of the county, appears to be a nexus of communication for the selected foster families. Certain clusters, such as Webster Township's three foster families, speak to the power of transference of information and joint decision-making. Attending the same church, going to Webster City on market days or reading the local paper would be ways information was exchanged.

Bibliography

Unfortunately the 1890 United States census, which might have identified many of the children in New York City, was destroyed after a fire on an upper floor resulted in the records, stored in the basement, being water-soaked and eventually thrown away. Two census substitutes exist:
1. 1890 Police census. Taken in September and October, the census missed enumerating any child that left in August or October for Hamilton County. All names were checked and none of the Hamilton County children were enumerated.
2. 1892 state census of Kings County, New York. This enumeration could eliminate a child candidate if that child was still living in New York in 1892.

RESOURCES
Advantage Archives, now called *Community Archives.* A superb Midwestern newspaper resource
    Boone County, https://boone.advantage-preservation.com
    Hamilton County, https://hamiltoncounty.advantage-preservation.com
    Hardin County, (only available in the Hardin County Library)
    Kossuth County, http://algona.advantage-preservation.com
    Story County, https://ames.advantage-preservation.com

American Experience, "The Orphan Trains." Public Broadcasting System, 1997.

Ancestry, primarily used for draft registrations, federal censuses, probate records, public trees, https://www.ancestry.com

Asylum Projects, https://www.asylumprojects.org.

Bellingham, Bruce. " 'Little Wanderers': A Socio-Historical Study of the Nineteenth-Century Origins of Child Fostering and Adoption Reform, Based on Early Records of the New York Children's Aid Society", Ph.D. dissertation, University of Pennsylvania, 1948.

Birk, Megan. *Fostering on the Farm: Child Placement in the Rural Midwest.* Chicago: University of Illinois Press, 2015.

Brace, Charles Loring. *The Dangerous Classes of New York and Twenty Years' Work Among Them.* New York: Wynkoop & Hallenbeck, 1872. Internet Archive: https://archive.org/details/dangerousclasse00bracgoog.

Boyken, J. Clarine J. *Echos of Spring Valley.* Internet Archive, https://archive.org/details/echoesofspringva00boyk

Bureau of Land Management, General Land Office. Homestead claims. https://glorecords.blm.gov/search/default.aspx

Children's' Aid Society. Paul Clarke, Archivist. https://www.childrensaidnyc.org/

Close, Harriet Bonebright. *The Story of Newcastle.* (Historic name of Webster City, Iowa.)

Colorado. Carnegie Library, Boulder. Mining claims.

Chrastil, Rachel. "Not Having Kids Is Nothing New." *The Washington Post*, 5 September 2019. https://www.washingtonpost.com/outlook/2019/09/05/not-having-kids-is-nothing-new-what-centuries-history-tell-us-about-childlessness-today/

FamilySearch, various records including all Iowa state census records and many marriage and death records, https://familysearch.org .

-----, FamilySearch Wiki, https://www.familysearch.org/en/wiki/Main_Page

FindAGrave. "Memorial Pages." https://findagrave.com.

Flickr, "Children's Aid Society Records," https://www.flickr.com/photos/nyhs/collections/72157623964464144/. Administrative records starting in 1854 and photos.

Goldin, Claudia and Lawrence F. Katz. 2000. "Education and Income in the Early 20th Century: Evidence from the Prairies." *The Journal of Economic History* 60(3): 782-818; JSTOR, permalink: https://www.jstor.org/stable/2566438

Greteman, Kristen A. "Lost Lake: A Deep Map of a Farm Field," MA diss., Iowa State University, 2020. https://dr.lib.iastate.edu/entities/publication/b391b458-30e8-45e0-a5b4-9ec10c437e5d/full

Hamilton County, Iowa, Court Clerk's Office, for probate, criminal, civil records. https://www.iowacourts.gov/iowa-courts/district-court/judicial-district-2/district/2/county/hamilton

———, Recorder's Office, for deeds, and Coroner's Report
https://www.hamiltoncounty.iowa.gov/departments/recorder/index.php

IAGenWeb. "The Orphan Train Project."database, Madonna Harms. http://iagenweb.org/hamilton/.

Illinois Regional Archive Depository (IRAD). Click on Databases: https://www.ilsos.gov/departments/archives/IRAD/home.html

Iowa State Historical Society. Des Moines. https://history.iowa.gov/history/research/research-centers

Iowa's County Schools: Landmarks of Learning. Parkersburg, Iowa: Iowa State Education Association and Mid-Prairie Books, 1998; Internet Archive.

Italian Genealogy Group (IGG), index to NYC vital records, https://www.italiangen.org/

Keene, Michael T. *Abandoned: The Untold Story of the Orphan Trains, Second Edition.* Pittsford, New York: Ad Hoc Productions. 2017. Stories from the orphans or their descendants.

Lebergott, Stanley. "Labor Force and Employment, 1800 -1960," Dorothy S. Brady, editor, *Output Employment & Productivity in the United States after 1800.* n.p.: National Bureau of Economic Research, https://www.nber.org/system/files/chapters/c1567/c1567.pdf

Lee, J. W. *History of Hamilton County Iowa,* vol 1. Chicago: S.J. Clarke Publishing, 1912. Google Books, https://www.google.com/books/edition/History_of_Hamilton_County_Iowa/GHwUAAAAYAAJ

Lyon, Bessie L. *Early Days in Hamilton County, Then and Now.* Webster City, Iowa: Freeman Journal Publishing Co., 1946.

McOilough, Verlene. "The Orphan Train Comes to Clarion." *The Palimpsest* 69 (1988), 144-150.
https://ir.uiowa.edu/palimpsest/vol69/iss3/7

Minnesota Historical Society. Vital records of events in Minnesota. Minneapolis, Minnesota, https://www.mnhs.org/library

MOMS, Minnesota Official Marriage System Birth and Death. https://moms.mn.gov/

Morelli, Jill, CG. "The NYC Irish Orphans & their Midwest Families." (Working title) *The Septs.* Vol 45: 4 (October 2024).

MyHeritage, Index of NYC Historic Vital records, https://myheritage.com.

National Center for Health Statistics (U.S.) "100 years of marriage and divorce statistics, United States 1867-1967," no. 24, 1973. https://stacks.cdc.gov/view/cdc/12831/

Nelson, Kristine E., "Child Placing in 19th Century: New York City and Iowa," *Social Services Review*, 59:1 (1 March 1985), p. 107-120.

New York City Municipal Archives, *New York City Historical Vital Records*; https://a860-historicalvitalrecords.nyc.gov/digital-vital-records

New York Historical Society Museum & Library. Finding Aid, Victor Remmer Collection. http://dlib.nyu.edu/findingaids/html/nyhs/childrensaidsociety/

New York Public Library "Victor Refer Historical Archives of the Children's Aid Society, 1836-2006, MS 111, finding aid, https://findingaids.library.nyu.edu/nyhs/ms111_childrens_aid_society/

O'Connor, Stephen. *Orphan trains: The Story of Charles Losing Brace and the Children He Saved and Failed*. Boston; Houghton Mifflin Company, 2001.

Parkway, Greg, "True Stories" blog https://markwayblog.com/?fbclid=IwAR00Gkd2-S-nDyEXQ5ViE-QbZYTTyF70mBjrqifqnzIUInlgq_fhWhhZU_4

Riley, Tom. *Orphan Train Riders: A Brief History of the Orphan Train Era (1854-1929) with Entrance Records from the American Female Guardian Society's Home for the Friendless in New York, vol 1*. Berwyn Heights, Maryland : Heritage Books, 2014.

Riley, Tom. *Orphan Train Riders, vol. 2*. Berwyn Heights, Maryland : Heritage Books, 2008. List of children.

Rocca, Mo. *Mobituaries with Mo Rocca*, podcast, "Revisiting the Orphan Train: An American Odyssey." 20 December 2019. https://podcasts.iheart.com/LVl2r6gs Interview with last known living orphan train rider Beatrice Polak, 97, of Wharton, Texas.

Sanborn Fire Insurance Maps, Webster City, Hamilton County Iowa, 1892, Library of Congress. https://www.loc.gov/collections/sanborn-maps/about-this-collection/

Seattle Public Library. https://spl.org. Seattle newspapers.

Thurston, Henry W. *The Dependent Child*. New York: Columbia University Press, 1930. Internet Archive. https://archive.org/details/dependentchild0000thur

Tourist in the Land of Reason, "The Cherokee State Hospital for the Insane, 1902 to Present," https://www.youtube.com/watch?v=WQLYCW4Awuc

Weill Cornell Medicine, Samuel J. Wood Library, "Historical Patient Records," for New York Infant Asylum (1871-1901) and New York Asylum for Laying Women, (1854-1899). https://library.weill.cornell.edu/archives/historical-patient-records

Additionally, I anticipate two articles in 2025 for the Utah Genealogical Association's periodical *Crossroads*. Titles to be determined, but topics are finding parents of orphans in New York City and self-publishing your work.

Index

The following were not indexed:
- The front matter, including the dedication and the preface
- Footnotes
- Tables and their footnotes
- Map
- Captions
- Bibliography
- Common names, places etc. that would have hundreds of references, e.g. Hamilton County, Iowa, CAS, Webster City, New York, New York City, orphan, etc.

Other items of note

The orphans are indexed according to their primary name. The page number reference in bold is the first page of their chapter. All names used by the orphans are indexed, including aliases & married names; all refer back to the primary name. Spelling variations are not indexed.

Female spouses of orphans are indexed under their birth and their married name, but refer the reader to the name used when married to the orphan.

Other women, e.g. foster mothers, are indexed under the name by which the orphan would have known them.

Place names are listed in order by large to small jurisdictions, even if all jurisdictions were not used in the referred narrative. Look for the state first.

Where the individual is named in a narrative footnote, but aggregated in the narrative, the reference form used is page #, n, followed by the footnote number, e.g. 219n726 is found on page 219 in footnote 726.

This index was done by the author, please forgive any inconsistencies, errors and omissions—they are all mine.

--?--, Rosa (*See* Rosa Breakfeldt)		Blackwell Island	3
"Gretna Green"	143	Board for Certification of Genealogists	241
"Old man's draft'	111		
"Old Mexico"	116, 117	**Bodger, John (*See* John Bodger Bringolf)**	
107th Infantry, Company E	167	Bohning, Lillian	199
157th Depot Brigade	167	Bonk, Etta	13, 14
A. M. Railway Company	20	Bonk, Jennie	13, 14
Adams, Elizabeth	153, 158	Booth, Mrs. Ella (neé Hogen) (See Ella Thompson)	
Adams, Joseph	153, 158, 219n726	Boozel, Eva	115
		Boozel, Luther	115
Adultery	76, 224, 230, 235	Borea Evangelical Lutheran church	71
Alexander, Charles	148		
Allison, Anna	15	*Boy's Life on the Prairie, A*	214
Allison, William	**13,** 224, 228, 234	Brace, Charles Loring	3-5, 230
Anderson Hays Motor Company	99	**Breckfeldt, George**	**33,** 215, 218n724, 226, 234
Angell, Emma Marie (See Emma Bringolf)		Breckfeldt, George (father of George)	33, 36-38
Angstrom, Eva	33, 34		
Angstrom, Olaf F.	33-35, 38, 219n726	Breckfeldt, Mary (neé Cusick)	33, 36-38
		Breckfeldt, Rosa (neé —?—)	34, 38
Arends, Albert	199	Brennan, Rev.	239
Ashpole, Elich Alexander	8, 247	Briggs, Ellen	180, 187
Ashpole, Elizabeth	17	Briggs, Frank	159, 165, 179, 180, 187, 219n726, 222, 235
Ashpole, Fred	9, **17,** 219n726, 234		
Ashpole, Frederick	8, 17, 222	Briggs, Thrisda	180
Ashpole, Glenna Fern	247	Brigham, Irene	70, 71
Ashpole, Lucy	17	**Brigham, Lucy (*See* Lucy (Johnson) Fay)**	
Baker, Eveline	127	Brigham, Wilfred J.	70, 74
Baldwin, James Garfield (Johnson)	9, **19,** 218n724, 224	Bringolf, Charles Wesley Bodger	42, 43
Baldwin, Lavanche	19, 20	Bringolf, Clara	39, 40, 43
Baldwin, Loretta (*See* Loretta McCabe)		Bringolf, Clarence Bodger	42, 43
Baldwin, Perry O.	19, 20	Bringolf, Emma	40, 41, 43
Baptist	26, 80	Bringolf, Ida Louise	43
Bateman, Orle	200	**Bringolf, John Bodger**	9, **39,** 213, 219, 228, 233, 250
Bauman, August	89		
Beck, Harley	161	Bringolf, Merlin G.	43
Bernnake farm	204	Bringolf, William	39-40, 43, 229, 233, 250
Bishop, Calla (*See* Calla Lyons)		Brunkhorst, John	180
Bishop, Joseph A.	98	Bugbee, Florence Dorothy (*See* Florence Dorothy Lyons)	
Bishop, Sarah, J.	98	Burcham, Frank H.	17
Bittner, Harry	9, **25,** 213, 217n723, 223, 228	Burnett, Eva (neé Butler)	46, 50
		Burnett, John Henry (Murtha)	**45,** 213, 224, 226, 230, 236
Bjustrom, Arthur "Charles"	**27,** 218n724		
Bjustrom, Joseph	27-29, 32, 219n726	Burnett, John M. (foster father to **John**)	45
Bjustrom, Lucy	28, 32	Burnett, Mary	45
Bjustrom, Mathilda	27-29, 32		

Busing, Aalderk	8, 51, 52, 219n726	Closz, Charles	6
Busing, Grietje "Grace" (neé Bloem)	51, 52, 219n726	Colorado	132, 133, 135, 179, 183, 185, 188, 190, 235
Busing, Minnie Everhardina	**51,** 213, 219, 218n724, 228, 234	Colorado, Boulder County, Ward	179, 183
		Colorado, Jefferson County	182, 183
Busy Bee	34	Colorado, Jefferson County, Golden	182
Butler, Eva (see Eva Burnett)			
Butto, Frank	180	Colorado, Larimer County, Loveland	133
California, San Mateo County	21, 97, 99, 101		
California, San Mateo County, Belmont	99, 101	Colorado, Moffat County	132, 135
		Colorado, Ward Mining District	183, 190
California, Campbell's Sanitarium	99	Courter, Charles	119
California, Del Norte County, Crescent City	190	**Crane, Anna (*See* Anna McIntyre)**	
		Crane, Frances E.	103
California, Dos Palos	19, 20	Crane, Mary A.	103-105, 108, 219, 222
California, Hollister	90		
California, Long Beach	39, 41, 43	Crane, Robert	103-105, 108, 219n726, 222
California, Marin County, San Quentin	15		
		Crisis/crises	2, 47, 56, 223-225, 230, 234, 235
California, Merced County	19,23		
California, Oakland	20	Cuba	63-66, 68
California, San Francisco	19- 21, 23, 99	Cusick, Mary	33, 36-38
California, San Mateo County, Brisbane	99, 101	Dangler, Cecil T. (*See* also Cecil Wise)	148, 152
California, San Mateo County, Holy Cross Catholic Cemetery	21	Dangler, Earl	148
		Dawson, Harry (*See* Iris Doutrich)	
California, Stanislaus County	133, 135	De-culturalization, Native American	5
Canada	103, 199-201, 219, 223		
Canada, Quebec Province, Montreal	199-201	Delaney, Mrs. M. M.	197
		Delivery, first (August)	1, 8, 75, 85, 95, 137, 159, 165, 221, 237, 247-249
Caneo, Myrtle	21		
Cannon, Ben (son of Benjamin)	70, 71	Delivery, second (October)	8, 9n22, 19, 23, 27, 32, 39, 45, 55, 63, 69, 131, 135, 137, 140, 159, 165, 177, 179, 187, 193, 197, 199, 201, 212, 221, 238, 247, 250
Cannon, Benjamin Edward	70, 71, 74		
Cannon, Glenn	70, 71		
Cannon, Lucy (*See* Lucy (Johnson) Fay)			
Caroon, Harry	239		
Caroon, Patrick & Ellen	239		
Carrie B. (in Nels Jensen household)	119	Delivery, third (November)	8, 55, 141, 147
Cash & Lenhard	80	Denmark	119, 223
Children's Mission to Children of the Destitute	3	Devine, James	167
		Dickman, Paulina (Rosenau)	249
Christenson, S. A.	120	Dickman, Rev. P. H.	8, 193, 249
City Restaurant	126	**Doutrich, Iris (alias Harry Dawson)**	55, 105, 224, 228, 233
Closz & Howard Sieve Manufacturing Company	6, 120, 204, 208		
		Doyle, Annie (neé Newall)	63, 64, 66, 68
		Doyle, Irene	66

261

Doyle, John W.	63-66, 64, 68
Doyle, Minnie (neé Runyon)	65, 68
Doyle, Richard	**63**, 211-213, 226, 228, 236, 250
Doyle, Sadie	64, 65
Doyle, William	64
Dubert, Jacob	137-140
Durall, Athol	144
Eckhoff, Belle (*See* Belle Wientjes)	
Eckhoff, Dick	194, 195, 197, 230, 234
Eldora Training School for Boys	39, 56, 57, 224, 228, 233
England	5, 17, 46, 68, 103, 172, 223
Essig, Elizabeth	203, 208
Essig, John	8, 203, 208, 219n726,
Fay, Hester (neé Parisian)	**69, 72,73**
Fay, Lucy (Johnson)	69, 213, 217, 220, 222, 226
Fay, William Henry	69, 72, 73
Fee, Emily	46
Fee, Florence	73
Fee, Hester (neé Parisen) (*See* Hester Fay)	
Fee, William Henry (*See* William Henry Fay)	
Ferrell, Garfield	200
Fink, Arthur	120
Fisher, W. T.	204
Fitzgerald, Delos	172
Follett, Catherine E.	154, 158
Follett, Donald H.	158
Follett, George M.	154, 158
Follett, James L.	158
Follet, Julia (*See* Julia M. Sumpter)	
Follett, Louis	154, 155, 158
Ford, John L.	8, 248
France, Brest	167
France, Charles Marston	8, 248, 249
France, Myrtle	248, 249
France, Rachel	248, 249
Fry, Mr.	194
Fuller, Alonzo	116
G&K Study	213, 215
Galloway, Dr. M.B.	80
Garland, Hamlin	214
Georgia, Camp Gordon	166 167
Gerber, Charles	159, 165, 187, 188, 219n726, 235
Gerber, F. A.	188
Gerber, Mary	159, 165, 187, 188, 235
Gerber, William (*See* William Weber)	
German (First) Presbyterian Church	14, 51, 75, 224, 234
Germany	13, 38, 86, 125, 138, 157, 158, 188, 194, 199, 203, 223, 234
Glacial intrusions	6
Golden Eagles baseball team	40
Goulden, Dean	80
Goulden, Katie (*See* Katie (Mickle) Hines)	
Goulden, Fredrick	80
Goulden, John	80
Goulden, Joseph H. "Joe"	80, 81, 84
Graham, Edward (*See* Edward Pruismann)	
Gray, Geraldine "Ina"	135
Gray, Gilford	133, 135
Gray, Howard	133, 135
Gray, John Bennett	132, 133, 135
Gray, Lillian (*See* Lillian Florence Lingreen Roop)	
Gray, Paul	133, 135
Great Depression	7, 29, 41,47, 81, 87, 111, 121, 123, 127, 133, 162, 189, 195, 197, 208, 218, 223, 234, 235
Grensberg, Grietje "Grace" (See Grietje Busing)	
Grensberg, John	51, 52, 222n717
Guseka, Harry (See Harry Guseka Moore)	
Hamilton County Hospital	119, 121
Harms, Madonna	237
Harvest Home Festival	126
Hassebroek, Geerd	8, 13, 14, 219n726, 222, 224, 234
Hassebroek, Harriet "Etta" (neé Bonk)	23, 14, 222
Hassebroek, Jennie (neé Bonk)	13, 14, 219n726
Hayes, Isaac	28, 32
Hayes, Lucy (Allison) (See Lucy Bjustrom	
Hellen, N. H.	9
Hill, Leonard	63, 250
Hinderks, Aeilt	75, 78, 224, 234
Hinderks, Henry Aeilt	75, 224, 234

Hinderks, Hilke	75, 78, 224	Iowa, Boone County, Boone	27-30
Hinderks, Lulu Pearl (neé Kennedy)	76, 78	Iowa, Bremer County, Waverly	193, 195, 197, 201
Hines, Catherine Francis (*See* Katie (Mickle) Hines)		Iowa, Bremer County, Waverly, Mercy Hospital	195
Hines, Katie (Mickle)	79, 194	Iowa, Butler County, Parkersburg	110
Hines, Ellen (neé Leahy)	79, 83, 84	Iowa, Butler County, Washington Township	194
Hines, Francis "Frank"	79, 80, 82-84	Iowa, Calhoun County	25
Homestead Act	166, 223	Iowa, Cedar Falls	189
Hoover, Hugh E., Jr.	88	Iowa, Cerro Gordo County, Mason City	172, 173, 175, 239
Hoover, June Joyce (neé Kuchenreuther)	88, 90, 91	Iowa, Cherokee County, Cherokee Hospital	33, 35, 38, 39, 63, 66, 68, 153, 224, 224n730, 233
Horton, John	92		
Horton, Joseph Foster Ellery	92-95	Iowa, Clinton County	18, 79-81, 84
Horton, Sarah Lavinia (*See* Sarah Lavinia Mason)		Iowa, Dallas County	45,47,50
Hutchinson, Harriet "Mae" (*See* Harriet "Mae" Weber)		Iowa, Des Moines River	65
Hutchinson, Mary	188	Iowa, Dubuque	98, 101
Illinois Central Railroad	111, 120	Iowa, Grundy County	194
Illinois, Cook County, Evanston	141, 143-145	Iowa, Howard County	167
		Iowa, Kossuth County	29, 85, 86, 95, 160-162, 166, 224, 249
Illinois, Chicago, Illinois Central Hospital	195		
		Iowa, Northern District Court	58
Illinois, Lee County	142, 143	Iowa, Polk County, Des Moines	57, 116, 117
Illinois, Marian County	144		
Illinois, Ogle County	52	Iowa, Story County	34, 135
Illinois, Rock Island County, East Moline	51	Iowa, Story County, Ames	132
		Iowa, Story County, Cambridge	34
Illinois, Rock Island County, Watertown State Hospital	52, 54	Iowa, Story County, Story City	161
		Iowa, Thorton	58
Illinois, Stephenson County	52, 54, 249	Iowa, Webster County	65, 66, 159, 165
Immigrants	3, 214, 223	Iowa, Webster County, Dayton	35
Indentured servants	3	Iowa, Webster County, Fort Dodge	58, 131, 166, 167
Indian Famine Fund	180		
Indiana, Jay County	148	Iowa, Winnebago County	66, 214
Indiana, Lake County	143	Iowa, Wright County	132, 204, 208
Indiana, Richland County	148	Ireland	37, 46, 49, 59, 66, 68, 92, 97, 141, 152, 158, 160, 166, 223
Industrial Revolution	2		
Industrial schools	3		
Iowa GenWeb Orphan Train project	237		
		Jefferson, Thomas	4
		Jensen, George (*See* George Jensen Myers)	
Iowa Supreme Court	182, 185	Jensen, Nellie	119, 120, 123, 224
Iowa, Anamosa, Iowa State Penitentiary	57, 58, 161		
		Jensen, Nels	119, 120, 123, 224
Iowa, Aplington	195		
Iowa, Austinville, Christian Reformed church	194	**Johnson, James (*See* James G. Baldwin)**	
		Johnson, Johanna	70
Iowa, Bancroft	166	Johnson, John L.	69

Johnson, Lucy (*See* Lucy (Johnson) Fay)	
Johnson, Nels	70, 74
Johnson, Thea	69, 72, 222
Johnston, James (*See* James G. Baldwin)	
Kansas	219, 229, 233, 237
Kansas, Cowley County, Arkansas City	132, 135
Kansas, Leavenworth	38, 61, 105, 233
Kansas, Sedgwick County, Wichita	41
Kennedy, Lulu Pearl (*See* Lulu Pearl Hinderks)	
Kennedy, Margaret	76
Kennedy, Robert	76
Kentucky	110, 223
King, Minnie	247
Klaus, George	125
Klaus, Mary	125
Knox, Lulu (*See* Lulu (Knox) Strowbridge)	
Knox, Sarah M.	147, 148, 152
Knox, Thomas	147, 148, 152
Kraft, Adam	109, 110
Kraft, Cora May (neé Moore)	109, 110, 111
Kraft, Harry	110
Krohn, Charlotte "Lottie" (Roseneau)	85-87, 89, 95, 212, 219, 221, 224, 249
Krohn, Christ	8, 85-87, 90, 95, 221, 224, 249, 252
Krohn, Clara Lavinia (Mason)	85, 211-213, 219, 220, 224-226, 230, 249
Kuchenreuther, Anna	87
Kuchenreuther, Charlotte "Lottie"	87
Kuchenreuther, Clara (*See* Clara Lavinia Krohn)	
Kuchenreuther, Dorothy Lavinia	87
Kuchenreuther, Ervin/Irvin	87
Kuchenreuther, Hienrich/Henry J.	86, 91, 95
Kuchenreuther, Julia	87
Kuchneneuther, June Eleanor	90, 91
Kuchenreuther, Lena	87
Kuchenreuther, Mason	87
Laying-in hospital	3, 174
Lee, Emily (See Emily Fee)	
Lengren, Lillian (*See* Lillian Florence Lingreen Roop)	
Lindland, Frank	21
Lindland, James	21
Little Chicago Cafe	115
Loveland, George C.	143
Lucas, Harry M	105
Lutheran	71, 86, 127, 129
Lyon, Elizabeth "Lizzie" (*See* Elizabeth "Lizzie" Zahn)	
Lyons, Calla (neé Bishop)	98, 101
Lyons, Florence Dorothy (neé bugbee)	99, 101
Lyons, James Wilfred	97, 217, 217n724
Lyons, Kearnes E	97-101
Lyons, Mary	97-101
Mason, Annie (neé Robinson)	92, 94
Mason, Charles P.	92
Mason, Charlotte	92
Mason, Clara (*See* Clara Lavinia Krohn)	
Mason, Lavinia (neé Viele)	92
Mason, Robert A.	92, 94
Mason, Robert H. (son of Robert A.)	92
Mason, Sarah Lavinia	85, 90-95
McCabe, Anna	21
McCabe, Loretta A.	20, 23
McCarthy, Kate	197
McCollough Inc.	121, 127
McCendry, William (*See* William Thompson)	
McFarland, David	55, 56, 59, 219n726
McFarland, Eliza	55, 56, 59, 219n726
McFarland, Iris (*See* Iris Doutrich)	
McIntyre, Anna (Crane)	59, 61, 103, 217, 217n723, 219, 228, 234
Metcalf, Rev.	181
Methodist	121
Meyer, Anna (Busing)	52
Meyer, John (father to John)	52
Meyer, John (son of John)	52, 54
Meyer, Minnie (*See* Minnie Everhardina (Busing)	
Meyer, Viola	52, 54, 219
Michaelson, Sammie	65
Michigan	4, 120, 123, 224
Michigan, Newaygo County	120
Mickle, Elsie J.	79, 84
Mickle, Katie (*See* Katie (Mickle) Hines)	
Mickle, N. Jackson	8, 79, 80, 84, 219n726
Midwest	4, 37, 38, 51, 203, 218
Mine, Canton	183

Mine, Cardiff	183	Myers, Anna (neé Rabe)	120, 121, 123
Mine, Free Gold Mining Claim Survey	190	Myers, Dorothy Lorraine	121, 123
Mine, Gold Coin	183	**Myers, George Jensen**	119, 213, 220, 224, 230, 236
Mine, Gold Cord Lode	183		
Mine, Hill Top Lode	183	Nation, Clifford V.	143, 145
Mine, Janet Lode Mining Claim Survey	190	Nation, Mae (*See* Mary "Mayme/Mae" Smith)	
		Nebraska	34, 70, 74, 160
Mine, Lafayette Lode	190	Nelson, Burna	149
Mine, Lafayette Mills site	183	New City Electric & Light Power Company	180, 182
Mine, Valley View Lode	183		
Mine, Valley View Mill	183	New Jersey, Hoboken	167
Mine, Ward Mining District	190	New York Infant Asylum, 61st St. & 10th Ave.	37, 151, 152, 157, 158, 174, 226
Minnesota, Austin	173		
Minnesota, Blue Earth County, Lake Crystal	159, 162, 164	New York, Bellevue Hospital	84, 226
		New York, Brooklyn	49, 64-69, 73, 89, 92, 211, 240
Minnesota, Carlton County, Twin Lake	40		
		New York, Greenwood Cemetery	93
Minnesota, Crow Wing County	153	New York, Kings County Alms House	37
Minnesota, Faribault County, Pilot Grove Township	204		
		New York, Long Island, Jamaica	84
Minnesota, Hennepin County, Minneapolis	98, 99, 101, 116, 117	New York, Manhattan	45, 50, 53, 84, 91, 151, 158, 211, 240
Minnesota, Houston County, Money Creek	70		
		New York, Manhattan, Calvary Church	83
Minnesota, Lake Wilson	122		
Minnesota, Mower County, International Falls, Frederic Hotel	173	New York, New York City, Children's Home	33
Minnesota, St. Louis County, Lake Kabetogama	173, 175	New York, New York City, Free Home for Destitute Girls	151
		New York, Oneida County	79
Missouri, Macon County, Macon	46, 50	New York, Queens, Rockaway Beach	197
Missouri, Randolph County	46, 50		
Monarch Factory	121	New York, Richmond County (Staten Island0	125, 127-129, 151, 197, 211, 240
Montana	41, 166		
Moore, Alfred	109, 110, 113		
Moore, Harry Guseka	**109**, 219n726, 219	New York, Staten Island (*See* Richmond County)	
		Newsboy Lodging Homes	3
Moore, Sarah E.	109, 110, 113	Northwestern railroad	35
Morris, Fannie	250	Norway	177
Morris, Nelson	**115**	Nursery & Childs Hospital	90, 91, 94, 197, 226
Morris, Philip	39, 43, 250		
Motheral, James V.	171-173	O'Dell, Blanche	144
Motheral, Minerva	171-173	O'Neil, Agnes	141, 142
Moving Day	66	O'Neil, James H.	142
Muller, Arthur (*See* Charles Arthur Bjustrom)		O'Toole, John	183
		Ohio	110, 115, 147, 149, 223
Murtha, Emily (neé Lee)	45, 49, 50		
Murtha, John (*See* John Henry Burnett)		Olmstead, Lucy	25, 26, 223
Murtha, Patrick	45, 50	Olmsted, Hiram S.	25, 26, 223

Orphan Train Depot	237	Schroder, Anna (*See* Anna Witte)	
Orphan Train Movement	3, 3n5, 5	Scotland	172, 174, 223
Ostfriesens	234	Scott, Eunice	166, 168, 170
Out-placed orphan	59, 64, 68, 76, 97, 103, 105, 119, 120, 141, 148, 159, 165, 171, 175, 188, 203, 205, 209, 237, 249	Scott, Guy M.	166, 168, 170
		Segar, Benjamin E.	137, 219n726, 247
		Segar, Emmert	137
		Segar, Horace	8, 137, 247
		Segar, Maria	137
Out-placement	2, 3, 3n5, 4, 84, 209, 215, 218, 221, 225, 227, 230	Smith, Andrew	141, 145, 219n726
Peitsch, Bena	248	Smith, Andrew (son of Andrew)	142
Peitsch, Fredericka	248	Smith, Blanche	142, 144
Peitsch, William	248	Smith, Delbert	144
Pruismann, Anna	129	**Smith, Mary "Mayme/Mae"**	**141** 213, 217n724, 223, 230
Pruismann, Darlene	129		
Pruismann, Edward Graham	76, **125**	Smith, Mary	141, 142, 145
Pruismann, Emma (neé Rathman)	127, 129	Smith, Peter	142, 143
Pruismann, Frank	8, 125, 126, 129	Smith, William J.	142, 143, 145
Pruismann, Henrietta (married to Frank)	125, 126, 129, 219n726	Smith's Rink	2, 8
		South Dakota, Harrold	57
Pruismann, Henrietta (daughter of Edward)	129	South Dakota, Madison	59, 61
		South Dakota, Sanborn County, Woonsocket	58, 59, 61, 105, 108
Public auction	66		
Quinn Wire & Iron Works	28	South Dakota, Yankton, Hospital for the Insane	103, 106, 108
Rabe, Anna (*See* Anna Myers)			
Railroad Brotherhood	200	Spain	68
Ralph Study	209, 228-230, 235	St. Thomas Aquinas Church	98
Ralph, Georgia G. (*See* also Ralph Study)	5, 209, 227, 233	Steinman, Helen	90, 91
		Stevens, Lulu (See Lulu (Knox) Strowbridge	
Rathman, Emma (*See* Emma Pruismann)		Stevens, William Edward	149, 152
Rebekahs auxiliary	81	Strever, George	14, 224
Reagan (tailor in Madison, SD)	59	Strowbridge, Emma	147, 151, 152,
Reinhardt, Henry	116, 117	**Strowbridge, Lulu (Knox)**	**147**, 213, 217, 217n726, 224
Riemtema, Carrie	52		
Roop, Charles Henry	131, 132, 135	Sumpter, Annie	153, 157, 158
Roop, Lillian Florence Lingreen	**131**, 212	Sumpter, Charles	158
		Sumpter, Julia Mae	**153**, 213, 220, 224, 230, 234
Roop, Sophronia "Flora"	131, 132, 135		
Rouse, Pearl (*See* Pearl Tarrant)		Sumpter, Margaret	158
Royal Neighbors Camp	132, 154	Sumpter, Mary	158
Runyon, Minnie (*See* Minnie Doyle)		Tapper, Bena	248
Rupple, William	204	**Tarrant, Charles Joseph**	**159**, 165, 170, 179, 213, 219, 235, 248
Schloss, Benjamin	139		
Schloss, Fann	139		
Schlosshauer, Edward	138, 139	Tarrant, Duane R.	164
Schlosshauer, Katharina "Carrie"	137-140	Tarrant, Ellen	159- 162, 165, 166, 170, 221
Schlosshauer, William	**137**, 211, 247		
Schmitz, William J. (*See* William J. Smith)		Tarrant, Helen G.	164

Tarrant, Kenneth C.	164	Weber, Harriet Mae (neé Hutchinson)	188, 189, 192
Tarrant, Margaret C.	164	**Weber, Jacob "Fred"**	159, 165, **179**, 187, 188, 190, 192, 217n723, 222, 235,
Tarrant, Mary E.	164		
Tarrant, Paul C	164		
Tarrant, Pearl (neé Rouse)	160, 164		
Tarrant, Richard	159, 160, 162, 165, 166, 170, 221	Weber, Wayne	189, 190, 192
		Weber, William Louelette	159, 165, 179, 182-184, 187, 217n724, 235
Tarrant, William Anthony	159, 160, 162, 164, **165**, 179, 213, 217n723, 219n726, 224, 235, 248		
		Welch, Bella (*See* **Belle (Welch) Wientjes)**	
		Welch, Maggie	193, 195, 197
		Westway Club	154
Thompson, Barney	177, 219n726	**Wientjes, Belle (Welch)**	**193**, 211, 224-226, 230, 234
Thompson, Betsey	177		
Thompson, Ella (Booth) (neé Hogan)	172, 173, 175	Wientjes, Fred	193, 195, 197, 219n726, 221
Thompson, Maggie	171, 173, 174	Wientjes, Minnie	193, 197, 221
Thompson, O.W.	173	Williams Harness Shop	57
Thompson, Walter	10, **171**, 217n724, 225	Wilson, William Robert (W. R.)	63, 64, 219n726, 250
Thompson, William (McKendry)	**177**, 234	Wisconsin	85, 95, 199, 223
		Wisconsin Drift	5
Thurston, Henry W.	209	Wisconsin, Lafayette County, Belmont	70
Trott, Eli, Superintendent	2, 8, 13, 17, 25, 51, 75, 79, 125, 203		
		Wisconsin, Marathon	70
United States, Kansas, Leavenworth, Federal Penitentiary	58, 61, 105, 233	Wisconsin, Medford	69
		Wisconsin, St. Croix	99, 101
United States, Works Progress Administration, Toy Project	189, 190	Wisconsin, Superior	71
		Wisconsin, Taylor County, Greenwood Township	71
Valentine, Sadie (*See* Sadie Doyle)			
Veterans of Foreign Wars, Ladies Auxiliary	81	Wisconsin, Taylor County, Rib Lake	71
Vetter, Charlotte	207	Wisconsin, Waupaca County	70
Vetter, Fredricke (*See* Fredricke Zahn)		Wisconsin, Wood County,	71, 74
Vetter, Louisa	207	Wise, Cecil T. (also Dengler & Stevens)	152
Vetter, Mary	207		
Vetter, Reinhardt	207	Wise, Dwight	148,149, 152
Virginia	147, 223	**Wise, Lulu (***See* **Lulu (Knox) Strowbridge)**	
Voogd, Dick	195	Witte, Anna	199, 200
Warden, George R. (*See* **George R. (Warden) Witte)**		Witte, August	199-201, 219n126, 230
Warner, William A.	143	**Witte, George R. (Warden)**	199, 217n723, 219, 229
Washington Co-operative Egg & Poultry Association	88		
		Witte, Minnie	199-201
Washington, Cowlitz County	147, 149, 152	Women of the Moose	81
		Woodall, M.M.B.	109
Washington, King County, Seattle	85, 89,95, 96	Woolsey, William Clark	8, 159, 165, 248
Washington, Whatcom County	86-88, 95	Accident	116, 126, 1180, 188, 234, 235
Weber, Evelyn Dorthea	188		
		Wright, Julia (*See* **Julia Mae Sumpter)**	

Wright, William	153, 158
World War I	20, 35, 61, 65, 76, 99, 117, 161, 170, 188, 224, 235
World War II	41, 47, 126, 168
Wyoming, Laramie	200
Young, Charles H.	25, 26, 219n726
Young, Harriet	25, 26
Young, John E.	8, 248
Zahn, August Hilbert	70, **203**, 207, 211, 213, 214, 226, 228, 230, 236
Zahn, Elizabeth "Lizzie" (neé Lyon)	204, 208
Zahn, Fredricke (Vetter)	203, 205, 207, 208
Zahn, Louisa "Elsie"	204, 208, 228
Zahn, Wilhelm/William	203, 205, 207, 208
Zahn, William "George"	205, 207, 208

www.ingramcontent.com/pod-product-compliance
Lightning Source LLC
Chambersburg PA
CBHW050132170426
43197CB00011B/1802